AMERICAN STATES OF MIND

American States of Mind

Political Beliefs and Behavior among Private and Public Workers

CRAIG REINARMAN

Yale University Press
New Haven and London

Published with assistance from the Louis Stern Memorial Fund.

Designed by James J. Johnson
and set in Electra Roman type.
Printed in the United States of America by
Halliday Lithograph Corporation,
West Hanover, Massachusetts.

Library of Congress Cataloging-in-Publication Data

Reinarman, Craig.
American states of mind.

Bibliography: p.
Includes index.
1. Trade regulation—United States—Public opinion.
2. Capitalism—United States—Public opinion.
3. Public opinion—United States. 4. Truck drivers—
United States—Attitudes. 5. Social workers—United
States—Attitudes. I. Title.
HD3616.U47R1464 1987   330.12′2′0973   86-26752
ISBN 0-300-03817-8 (alk. paper)

The paper in this book meets the guidelines for permanence
and durability of the Committee on Production Guidelines
for Book Longevity of the Council on Library Resources.

1 2 3 4 5 6 7 8 9 10

Contents

Preface

The logic of laissez-faire, or the "free market," we are told with increasing frequency, is the answer. The question, however, is not entirely clear. Government in all its guises, the State, has been rendered suspect; a scant two decades ago, *it* was the answer. If this is true, what did people think and do to make it so? And what do they now make of the change? This book is about political consciousness in America. To be more precise, it is about the political consciousness of a dozen Americans—six private-sector truck drivers and six public-sector welfare workers—in the 1980s.

Our epoch is one in which political issues are known via nightly network newscasts, and citizens' beliefs about them are assessed in the aggregate almost weekly in national opinion polls. We routinely read that Americans believe this or that, that they support one or another candidate or policy, or that the American electorate has "moved to the right." Nearly a decade ago, I was prompted to begin the research reported here in part because I felt uneasy with such characterizations. Now that it is finished (or at least abandoned), I am even more uneasy.

The broad structural conflicts between state and market, workers and management, the little guys and the big guys, do not register clearly in the polls and at the polls. We hear much about welfare spending and taxes, government regulation and the health of industry. But what do such big issues look like in little lives? What forms do they take in the lived experience of *individuals*? I attempt in what follows to look not so much at these issues themselves but at how they appear through the lens of life history. I wanted to discover something about the ways in which work and private life inform political beliefs about capitalism and democracy and the master conflicts of the 1980s. I wanted to know about how such beliefs, as well as the everyday dissatisfactions and deep democratic values that animate them, come to be expressed in the voting booth. Was it, say, "false consciousness" that led members of the working class to support Ronald Reagan? What, concretely, do people mean when they lash out against "bureaucracy" or "welfare cheats"? What molecules of everyday experience make up the "tax revolt" or the "shift to conservatism" or "health care as a right"?

It is my hope that the people you will meet in the chapters to follow will serve as ideological windows through which to glimpse an array of answers to such questions. Indeed, my twelve subjects were chosen precisely because their beliefs were so varied that they could not help but provide such an array. C. Wright Mills once made a famous yet still neglected plea for the "sociological imagination," in which he argued that in the modern world one cannot understand personality apart from social structure, private troubles apart from public issues, or biography apart from the broader historical flow of which it is a droplet. In a very real sense my choice of problem or topic was inspired by his words. There is another sense, however, in which I have inverted his logic. Mills wanted scholars and citizens alike to understand their situations by paying attention to the ways in which huge institutional structures impinge upon the individual. While I have tried to infuse this work with that sensibility, I have also tried to find in the minute experiences of a few individuals the grand themes of our epoch. Thus, while I have endeavored to understand my subjects as members of a "social class," I have also tried to learn about social class through their biographies. My analysis is an attempt to study the macrolevel issues of a moment in our history by looking at how these are refracted in the microlevel mosaic of a life history.

If this turns out to have been a useful exercise, it will be because of the many people who have given me aid and comfort along the way. Intellectual debts can never be repaid in any real sense, but they can be acknowledged. First and foremost I thank the twelve people who so graciously and honestly shared their time, beliefs, and concerns with a stranger. To say that I am grateful seems a masterpiece of understatement. I hope only that I have done justice to their views.

Through her great wisdom and support, Miye Narkis made all my work much easier, and Lynn Thingvold typed what must have seemed like endless early drafts with great skill and convincingly feigned cheer. Many other friends doubled as mentors: Marc Beyeler, Sharon Carlsen, Jeff Fagan, Victoria Hatfield, Ellen Hickey, David Keown, Tom Koenig, Ron Lembo, Clarence Lo, Pat Morgan, Sheigla Murphy, Judy Rothschild, Grace Schrafft, Susan Shapiro,

Mark Temple, David Wellman, Jack Whalen, and, *dulcis in fundo*, Chris Pugliese. Special thanks are due those who gave the extraordinary gift of their time and critical capacities in reading earlier drafts of this book: Bob Alford, Stanley Aronowitz, Jim Baumohl, Bennett Berger, Bill Domhoff, Jim O'Connor, Frances Fox Piven, and, especially, Rob Rosenthal.

Rosemary C. R. Taylor gave me the chance to test the waters with some of the early research at the 1982 meetings of the American Sociological Association. Troy Duster arranged for me to spend a year as Visiting Scholar at the Institute for the Study of Social Change at the University of California, Berkeley, where I first tried out some of the ideas reported here. I was fortunate as well to have a postdoctoral fellowship at the Alcohol Research Group of the School of Public Health at Berkeley. Although my work there had nothing to do with this book, Robin Room and Connie Weisner provided such support and stimulation that I found it easy to smuggle in my writing in the evenings. Similarly, Dan Waldorf of the URSA Institute in San Francisco kindly looked the other way when this work distracted me from our other research tasks.

The very early stages of the research were supported by a Charlotte W. Newcombe Doctoral Dissertation Fellowship from the Woodrow Wilson National Fellowship Foundation. My official graduate school mentors also doubled as friends—no doubt the reason I learned so much from them. Donald R. Cressey gave unstintingly of his time, his sense of the sociological enterprise, and his sharp blue pencils, and in so doing taught me much of the discipline of the writer. Don Zimmerman generously delved with me into issues new to us both and taught me the value of ethnomethodology—a powerful way of seeing social structure under construction in social interaction. My debt to Dick Flacks is evident throughout these pages. His gentle insistence upon building a social science capable of grasping both the mechanisms of ideological domination and the capacities of ordinary people for autonomous thought and self-development has been an essential nutrient in my growth as a scholar and a person. The ideas and the humanity he shared with me for six years in a seminar on political consciousness at the University of California, Santa Barbara, will forever infuse my intellectual and political sensibilities.

I must also thank Gladys Topkis of Yale University Press, whose patience and support throughout gave me the confidence I needed to finish, and Cecile Watters, whose editorial gifts have made this book infinitely more organized and readable than it otherwise would have been.

Finally, I dedicate these pages to my parents. It was my mother's fervent morality that led (in ways of which she did not always approve, yet somehow always encouraged) to my sense of social justice. It was her passion for learning and ideas that (finally) infected me, and her abiding respect for the beliefs of others that informs both question and method in this book. My father, having tired (remarkably slowly) of political arguments with his son, quoted to me the wisdom of Samuel Butler (1612–80), from which I continue to learn: "A man convinced against his will is of the same opinion still." From him I also gained a sense of craft and an understanding that one gets the job done by staying with it— brick by brick, paragraph by paragraph. What is of value in this work is due to their efforts as well as my own.

1

State and Market in the Public Mind: An Introduction

OMETHING was happening. No one seemed quite sure what or why, but by the end of 1980 it was clear that the winds of political change were blowing across America. The most conservative president in half a century had won office by a wide margin after frontally attacking a form of capitalist state that not long before had been taken for granted as central to prosperity and stability. This book is about what happened, or, more accurately, about how a dozen citizens *thought about* what happened: how they formed and used their political beliefs, what this had to do with their working and nonworking lives, and why, in the shifting circumstances of the late 1970s and early 1980s, they thought and believed and voted as they did. Before I introduce them, however, it is necessary to sketch the historical context in which they and the issues I asked them to talk about were situated.

Whether the 1980 presidential election was a "critical" election, involving a long-term realignment of the electorate under the Republican party, remains a matter of intense debate. What is not in doubt, however, is that it was a critical juncture in American political life. The period from the end of World War II to the end of the 1960s has been called the golden age of the welfare state (Gough 1979). Whatever else history may deem significant about the first Reagan election, it clearly defined a new terrain for political battle, what Katznelson aptly names the crossroads of state and market (1981, 313). Further, the election resuscitated the nineteenth-century laissez-faire notion that the state is inherently bad for the health of the market *and, therefore,* for the populace. The rival ideology, which had held sway since the 1930s, was that the success of capitalism requires an active state. Roosevelt had convinced even some conservatives that

1

welfare state liberalism and regulation are the best long-term defenses for private property and free enterprise because they counter the injustices of capitalism and thus defuse criticism. Later Democratic presidents built their coalitions and policies on this foundation, and neither Eisenhower nor Nixon succeeded in shaking it.

The domestic tranquillity and legitimacy forged in the New Deal and brought to fruition in the postwar years had two pillars. The first can be called Fordism. Rather than continue to maximize profits by paying workers as little as possible, many business leaders came to accept Henry Ford's idea that steadily rising wages would not only reduce economic conflict in the sphere of production but also allow more workers to purchase more goods. This strategy broadened the proportion of the population who could participate in mass consumption, thus increasing profits by expanding domestic markets at the same time that it presumably satisfied more human wants (see, for example, Aronowitz 1973; Ewen 1976). The Wagner Act of 1935 helped institutionalize this wage-price compromise between business and unionized workers by legalizing collective bargaining or institutionalizing a "democratic class struggle."

The second basis was the so-called welfare state, perhaps more accurately called the regulatory welfare state, born of the protests of the Great Depression. Following Keynesian economic theory, an array of income support programs was established (Social Security, public assistance, unemployment insurance, and so on) during and after the New Deal. Such programs eased the suffering caused by troughs in the business cycle and stabilized demand by putting a floor under consumer spending. While various forms of government regulation in key industries helped prevent wild swings in the market, the welfare state smoothed enough of the other rough edges of American capitalist society to avert most of the class conflict found in other industrial democracies.

Although the welfare state and the Fordist bargain between capital and labor were instrumental in postwar prosperity, both were predicated upon continued economic growth. The United States emerged from the war militarily and economically unscathed relative to Europe and remained the dominant actor in an expanding world market for two decades. Growth became problematic, however, when, almost simultaneously, the rebuilding Japanese and German economies became competitive, the civil rights movement successfully pushed for expanded state funding of the War on Poverty and Great Society programs, and spending for the Vietnam War began to inflate the U.S. economy. Under the low-growth conditions that began in the late 1960s, inflation began to take a toll on financial markets and the international monetary system. The oil crises of the early 1970s further strained Keynesian macroeconomic policies, and the "politics of growth" coalition that had governed since the 1940s began to show signs of wear.[1]

The unparalleled economic growth of the postwar years allowed both rising wages and living standards and expanded state services. When this growth faltered, signs of the 1980 electoral earthquake began to appear. Popular expectations for "the good life," or at least a "decent" life, arose alongside the high wages of Fordism and the expansion of the welfare state. But by the mid-1970s, an army of business lobbyists began to argue that the economic costs of such expectations were a fetter on capital accumulation. What amounted to an investment strike began. Rather than invest in research, development, and new factories, many corporations put their capital in low-wage developing nations or into mergers. This further lowered the relative productivity of U.S. industries, exported jobs, and increased unemployment. Many industry organizations began ideological offensives against state regulation and social spending in which government was held to be solely responsible for stagflation (O'Connor 1981). In October 1974, *Business Week* editorialized candidly about the mounting accumulation crisis:

> It is inevitable that the U.S. economy will grow more slowly than it has. . . . Some people will obviously have to do with less. . . . Indeed cities and states, the home mortgage market, small business, and the consumer will all get less than they want. Yet it will be a hard pill for Americans to swallow, the idea of doing with less so that big business can have more. Nothing that this nation, or any nation, has done in modern history compares in difficulty with the selling job that must now be done to make people really accept the new reality.

President Carter beat a Watergate-tainted President Ford in 1976 by campaigning on more or less traditional Democratic themes, even proposing national health insurance. However, declining U.S. predominance in the world market, a continuing energy crisis, balance-of-payment problems, and worsening stagflation led him to change his political tune. What Wolfe has called Carter's conundrum (1981, 200) began before the hostage crisis in Iran. Simply put, without sustained economic growth, the Keynesian macroeconomic formula by which liberalism had traditionally reigned was less and less available to him. By the middle of his term, Carter was sounding more and more like a Republican. He admitted to the nation that austerity needed to be imposed, that an unemployment-riddled recession had to be induced to wring inflation out of

1. For a variety of theoretical perspectives on these developments, see O'Connor (1973, 1984), Crozier, Huntington, and Watanuki (1975), Barnet (1980), Castells (1980), Vidich (1980), Wolfe (1981), and Calleo (1982).

the economy. In light of the accumulation crisis, he backed away from even the ideal of full employment, which had become bad for "business confidence" and the "investment climate."

Although such conditions intensified the need for income security from public aid programs, Carter could not overcome the fiscal crisis besetting the welfare state. Corporations were demanding lower taxes as well as fewer regulations in the name of renewed profitability and growth. Nor would the middle class, whose living standards already had been seriously squeezed by inflation, stand for higher taxes. In 1978, the California tax revolt sparked by Proposition 13 began to spawn similar movements in two dozen other states, most of them rife with the raucous rhetoric of welfare state bashing (Kuttner 1980).

By 1980 candidate Carter spoke no more of national health care but instead boasted of his efforts toward deregulation. He also halved capital gains taxes, to the benefit of investors and corporations, while raising Social Security taxes for everyone earning under twenty-eight thousand dollars a year. Even while he nodded at the Democrats' traditional totem of fairness, he seemed to genuflect at the Republican altar of profitability. He failed in his attempt to fight on Reagan's ideological turf and thereby to capture the electoral center. The degree to which Carter's political demise can be blamed on the Iran debacle is debatable. What seems less debatable is that Reagan's margin of victory signaled a shift. Although it was not the revolution the Right quickly claimed it to be, the economic, political, and cultural templates upon which postwar America sat had experienced a jolt that measured jarringly high on the social Richter scale.[2] The welfare state, once held up as the savior of capitalism, was now cast as the villain who was ruining it. The New Deal–Great Society state was symbolically transformed into a Democratic party vice while its elimination, or at least amputation, became a Republican party virtue.

Of course, the notion that welfare state programs enacted *in response to*

---

2. Clearly there is more to the Reagan victory in 1980 than this sketch of the state-market core implies. Edsall (1983) finds many elements in what is often spoken of as a simple ideological shift in the electorate: the marriage of ideological (cultural) conservatives and increasingly powerful corporate political action committees; the decline of trade union membership; the diversity of Democratic party constituencies (a source of strength in times of growth but a vulnerability during contraction or crisis); the effects of inflation on tax bracket creep, which pushed many former welfare state supporters toward antistate positions; and the continuing decline in voter turnout among potentially Democratic voters. Shoch (1985) links such diverse developments to the transition to a postindustrial economy, in which one social structure of accumulation, and attendant class configurations and political relations, is being replaced by another. New technologies, for example, have reduced the size and power of unions, while workers' support for New Deal welfare state programs was weakened by postwar prosperity, which made many of them into middle-class suburbanites (see O'Connor 1981). Perhaps the richest critical analyses of the meaning of 1980 are Ferguson and Rogers (1981) and Piven and Cloward (1982). For an intriguing conservative view, see Phillips (1982).

failures of the market were the *cause* of those failures is difficult to swallow. But the important issue is why that notion became appealing to so many. It had not always been so. Throughout the 1950s a residue of affinity for government remained from the successes of the New Deal and World War II. In 1960, the Report of the President's Commission on National Goals found majoritarian support for expanding the size and scope of government and raising the pay of government workers (for example, Wriston 1960). There was also strong popular backing for the Kennedy-Johnson War on Poverty in the mid-1960s. Thus, scarcely a decade before the rise of Reaganism, it credibly could be said that Americans believed that the state not only could but should solve social ills (see, for example, Lane 1962, 190–92).

By 1968, however, the Democrats were hurt by, among other things, the growing schism over Vietnam. Nixon's budding conservative renascence was nipped by a Democratic Congress and the Watergate scandals. But the "crisis of confidence" and "malaise" of which President Carter was soon to speak afflicted both major parties. Government in general seemed increasingly discredited, but particularly, in a context of stagflation and creeping taxation, the welfare state. Without economic growth—to keep the promise of opportunity that is the essence of America and to finance the public programs that sustained those for whom that promise was unkept or broken—politics grew into what Thurow (1980) called a zero-sum game. More demands were made on a state less able to meet them. In a situation of fiscal crisis, one group's successful claim on the state was another's loss. Without growth, the Keynesian consensus cracked, and the liberal-labor coalition that had supported it began to disintegrate.

All this provided fertile political soil for the rise of the Right. In the aftermath of the 1960s, Vietnam, and Watergate, the right wing of the Republican party brokered a marriage between economic conservatives who wanted business to have free reign and social conservatives upset about what modernity had done to "traditional values." As liberalism crumbled, this marriage broadened the popular base of the Right. By 1980, Reagan managed to convince nearly all conservatives and more than a few moderates and weak liberals that the problems facing the United States constituted a crisis not of capitalism but of Keynesianism. The market, he assured the electorate, would solve all America's problems if only the state would get out of its way. His ability to roll back the regulatory welfare state has been constrained and partial, but he has had remarkable success at the level of symbolism. The outsider versus the establishment and the little guy against the powerful are enduring motifs in American culture. Yet, where earlier populists fought against banks and railroads, "Wall Street" or "big business," Reagan managed for the first time to redefine populism as *pro-business*. It did not seem to matter that the market under Reagan was characterized by a concentration of capital into larger and larger corporate units while the rates of small-business failure and unemployment reached heights known only in the Great Depression. What seemed to matter most was that for the first time since the 1930s, government was seen by many as a force for evil rather than good. The development of the welfare state was not, as theorists of many stripes had assumed, inexorable.[3]

This attempt at a historical overview surely omits or oversimplifies much of significance. I do not mean to imply that the so-called Reagan Revolution has *unequivocally* triumphed. For instance, Reagan had surprisingly short coattails in his first election and nearly none in his second. His personal popularity did not extend far enough to garner a Republican majority in Congress. This often made for stalemates on foreign policy and legislative issues. For all his self-proclaimed fiscal conservatism, Reagan has run up the largest budget deficits in the country's history.[4] Polls throughout both terms have revealed huge personal approval ratings for Reagan *and* disapproval of many of his basic policies and spending priorities. In a thorough review of recent survey evidence, Lipset and Schneider (1983) show, for example, that Americans back free-enterprise competition but remain critical of its consequences, just as they support government regulation and hate bureaucratic red tape (see also Schneider 1984). If what Reagan signified and accomplished can be seen as a transformation, it was a truncated one. What Antonio Gramsci said of a different society in an earlier era somehow

---

3. The view that the development of the welfare state is integral to the development of advanced capitalism, once held by scholars of many political persuasions, is now being questioned. See, for example, O'Connor's (1973) path-breaking study on the fiscal crisis of the state; Katznelson (1981) for an excellent overview of this issue vis-à-vis the 1980 election; Skocpol and Orloff (1984) for a historical cross-cultural study that casts doubt on theories that assume the inevitable growth of welfare states in advanced capitalist societies; and Gough (1979) and Offe (1985) for solid, neo-Marxian analyses of the nature of the welfare state under capitalism.

Although it is beyond the scope of this work to analyze the efficacy of regulatory-welfare states in reducing suffering and inequality, it should be mentioned that there is evidence that state intervention in economies does work toward that end. Stack's (1978) research on thirty-two nations found this to be the case, independent of levels of development and growth; and Piven and Cloward (1971) and Jencks (1983) offer similar evidence on the United States supporting this point.

4. By the second year of Reagan's second term, when his sixth record-breaking deficit budget was submitted to Congress, it became apparent that these were, so to speak, designer deficits. Despite attempts to blame them on profligate welfare state liberals, the deficits were largely the consequence of huge increases in military spending. By late 1985, prompted by a letter to the editor of the *New York Times* by Senator Daniel Patrick Moynihan, administration aides began admitting privately to the press that the deficits were a deliberate attempt to saddle future administrations with levels of debt and interest payments that would preclude new federal spending initiatives in the foreseeable future. Deficit spending thus combined with new weapons systems to form a unique tactical Trojan horse for the Right: unable to dismantle the regulatory welfare state legislatively, they could go a long way toward that end budgetarily.

seems apropos: "The old is dying and the new cannot be born; in this interregnum a great variety of morbid symptoms appear." (1971[1930], 276).

Partially hidden within all these recent developments lies a metaissue that, at least since the democratic revolutions of the eighteenth century, has been at the heart of Western political and economic thought. It has to do with what I will call *the state-market relation*. The people introduced in the next chapter never spoke of it as such, nor did they entertain the idea that their beliefs and policy preferences had much to do with the grand themes of history. Yet the major and minor political debates that were part of their daily lives were fundamentally about the nature of the proper relation between state and market. Their political talk, I hope to show, was continuous with Rousseau's discussion of the tension between liberty and equality in *The Social Contract* (1761). Although it has been difficult indeed to improve on his finding that neither liberty nor equality can be had without the other, this has not discouraged citizens or scholars from trying to do so ever since.

In the year the American Revolution began, Adam Smith published *The Wealth of Nations* (1937 [1776]), in which he made an eloquent moral case for the notion that only liberty could yield equality. In contrast to the uses to which his philosophical treatise is now put, Smith saw it as a weapon against the utterly undemocratic feudal and ecclesiastical institutions that controlled commerce and virtually all other forms of social life. To the cheers of the mercantile and industrial class then battling lords and popes, Smith laid out a laissez-faire theology in which only the famed "invisible hand" of the free market was capable of boosting production and exchange, improving the material lot of societies, mediating conflicts, balancing liberty and equality. Capitalists were delighted to see their interests elevated to "natural law." A careful reading of *The Wealth of Nations*, however, shows that the economic actors Smith had in mind were independent artisans and farmers rather than, say, the real estate speculators and conglomerate chieftains who now invoke his work as a weapon in their ideological combat with government regulators and union negotiators. Presaging Marx, who used him to great scholarly advantage, Smith feared that the inequalities of power between owners and workers might lead to something less than the distributive justice and social harmony predicted in his ideal-typical map of a market world.

Whether we look at the world before Smith and Rousseau or after the 1980 presidential election, I want to suggest that politics was and is centrally concerned with negotiating the nature of the state-market relation. From the thirteenth through the sixteenth centuries, peasant rebellions, riots, and other popular uprisings routinely accompanied recessions (Wallerstein 1976, 20–23).

These have often been portrayed as spasmodic or compulsive mob phenomena rather than rational or strategic forms of political expression (see Rude 1980 for a critique of the former). In a classic essay, British historian E. P. Thompson reinterpreted the bread riots and other forms of primitive protest among eighteenth-century English crowds and found in them an implicit politics. His central concept was the notion of *moral economy*, which I will borrow often in this book to explicate the meaning of the state-market relation and the struggle over it. He defined this as the "popular consensus" about what are and are not legitimate market practices, a consensus "grounded upon a consistent traditional view of social norms and obligations, of the proper economic functions of several parties within the community." This moral economy "supposed definite, and passionately held, notions of the common weal . . . [which] impinged very generally . . . upon government and thought." Thompson found in early crowd actions some "notion of legitimation" informing the basic beliefs of protesters, notions that "they were defending traditional rights and customs" that were "supported by the wider consensus of the community" (1971, 78–79; cf. Tilly 1985).

American history, too, has been full of fights over the state-market relation and the nature of the moral economy. The United States has not had only one form of democratic state since its inception but rather several successive ones characterized by the varying degrees to which democratic constraints have been imposed upon market mechanisms. In Jeffersonian America, for example, democracy was limited to the propertied, and public policy served largely to protect the market distribution of property. As the have-nots struggled over the years, first for the vote and then with it, in an attempt to make the market fair to the nonpropertied, the laissez-faire moral economy here and there gave way to a broadening of democratic rights. These rights came to be ensconced in norms and later in law and public policy—that is, in the state. Wolfe (1977) argued that there have been six stages of American government, each characterized by a distinct mode of resolving the tensions between capitalism and democracy. These have included an "accumulative state," organized at the dawn of industrialization to facilitate capital accumulation, and, later, "harmonizing" and "expansionist" states that developed in response to the democratic demands made on the market system after immigration and unionization (cf. Macpherson 1977).

Relative to European industrial democracies, the United States has not had a politicized working class or a labor party, and thus the American moral economy is characterized by a relatively undeveloped welfare state. A variety of notions has been advanced to account for this American exceptionalism. These include the absence of a feudal legacy, which might have inhibited social mobility and thus exacerbated class conflict; a rich and expansive frontier, which served as a safety valve; foreign expansion or imperialistic ventures, which helped sustain growth and mobility; ethnic, cultural, and religious cleavages among an uncommonly heterogeneous working class; and the extension of voting rights prior to the rise of overt industrial class conflict.[5] To these might be added theories of postindustrial domination that stress the cooptiveness of mass-consumption culture. Here the combination of higher living standards and ideological manipulation integrates workers into the middle class and so diffuses more radically democratic demands (cf. Mills 1956; Marcuse 1964). Most of such accounts of American exceptionalism have been criticized if not discredited.

According to Piven and Cloward (1982), a laissez-faire moral economy persisted in the United States long after European nations had moved toward a new democratic moral economy with strong welfare states, and after the granting of voting rights had established political democracy in America. They attribute its staying power to institutional and ideological "walls" (for example, structures of government, cultural individualism) that blocked popular understanding of "the market" as a set of *socially constructed* relations sustained by the state rather than simply as part of the natural order. Such walls developed cracks during the economic crises of the Progressive Era and began to crumble during the depression, when chaotic unregulated competition and speculation led to massive middle-class poverty, putting the lie to the laissez-faire "law" that hard work and the invisible hand would yield economic well-being. The New Deal gave birth to the modern regulatory welfare state and in so doing established more firmly than ever before in American history that because the economy was a *political* economy, subsistence is not a matter for the lone individual to struggle for in an impersonal market.[6] Since then, the federal government has been so much a part of the economy—both in making the market profitable with tax laws, business loans, induced recessions, and foreign policies that protect private investments and in mediating the social impact of market activity by protecting the poor, the sick, consumers, or the environment—that the walls that had for so long symbolically separated state and market lay "in ruins" (1982, 150).

5. For contrasting treatments of American exceptionalism as it pertains here, see Bell (1960), Aronowitz (1973), and Piven and Cloward (1982).

6. Ignatieff (1985) rightly points out that the welfare state originating in the New Deal was not seen as a permanent means of meeting human needs. It had legitimacy in part because so many middle-class citizens found themselves poor, and these people were expected to rise again when the emergency of the depression passed. However, that no formal obligations to the poor are written into the Constitution and that Congress legally could have scrapped New Deal programs at any time suggest that the welfare state is sustained by the momentum of political culture, like the notion of a new moral economy. Another reason welfare state programs persist is that, contrary to folklore, for every dollar spent on means-tested programs for the poor, nine dollars are expended on programs serving the nonpoor (Jencks 1985; cf. Gilbert 1983).

A core theme in Piven and Cloward's thesis is that democratic political rights historically have been used to make the state ensure the right to livelihood or at least subsistence. As the state has increasingly become the locus of demands from both business and the mass public, they argue, we have undergone an "ideological transformation" in which the state's role in sustaining livelihoods *and* profits has become transparent.[7] There is evidence that a new moral economy, or at least one that seriously contends with laissez-faire, has evolved as part of this transformation. Business-backed offensives against the "culture of entitlement" and the "excess of democracy" (for example, Crozier, Huntington, and Watanuki 1975) imply that a substantial proportion of the American public believes there are such things as economic rights.

If culture may be understood to be that which is taken for granted, and if that which is contestable falls in the realm of ideology, then the trajectory of the United States in the twentieth century has been toward a moral economy that is not restricted to pure laissez-faire precepts. In 1985, for example, the Conference of U.S. Catholic bishops wrote a pastoral letter, to be read in thousands of churches, arguing that unrestrained capitalism often exacerbates injustice and that economic and social policy should therefore show more concern for the poor. This unsurprising moral appeal, in draft form and prior to publication, provoked surprisingly vociferous opposition from conservative Catholics and corporate spokesmen. The level of outrage from the leaders of the Right made it apparent that they felt capitalism *needed to be defended*, that it could not be taken for granted.

A debate on ABC's "Nightline" (February 14, 1986) offers another telling illustration. Anchor Ted Koppel threaded his way between a banker and a farmer arguing over the crisis of the family farm. The banker concluded that the increasing frequency of farm failures was an unfortunate but necessary part of the market system, and that "Americans have got to be prepared to see a shakeout" in which many "less efficient" farms would "go under." The farmer replied, "I am a *farmer*, not just a commodity. Farming is a way of life as well as an industry." He closed his critique of the administration's imposition of free-market discipline by

---

7. O'Connor (1978) offers a compelling case for this same point. Because the state has increasingly implicated itself in daily life through policies and spending for both accumulation and legitimation, it has become *the* arena of class (and other) conflicts in advanced capitalist societies. State attempts to rationalize social life to reduce the costs of reproducing the social relations required by the economy (for example, transportation, education, health care) have only increased the visibility of the state in the economy and further politicized hitherto private issues. For O'Connor, the current gamut of localized, particularistic demands on public agencies constitutes a popular, albeit often inchoate, movement to democratize the state—to make it responsive to human and community needs rather than to the imperatives of capital (cf. Crozier et al. 1975; Lindblom 1977; Castells 1980).

predicting that "Ronald Reagan is gonna go down as the Jim Jones of American agriculture."

What struck me about this exchange was not so much who won or lost which points but that it took place at all and that the two contenders were presented as having equal claims to credibility. Philosopher Jurgen Habermas (1973) has defined "truth" as that about which a rational consensus might be reached in an "ideal speech situation." Although "Nightline" is some distance from the sort of situation Habermas outlines, it is worthwhile to examine it as an exemplar of the formal public speech situations in our culture that are construed as fair or approximating the ideal. In this light, the pretense of "Nightline" to objectivity required that equal time and legitimacy be granted to the analyses of farmer and banker alike. Such epistemological equivalency implies that what counts for truth in America in the 1980s is something other than uncontested laissez-faire discourse. Our values and our views of what is true and possible and natural now seem to incorporate the visible hands of Keynes and Kennedy along with the invisible hand of Adam Smith. As historian Barrington Moore has put it, "The nineteenth-century notion that society bore no responsibility for the welfare of the population, that it was both especially futile and quite immoral to expect the chief of state to take effective action countering threats to the general welfare, now looks like a minor historical aberration" (1978, 22).

Yet, Moore wrote before Reagan and the New Right rose to political prominence—a rise that was due in no small part to their contrary assertion that the very reforms, regulations, and public programs that have accumulated since the 1930s to protect the general welfare from the vicissitudes of the market are the *cause* of current crises in the market. The Reagan administration has consistently attempted to scale back or eliminate both welfare and regulatory facets of the state and to institute "supply-side" (or, in the older argot, "trickle-down") economic policies that redistribute income upward so as to spur investment. Piven and Cloward argue that these policies fly in the face of the new moral economy that has evolved since the New Deal, and that because so many people have benefited from government programs and regulations, *the state and the new moral economy will be defended*. In broader historical terms, they say this defense will occur because capitalism itself has shown that human action has unlimited potential to transform the world and that, therefore, neither market outcomes nor anything else are understood as inevitable. The historical trajectory they trace thus takes an ironic shape: the market's successes have helped undermine the authority of the traditions of belief that undergird the social order of the market; the very democratic forces unleashed by capitalism are now taming it. [8]

8. I have reluctantly circumvented the reform versus revolution debate running through neo-Marxian work on the capitalist state, which stimulated much of my thinking. That debate too often

When I began the interviews for this book, I wanted to know whether such a defense of the new moral economy was in fact occurring and, if so, what forms it was taking. I soon discovered that this research problem was more easily stated than solved, or even addressed. Throughout the early backlash against the welfare state, the tax revolt, and the Reagan years there remained evidence of support for both the welfare and the regulative functions of the state (Lipset and Raab 1978; Yankelovich and Kaagan 1979; Lipset and Schneider 1983). Even in 1980, as Reagan was being elected by a wide margin, rent control measures were passed in several California cities by many of the same voters who elected him. And, despite the president's best campaign efforts, voters continued to elect Democratic congressional representatives who vowed to block many of the administration's initiatives against the state.

It was not clear, however, that these phenomena constituted an actual defense of an existing moral economy. Whatever the depth of support for the state from the New Deal through the Great Society, surely there was a tradition in America of skepticism toward government (particularly "big government"), and the clear success Reagan had in drawing upon and mobilizing it suggested that such a defense is at least contingent and problematic. The trajectory toward greater democratic economic rights has not been a straight line, nor has support for state intervention remained steady. In the early 1960s, political scientist Robert Lane found a base of support for the state, which, although tempered by notions of limited noninterference, seems remarkable in the 1980s:

> The government is charged with unlimited responsibility for the general welfare. . . . Today it is embodied in law (the Full Employment Act of 1946), and [the community], in a rather vague, backdoor fashion, accepts this as approved doctrine. This is part of a more general belief that the

---

does not ask whether democratic constraints on the market and reforms that insulate vulnerable groups from it have progressive significance in culture and daily life. Rather, the state as a whole is often seen as inevitably doing what capitalism needs to preserve itself, whether because the capitalist class actually dominates the state (instrumentalism) or because whoever runs the state must meet those requirements (structuralism). This theoretical corpus tends to ask only whether a reform will help preserve capitalism or lead to revolution. It therefore often precludes the analysis of the uses of reforms in present and future struggles and their cumulative significance (see Miliband 1969, 1977; Poulantzas 1973; Gold, Lo, and Wright 1975). For understanding politics at a given juncture, I assume that such issues cannot be assessed in advance (see, for example, Esping-Andersen, Fried-ling, and Wright 1976; Thompson 1978; Wright 1979; Skocpol 1979). Implicit here is the belief that it is erroneous to read Marx as saying that the transformation of capitalism into socialism would inevitably and everywhere and at each stage occur by revolutionary rupture (see Stephens 1979), and that social-democratic welfare state forms may be preferable to existing forms of communism or to a return to protocapitalist forms.

government is responsible for discovering and seeking solutions for *all social ills*.

The problems will yield to appropriate government action. . . . [The community] believes that man, through government, can improve his lot in almost any direction; he can change economic laws, and need not be a slave to any circumstance. (1962, 191)

Support for the state looked strikingly different by the mid-1970s. Compare Lane's description with that of Owen and Schultze:

After conquering the Depression, winning World War II, achieving post-war full employment, and constraining Soviet expansion in the Cold War, the American people had by 1965 concluded that the federal government was an effective instrument for accomplishing important and useful ends. That belief has been sharply eroded in the last ten years—partly because of failures (Vietnam and Watergate) and partly because of semisuccesses (the Great Society and détente) that failed to fulfill exaggerated expectations. Skepticism about government's ability has been accompanied by suspicion about government's intentions. (1976, 1; see also Nie and Andersen 1974 for an important analysis of survey data supporting this point)

Whether one looks at such shifting sentiments toward government, the decline of the Democrats' liberal-labor coalition, the rise of Reagan and the New Right, or the processes of renegotiating the American moral economy that is present in all such developments, it seems safe to say that the legitimacy of the regulatory welfare state from the late 1970s through the mid-1980s has become at least ambiguous. This conjuncture of political-economic problems has prompted theorists of varying ideological persuasions to write of the potential for a "legitimation crisis."[9] This concept is a slippery one, however. Citizens can be dissatisfied with a specific regime, with the basic values or the dominant ideology in a culture at a given time, or with the justice and efficacy of a society's master institutions (Yankelovich 1972; Friedrichs 1980). Moreover, perceptions of all three modes of delegitimation may be widespread and still not lead to any identifiable crisis. The forms of delegitimation *experienced* and the passions attached to them typically vary across the population. History is rife with examples of brutal, corrupt, and unjust regimes and political-economic systems that have limped along for decades with only cultural momentum and the support of key strata on their side.

Just as W. I. Thomas taught us that if people define situations as real they

9. For different slants on the notion of legitimation crisis, see Yankelovich (1972), O'Connor (1973), Habermas (1975), Crozier et al. (1975), Janowitz (1976), Wolfe (1977), Denitch (1979), Thurow (1980), and Castells (1980).

will be real in their consequences, so Habermas (1975) has shown that subjective perceptions of legitimacy are an intrinsic component of objective crises. Between the social-structural roots of problems and their behavioral-political consequences lie the murky realms of perception and cultural articulation. Unless discontent and delegitimation become intersubjectively shared perceptions, they may not register at the social-system level. [10] In this sense, both "legitimacy" and "crisis" remain relative, particularly in a historical context characterized by crisis and change, and depend fundamentally upon the way in which grievances are experienced and expressed. This, in turn, depends upon how issues are framed, organized, and mobilized so that they come to have a specific ideological valence or partisan political charge. Although this work is hardly done democratically, from the masses up to elites, I do not wish to imply that ideologies are simply spoon-fed from above. Historically, popular discontents have taken on a great variety of ideological hues, but they have remained concrete and particular, bonded to specific experiential referents that are embedded in specific life histories. Although elites clearly do try to define issues and/or construct the frames through which problems will be perceived, these must *resonate* with voters in order to be effective (Fromm 1941; Lane 1962; Geertz 1973, 193–233; Mepham 1977; Moore 1978). Citizens more or less actively appropriate such frames and issues into their own political belief systems, or at least act to position themselves strategically among the belief systems extant in the political culture of which they are part (Bourdieu 1977; Wellman 1977; Aronowitz 1981).

All this leads into the somewhat vague arena of political consciousness that will be explored in the dozen depth interviews that follow. If there is conflict over the state-market relation, if the moral economy is being renegotiated, and if political alliances are being built up and torn down accordingly, then both the causes and the effects of such macrolevel phenomena must have their microlevel counterparts in the political consciousness of individuals. If the elites, electoral and otherwise, who are contending for the ideological souls of citizen-voters in this time of transition must make their beliefs resonate with "the people," what

10. I am indebted to Don Zimmerman for pointing out the importance of intersubjectivity in this context. Also, I must offer here an attempt at ideological work that may preempt some structuralist critics. If the forms of consciousness I will be examining may be seen as "false," then what I am proposing to study is how those living within them create their phenomenological "truth." Erving Goffman introduced his book on the organization of individual experience, *Frame Analysis*, by agreeing that such a focus was tacitly conservative in that it did not address, in fact distracted attention from, social-structural concerns. But, he added, "I can only suggest that he who would combat false consciousness and awaken people to their true interests has much to do, because the sleep is very deep. And I do not intend here to provide a lullaby but merely to sneak in and watch the way people snore" (1974, 14). In lieu of such a literate disclaimer I substitute the hope of learning how individual experience is informed by and comes to affect social structure.

do "the people" make of it all? If newspaper headlines and network news stories give us day-by-day, blow-by-blow accounts of political change, and if scholars interpret its objective historical significance, what do such changes look like at the level of *lived experience*, which is where, democratic societies like to believe, all such changes originate?

A Note on Method

Having settled on this general topic area, I was faced with how to organize an investigation that might lead to worthwhile data and findings. The dominant methodological paradigm for the study of political beliefs in the social sciences— structured surveys and opinion polls of randomly selected samples—offers great breadth and generalizability. There is no equal to systematic questions asked of national probability samples for assessing short-term shifts in political attitudes and affiliations.[11] Yet such methods are deaf by definition (if not by design) to the *texture* of belief systems, to the nuance and complexity found in virtually every study that looks up close at the moving target of ideology as it exists in everyday life.

In his classic and now controversial survey of political belief systems, Phillip Converse (1964) found that contradictory beliefs and ideological inconsistencies are often the norm among most segments of the electorate, although subsequent research has shown this to be the product of how existing attitudes interact with the emerging events and conditions shaping the political environment (for example, Nie and Andersen 1974). Yet, in countless conversations about political issues, I had never met people who *thought* they held contradictory beliefs. I became intrigued by the possibility that beneath the objective inconsistencies measured in quantifiable, forced-choice survey questions there might be forms of subjective consistency that were important for grasping why people believe and act as they do. My leanings toward a qualitative approach got a push during a preliminary interview in which I asked a thirty-year-old tenant what she thought about housing problems and the rent control initiative in her city:

> I lived in Hawaii before I moved here two years ago, and landlords there were ripping people off so badly I couldn't afford to live there anymore. Since I've been here I've had two big rent increases—*after* my landlord's

11. The early exemplars of the dominant paradigm and their most sophisticated successors are Lazarsfeld, Berelson, and Gaudet (1948), Berelson, Lazarsfeld, and McPhee (1954), Campbell et al. (1964), Free and Cantril (1967), and Nie, Verba, and Petrocik (1976). For important revisionist or critical treatments of the same materials or methods, see Hamilton (1972), Wright (1976), and Gitlin (1978).

taxes were cut in half by Prop 13—and he doesn't do a damn thing to keep the place up. I'm afraid I won't be able to live here much longer either.

Q: Sounds like you'd be supportive of the upcoming rent control measure then?

No way! Absolutely not. I don't believe in those kinds of controls. It would just be wrong in this country.

As I walked away from her doorstep and down the block, growing more stunned with each step by the distance between her ideology and her material interests, it became clear to me that in addition to my interest in *what* people's political beliefs were, I wanted to know *where* they got them and *how* a response like hers was possible. This called for qualitative methods such as securing life histories and conducting depth interviews.

I have therefore drawn upon a rich and growing tradition of qualitative research on political consciousness and ideology. Although life histories and depth interviews have been used to great advantage by Chicago School sociologists since the 1920s, their use in the study of political beliefs was established by David Riesman (1952) and Robert Lane (1962). Under their close-up lenses, the ambiguities and inconsistencies uncovered in surveys took on new meaning. Lane's largely Democratic working-class men, for example, expressed only tepid support for the welfare state's egalitarian social policies, which they might have been expected to support. Because they subscribed to the American tenet that everyone is created equal, and because they felt there was enough, if not equal, opportunity, they held that each person was the master of his or her own fate. These men had little hope of climbing out of the working class, but their hard work had allowed them to live "better than their parents." Mobility was therefore perceived as possible, so the idea that others might approach their "tenuous hold on respectability" with government aid bordered on a moral affront. For these otherwise charitable men, welfare programs threatened to rob their own efforts of meaning.

The Lane lineage was extended a decade later by Sennett and Cobb (1973). In their study of working-class families in Boston, they uncovered a subtle syllogism that also had to do with the limited permeability of class lines. If success and upward mobility are possible for even some people, then those who do not succeed and move up to the middle class must be responsible for their own failures. In this way the *presumption* of dignity for all was precluded by the *possibility* of dignity for the few achievers. Although these men and women deeply resented the injustices of class society, their feelings got expressed in strange and circuitous ways and their vision of the moral economy was affected accordingly. The fact that at least some of their peers had made it led them to blame themselves for their own plight. At the phenomenological level, the only antidote they could imagine was continued sacrifice. Thus the very self-pre-scribed medication thought to heal the "hidden injuries of class" also seemed to inoculate against the appeal of state policies that might mitigate such injuries.

Using the same in-depth approach, Lamb (1974) studied ostensibly conser-vative California suburbanites. He too found political beliefs that did not make sense on the surface. Most members of the twelve families from the affluent Republican stronghold he studied were fans of the free market in principle. But unfettered urban development had encroached upon their little corner of Eden just enough to render their belief in property rights less than absolute, so they tended to favor strong land use and environmental regulations. Some aspects of the new moral economy had seeped into their otherwise conservative belief systems.

In each of these studies as in others in the qualitative tradition (for example, Wellman 1977; Botsch 1980; Berger 1981; Hochschild 1981), surprising ideo-logical patterns were both discovered and made comprehensible by seeing how beliefs originate and operate in situ. If my goal was to understand how political beliefs about state and market worked as part of lived experience in the 1980s, this was the sort of study I had to do. This approach, however, demands a small number of subjects, and as I was not attempting to draw a representative sample, I could not rely on the rules for choosing randomly. I was left with the problem of *which* handful of people to interview.

My choice of subjects was made with a very old question in mind: namely, the relationship between work and class position on the one hand, and political beliefs and behavior, on the other. Social scientists since Marx and Weber[12] have studied this issue, and no doubt others are doing so as this is being written. Indeed, it is difficult to conceive of a sociological study of ideology that does not examine beliefs in relation to work experience. I tried to combine this classical theoretical concern with my substantive interest in beliefs about the moral economy and the state-market relation. I conducted field research in an intensely

12. Social psychology has long been the Achilles heel of Marxist theory, in part because his early neo-Hegelian writings were not translated until rather recently and in part because many Marxists and most critics selectively imported from Marx's writings only his ideal-typical, di-chotomous model of false consciousness–revolutionary class consciousness. However, in his empiri-cal case studies, Marx argues that the latter develops *in the process* of class struggle and social change, and he identifies various conditions, usually tied to the labor process, that inhibit or enhance that development (for example, Marx 1967, 243–302, 1974). Weber's argument—that status groups, conceptions of honor, and styles of life all complicate and mediate the relation between class membership, consciousness, and political action—is very useful here for grasping the ways in which there is more to lived experience than labor or class position, although surely Marx, too, recognized this.

profit-oriented, private-sector business, "National Delivery Corporation," and, in the belly of the state's bureaucratic beast, in a local welfare office, "City Social Services." After enough visits to learn the lay of these lands and the casts of characters, I selected six workers from each setting for a series of depth interviews. (Like the company, the agency, and the town, the workers have been given pseudonyms to preserve their anonymity.)

Aside from asking about their life histories and work experience, I explored a wide range of questions about political principles and policy preferences, many taken from polls and surveys, and the reasoning behind their voting decisions over the past several elections. The overarching theme I hoped to get at was their sense of what may be called the *social charter*. Webster's defines *charter* as a "grant or guarantee of rights, franchises, or privileges from the sovereign power of the state." The notion of social charter thus provides a more accessible handle on what I have been calling the state-market relation and the moral economy.[13] I tried to get at their visions of what was and was not legitimate about the state vis-à-vis the market. Operationally, this meant probing their spending preferences on a variety of government programs and their support for or opposition to various forms of state regulation of the marketplace. By analyzing for each individual and group the links among life history, work experience, and political beliefs and behavior regarding the social charter, I was able to describe features of the social organization of lived experience that help account for what ideologies resonate and why and how beliefs take hold and get tailored, used, and changed to suit the shifting personal circumstances of their holders in the shifting political circumstances of the 1980s.

What can a mere dozen people (and from California!) tell us about political-economic matters? If it is not enough to cite the great insights of Riesman, Lane, and the many others who have followed in their methodological footsteps by garnering a mass of data on a minuscule number of subjects, and if those skeptics of quantitative bent remain unsatisfied after reading that my purpose is to *explore* rather than to test this or that hypothesis or to prove a theory, what can be said? I am not comfortable simply asserting the authority of Margaret Mead (1953, 41–49), who argued that a sample of one will do because all individuals are socialized in terms of their specific culture and thus reflect it; although this is

13. I have borrowed heavily here (and more generally for purposes of defining my problematic) from the works of Richard Flacks (1976, forthcoming). He argues that a "cultural charter" exists in which indiviudals exchange role conformity in the sphere of work for the economic security afforded by a steady job at decent wages. The ends of this exchange, however, are free space and a private life in which one's projects are one's own. While this charter, like my social charter, is nowhere written, the tacit rights and expectations that compose it have been central to the legitimacy of the U.S. political economic system throughout the postwar era. In this light, commitments to private life have a political dimension, and people's perceptions of state and market take on substantive significance.

true, each sample of one offers its own unique reflection. In fact, I feel shy about using the term *sample* at all, for as my friend Donald Cressey reminded me, "You don't have a sample, you've got a bunch. Call them 'a bunch.'"

No pretense of traditional representativeness or generalizability is implied in this book (although I frequently could not avoid the temptation of contrasting the ideas of my subjects with those found in national surveys and polls). It should be apparent to readers, however, when my subjects' views of the social charter are shared by millions of others and when they are anomalous. And because the dozen Americans described below *are* part of a common political culture, both the variations of belief among them and the concerns they share *can* tell us something of value, even if the magnitude of this something among larger collectivities cannot be known without doing additional and very different sorts of research.

Though qualitative researchers pay a steep price in lost generalizability, they get something in return. The particular, idiosyncratic, and local facets of opinions, as well as much of their subjective meaning, are either lost or glossed in large representative samples, whereas these are precisely what qualitative studies bring to center stage. "To an ethnographer," Clifford Geertz has written, "the shapes of knowledge are always ineluctably local, indivisible from their instruments and their encasements. One may veil this fact with ecumenical rhetoric or blur it with strenuous theory, but one cannot really make it go away" (1983, 4).

In what follows, I have attempted to render the localness of political beliefs—in all their fractal shapes, their stitches and jagged edges showing. My analysis elicits from a small number of subjects a different sort of representativeness through the greater richness of detail of what little *is* observed: the sort of representativeness possible only through ongoing comparisons, constant searches for the negative case, continuous revision of the hypotheses generated, and attention to quibbling qualifications and subtle variations (Glaser and Strauss 1967; Katz 1982). This method, too, then, is capable of identifying links between the local and the world beyond it. It is capable, if used well, of providing what Howard Becker (1970) has called a touchstone for theories grand and otherwise—capable, that is, of showing us how well our abstract ideas about social life work in accounting for concrete social lives. It is for these reasons that "soft" research on small groups of subjects has its place in the scientific mosaic.

Whether this book lives up to such claims is another matter. In chapters 2 and 3, a workplace niche in the market world is described by its workers. One is a former 1960s radical who makes it a point of pride never to vote and who is among the most "procompany" of her coworkers; another is an extreme right-wing born-again Christian who voted against Reagan in 1984 for selling out the conservative cause and whose scathing critique of the corporate profit motive has led him to embrace workplace democracy. In chapters 5 and 6, a public-sector welfare office is described, and six of its workers are introduced. Among them are a left-wing democratic socialist union leader who favors increased spending for law enforcement and prisons and a yuppie landlord who voted against the Proposition 13 property tax cut and for rent control. If my attempt at "thick description" (Geertz 1973) has been successful, such seeming oddities and what they may imply about political life in the 1980s will be comprehensible.

I have attempted through the use of a reflexive (confessional?) style and the first person singular to let readers in on why I chose to describe what I do and to help distinguish that description from the analyses and inferences I have drawn from it. If my interpretations wander from the points of view of my subjects, their own words can provide a check on how far and in what direction I stray. This approach is based on *my* belief that the only road approaching scientific objectivity is the one passing explicitly through the scientific traveler's subjectivity. To be sure, this is a work of sociological impressionism. But I have tried to make my brush strokes clear so that others will at least be able to see that *I* have made them. This way critics may charge me with poor painting but not forged photography.

2

National Delivery Corporation: Paragon of Productivity

ONE of the most striking aspects of recent political change in the United States has been the erosion of working-class support for the Democratic party. Although there were signs of such shifting loyalties in Nixon's victories over Humphrey in 1968 and McGovern in 1972, the stigma of the Watergate scandals seemed to stem the Republican tide. By 1980, however, it was clear that the defection of many traditionally Democratic workers was a decisive factor in Reagan's win over Carter. Despite a sophisticated national campaign by the AFL-CIO in 1984, exit polls showed that a majority of blue-collar voters helped Reagan win a second term. Even among union households, labor's candidate Mondale edged the unabashedly probusiness conservative Reagan by a slim 52 percent to 48 percent, a margin narrower than Carter's four years earlier. Reagan's claim to a landslide and thus to a laissez-faire mandate was made possible in large part by union workers who had supported Democratic presidential candidates by 20 to 30 percent margins since the New Deal.[1]

The field research reported in this chapter began in 1979, when many of these trends first gained momentum. The success of California's tax revolt was interpreted, at least by its proponents, as clear evidence of a backlash against the welfare state and government in general. The Democrats' traditional coalition of constituencies increasingly seemed in disarray under Carter. The rise of the New

---

1. "Long-Range Hopes for Republicans Found in Poll: No Sure Policy Mandate," *New York Times*, November 11, 1984; G. Gallup, "Dramatic Changes in Voting Pattern," *Los Angeles Times*, November 9, 1984.

Right and the so-called shift to conservatism were everywhere in the news. I set out to find a private-sector company likely to employ the sorts of unionized, high-wage workers said to be swirling in this ideological vortex. If my goal was to learn something of changing beliefs about state and market, such workers could well be ideal teachers.

While complaining to friends next door about the difficulties of finding such a business and getting to know its workers, it dawned on me that these very neighbors had made me privy to years of shop talk about and deliciously detailed portraits of the cast of characters who worked with them at the local branch of the National Delivery Corporation (NDC). I had learned that NDC was a staunchly capitalist enterprise in competition with the U.S. Postal Service and that its employees were hard-working, well-paid members of a large conservative union. Thus, NDC seemed as good a site as any for my research purposes, and my friends could provide me with background information, access to the NDC center, and introductions to a pool of potential interview subjects.

Between 1979 and 1984, I made field observations and conducted a series of depth interviews with six NDC workers.[2] Their life histories, political beliefs, and voting decisions are presented as individual case studies in the next chapter. This chapter introduces NDC and the industry in which it is situated and provides an ethnographic sketch of the Santa Theresa center and what its work looked like to six of the people who did it. I begin with the workplace not just because my subjects spent half their waking hours there making a living nor just because work has been given such significance in theories of class and consciousness but because it was there that I first came to know them.

For most of the years since World War II, NDC has enjoyed a near monopoly on the shipping of small parcels. Interstate Commerce Commission regulations stipulate that companies like NDC may ship packages of less than fifty pounds anywhere in the United States, but no more than a total of one hundred pounds per day to any one consignee. They are required to serve the general public, although it is well known within the company that they lose money on individual packages. Their bread and butter is small-business shipping. For a fee of two dollars per week plus normal shipping charges, NDC will make daily pickups as well as deliveries to any business within service areas that now include even most small cities in the country.

2. The initial formal interviews were conducted in the subjects' homes during the course of 1980 and 1981, with the NDC workers interviewed first and the public-sector welfare workers second. For each of the twelve respondents, approximately two hours were spent on life history and work experience, and another two hours on political beliefs and public spending and policy preferences. These interviews were tape recorded and transcribed. Follow-up telephone interviews on specific voting decisions and developments in their respective workplaces were conducted just after the elections of 1982 and 1984.

Because of the unique nature of its services and its management system, NDC has prospered. "Every package the guest of honor" is the corporate motto, one that workers read as an implicit attempt to play upon anxieties about the punctuality and safety of the postal service. The company guarantees a specific delivery date, usually one day for local, two days for intrastate, and about five days for cross-country deliveries. Although a national company with considerable assets, its stock is held privately by the original owner and by management personnel to whom it is given as part of a bonus plan. The more profitable a manager's center and the longer he or she stays with the firm, the more shares the manager will earn.

The firm's history of stable profitability and growth has been disrupted recently by changing political-economic circumstances. Recessions in the late 1970s and early 1980s depressed shipping volume, and deregulation—started under Carter and accelerated by Reagan—hastened the entry of competitors into the field. For example, eight thousand new trucking companies were chartered and two hundred others went bankrupt in the first eighteen months of deregulation. Yet, total truck tonnage in 1981 was down owing to slack demand in autos, housing, and related industries. When volume drops in an industry with such relatively high fixed costs, profits are squeezed. The industry suffered a shakeout: with demand dropping and competition climbing, rate wars began to force smaller and weaker firms under or into the arms of larger, more modern, and better capitalized operations—a process Schumpeter (1942) identified as capitalism's tendency to undergo periodic "gales of creative destruction." Further, several major airlines and large corporations entered the burgeoning air freight industry, offering overnight delivery of parcels and heightening competition. By the fall of 1984, the industry's ideological affinity for deregulation and a freer market had been tempered by its interest in a stable market, and its national association quietly began lobbying Congress for *reregulation* of new entrants and freight rates in the hope of curbing price wars.[3]

Transport workers faced their own difficulties. Union membership has dropped nearly one-third since the mid-1970s. More than 100,000 union members were unemployed in 1981, and the industry association asked to reopen contract talks to negotiate concessions like lower wage rates and relaxed work rules. Ironically, the union's ability to resist present industry demands had been undermined by its past success. Their national contracts traditionally had

3. "Hard Times for Truckers," *New York Times*, January 27, 1983; D. Moberg, "Recession a Third Party to Contract Talks in Trucking," *In These Times*, November 18–24, 1981; "UPS Delivers a Challenge," *New York Times*, September 25, 1982; "The 2-Tiered Wage System Is Damaging," *New York Times*, September 14, 1984; "To Regulate, to Deregulate, or, Now, to Reregulate," *New York Times*, October 29, 1984.

won high wages in part by agreeing to constrict members' grievance rights over local workplace issues. Thus, as in other large industries, the union's national power in contract years tended to reduce its day-to-day presence on the shop floor, to the detriment of rank-and-file esprit de corps.

In the spring 1983 contract talks, the industry association claimed that in the new economic environment small firms could be bankrupted by the usual increases, and union leaders knew this could cost them jobs and members as well as further concentration of the industry within the biggest firms. Yet, because the union's legitimacy had come to rest upon successive wage and benefit increases, any concessions entailed the heretofore rare risk of member discontent. The draft contract was a gamble: modest raises for current workers and sharp cuts for new workers, part-timers, and unemployed members called back to work. For the first time in decades, the membership overwhelmingly voted down their leaders' proposal.[4]

The company made two responses to these new circumstances. First, to stave off competition and preserve its market share, it entered the air freight business in late 1982. Relying on its long-standing reputation for reliable service and its existing network of local delivery centers, NDC began to offer reduced-price air delivery. Second, management took steps to increase worker productivity in a system already known for its high productivity. In addition to its own efficiency experts, the company retained consulting industrial engineers to conduct time-and-motion studies on every aspect of operations. The objective was to increase efficiency by computerizing route design and paperwork and reducing the standard times allotted for a given number of stops and parcels. The latter production changes in particular had a marked impact on the workers I met.

The NDC center in Santa Teresa is located just off the main north-south freeway in a suburban industrial district, ensconced between a medical equipment plant and the central post office, which backs up on a shopping center and low-income housing. It is a three-hundred-foot-long warehouse made of corrugated aluminum with four huge garage doors along either side. Behind each door sit three trucks so close together that their rearview mirrors have to be pulled in before parking. All trucks back up to the main artery of the plant, a four-foot-wide conveyor belt that runs the length of the building. Feeder trucks, the large

---

4. After members voted nine to one against the proposed two-tier contract, one union official noted, "You can be sure we won't do that again" (Paul Shinoff, "Unions' Major Shift on Two-Tier Pay: Some Who Accepted It in Pacts Now Are Sorry," *San Francisco Examiner*, March 17, 1985). The lesson was apparently short-lived; the terms of the subsequent tentative contract called for a similar two-tiered scale under which new workers would be paid 30 percent less than veterans ("Teamsters Pact Calls for Lower Starting Wage," *San Francisco Chronicle*, April 4, 1984).

tractor-trailers that carry all packages from regional centers to local ones, back up at one end of the belt. Their contents are emptied each night by off-loaders who wrestle the large and pitch the small parcels onto the humming belt. On-loaders then place ten of these packages per minute into the empty delivery trucks for the next day's runs.

The center also contains a drop-off counter for shippers, two small window-less offices for clerks and managers, a mechanics bay, and a locker room upstairs where workers gather before their 8:30 A.M. departures and where many stop briefly from 5:30 to 7:30 P.M. on their way home. The only occasion when workers are assembled in one place, the morning locker room ritual, is the scene of incessant joking and equally incessant complaining about the pressures of the job. Despite typically long hours, many of the workers arrive early in order to get ready slowly; as Margaret, a clerk, explained, "You need that time for mental preparation."

The work force at this NDC center consists of some two dozen drivers, about ten loaders, a half-dozen clerks who keep the books and handle faulty addresses and "send-agains," four utility workers who wash, gas, and help load and drive the trucks, and five supervisors and managers. These local managers are supple-mented by roving regional managers, auditors, and industrial engineers who make unannounced visits to all centers. "You can always spot 'em," a utility worker told me. "They're the ones with the briefcases and ties."

Most packages are picked up by drivers from regular shipping customers, although a few are brought to the center by "walk-ins." Each has an identifying number on its address label corresponding to the shipper's receipt. These num-bers are recorded by drivers on tally sheets where receiving customers sign for each package. If the addressee is not home, the drivers are supposed to try a neighbor. If the package is still undeliverable, a notice is left stating when a second attempt will be made.

What energizes these procedures is an incentive system, the defining feature of the NDC work process. The union contract guarantees full-time employees eight hours of work per day, but all routes are designed to take longer. Each route has a standard time computed by a complex formula that weighs the number of miles, stops, and parcels. Drivers earn time-and-a-half for all work beyond eight hours, but they are paid an incentive bonus—slightly higher than what they would earn in overtime—if they "break standard." The greater number of "tenths" (six minutes, or one-tenth of an hour) by which they break standard, the greater the incentive pay. "Beating standard" is the name of the game at NDC for two reasons. First, not only do their weekly paychecks show immediate results when they do beat standard, but their leisure time—par-ticularly valued given their long hours and high pay—also increases. Second, if they fail to beat standard more than occasionally, they face a pink slip, or warning from management. This carrot-and-stick incentive system is an ingenious managerial strategy. The firm offers high pay and benefits but in return gets the pressured pace and high productivity behind its history of steady profits. Although the contract specifies wages of fourteen dollars an hour, the incentive system in effect transforms hourly workers into individual entrepreneurs in a piecework system. They get extra pay *and* extra leisure in return for speed, so any tendency to gravitate toward their own pace, secure in the knowledge that they will be paid for however long the job takes, is mitigated if not extinguished.

On one of my early visits to the Santa Theresa center I saw a driver back his truck into its stall at the end of the day, grab his clipboard, and run to the time clock. He punched out and then walked back toward his truck, completing paperwork in what seemed a leisurely fashion. This surprised me. It was after 6:00 P.M. Why would this man *run* to punch out? Stranger still, why would he do so *before* finishing his paperwork? I asked Tori, the clerk in charge of "send-agains," why he had done this. She explained, in a tone suggesting that the answer should be obvious, that under the incentive system, beating standard was preferable to the twenty minutes of overtime he would have gotten had he waited to punch out until he was fully done. In subsequent visits I came to learn why behavior that appeared bizarre to me was seen as normal by the NDC natives. "Everything is percentages here—boxes per minute, you know; it's a real high-pressure job," said Joe Demski, a late-shift utility man who had been there five years. His coworker, Greg Larson, chimed in that NDC management finds it "cheaper to work the same twenty-four men to death than to hire additional drivers." In a later interview, Larson said that in his eighteen years at NDC this had always been the case:

> They're always down one, and generally two men. . . . They're doing it on purpose . . . [because] there's a certain bonus for the station manager if he can keep costs down. So it's cheaper to pay me overtime, all of us overtime, than to hire a person and have to pay his insurance and all that.

This strategy of using overtime to contain costs added to the pressures of the incentive system. Standard times included some overtime because virtually all routes were designed to take more than eight hours. Yet all drivers interviewed agreed that unless they wanted to spend ten or eleven hours on the road, they had to cut down or eliminate coffee and lunch breaks. By so doing, they could usually beat standard, earn bonus pay, and get home earlier. Drivers took great care on light days, however, to pace themselves so they never broke standard by too much, lest they invite the attention of management's computer. They believed that any sustained pattern of beating standard comfortably would ensure added work. This was the delicate balance drivers strained to strike. According to Larson, everyone disliked the pace and pressure inherent in this system:

> The other day one of the guys was saying, "My gosh, I worked all day, didn't stop for coffee, didn't stop for lunch, had like two hundred stops, maybe three hundred boxes, and I beat standard by three tenths," which is eighteen minutes. Now if you don't take [breaks] and you still don't beat your route by more than eighteen minutes, something's wrong. . . . You'd kill the company if you did it by the book. I'm debating about starting to take a lunch, but I'm afraid if I do that they'll switch my route around and I'll be right back where I started from.
>
> Q: Why would anyone not take a lunch break they had coming in order to work fewer hours?
>
> Well, that's kind of common knowledge. Everybody's into free time now; rather have off than work, you know? Nothin' they'd rather be doing, just being off. They'd all love to have three-day weekends and take a cut in money, or work a ten-hour day. . . . Even myself, I look at it sometimes and say, "Boy, what a bunch of idiots we are. We're the only company I've ever seen that works like this. The meanest sweatshop in town, they still stop and take their coffee, their lunch," you know? And here we are, supposedly a very respectable high-paid job, and we're worse than a bunch of laborers out in the field . . . the way we work. Crazy. I hate this job. . . . I'm overworked, which may sound trite or made up, but you know, I've been working until 7:00 or 7:30 at night—no coffee, no lunch, just startin' at 8:30 in the mornin' and punch[ing] out at 7:00 or 7:30—and that's going all day. The work doesn't kill me. I mean I can do the work. But the problem is, when I get home at 7:30 my kids are in bed, so I don't even see the kids now. And *that* really bothers me, you know? That's no way to live.

Although Greg's thoughts captured the main theme of his coworkers' complaints, there were variations. Sally Jones, a clerk who had worked at the center five years, had few complaints, prided herself on being "a good employee," and wanted more responsibilities that would challenge her "creativity." Unlike the others, she felt that management respected her, and she found the pressure stimulating. She felt she was "cheating the company" unless she was always working hard. Sally was atypical in this regard, however, and had a reputation for being excessively gung ho.

José Bustamante was a veteran driver who agreed with most of the others that there were problems with the NDC pace. He had developed his own solutions, however:

You can take your breaks if you want, no matter what. If you're too rushed, then there's gotta be something wrong with that route, right? . . . If you feel you're being rushed too much, you know, that guy should go and discuss this with the manager. Otherwise, the supervisor's not going to take any work off that guy because he's *doin'* it. They've tried to put some [extra work] on me, and if I feel it's more than I can handle, I'll tell them. 'Cause they know, they know already; I told them, "I don't want any extra—I feel my route is sufficient enough for me to make a good living. I'll help you out if you're really in a bind."

It's entirely up to the guy if he doesn't want to take his lunch, and when they say they can't take [it], it's because they don't want to. Not saying anything against the guys, you know, but I'm gonna take my breaks, I don't care, because if I didn't and came in early, [management] would say, "Wow, he could probably handle more work." If you don't take advantage of what they give you, they're gonna take advantage of you. . . .

There's three of us at work, we try to tell these people, "If you don't take [breaks], if you keep *doin'* what they give you all the time, they're just gonna stay with it and nothin's gonna change. But if you stop and take your coffee breaks, take your lunch break like you're supposed to be doin', they're gonna see you can only do so much in a certain time.

One of those who took his allotted breaks and often complained to management about extra hours was Buford Schmitt, the oldest of the drivers. He had been at NDC over twenty years. Like the others, Buford identified long hours as the biggest problem with his job, but his analysis of it moved beyond Greg Larson's:

Now, some guys want long hours, and I mentioned it to the manager the other day. I said, "I think it's a real crime to get a man adjusting his budget to a certain pay scale which is a false pay scale because of him [working overtime]. . . . And he has to stay on it because he may get himself into debt or his living standard be higher than it should be. So consequently he has to keep himself on that [pay scale], and when he gets older and he doesn't physically have the time, [it's] hard. Plus the fact that [overtime] is keeping him away from his family." Now, the purpose of a job is to bring in an income so that a man can do the things he wants to do. But I feel our company thinks that the purpose of a job is to bring in an income for the company. There's a conflict there, and I think the company ignores the man's personal life. . . . They want your complete allegiance. I think they want the man's allegiance to come before his family. I've seen it so many times. I've even told the manager that. I said, "You're puttin' this job before your family." And he said, "Well, I choose to do that. Later on I might be able to give them things." I said, "You're robbin' your family of time they should have now, your kids, when they're growin' up."

Implicit in such remarks are assertions about priorities. Union contracts and corporate policies notwithstanding, each of these men asserted the idea that people should *work in order to live, not live in order to work.* In their view, NDC was constantly on the verge of violating those unwritten rules that afforded them adequate private time to enjoy their earnings. Although most of them expressed no desire to leave NDC because of such infringements, most did agree with Greg—"something's wrong."

For two centuries Americans have repeated Ben Franklin's adage, "time is money." This remnant of the Protestant ethic has remained part of our culture as an unquestioned truism in corporate boardrooms and working-class taverns alike. Parents still use the saying to teach their children "good work habits." American tourists often are surprised to learn that in Europe and Latin America, many shops close at midday while workers and proprietors take long lunches and short naps.

What was striking about the NDC workers' comments about their jobs was the way they deviated from Franklin's aphorism. These men typically resented management practices that demanded more of their time, despite what they admitted was adequate recompense. Because they were relatively well paid and valued the joys of family life, the marginal utility of increased income paled in comparison to additional free time. Their priorities tended to stand Franklin's logic on its head—for them, "money was time."[5] They did not value free time as a symbol of status, as Veblen argued was the case with "vicarious leisure" and "conspicuous consumption" at the turn of the century. Given their long and pressure-packed work hours, leisure seemed less a means of esteem than an end in itself. The notion that money is time does have broader significance, however, insofar as it is emblematic of what Daniel Bell has called a core contradiction of capitalist culture: that Americans daily are expected to labor long and defer gratification in the work sphere *and* to indulge themselves with immediate gratification in the sphere of consumption. Indeed, the viability of our market economy has come to depend upon the ability of worker-consumers to juggle both these ethics in everyday life. But, at least for most NDC workers, the combination of hard work and high wages led them to place greater weight on leisure and comsumption.[6]

Complaints about the pressure at NDC may have been particularly acute

5. I am indebted to Professor Donald R. Cressey for this insight; personal communication, June 8, 1983.

6. See Thorstein Veblen (1899). Bell's analysis of such conflicts begins in Daniel Bell, *The Coming of Post-Industrial Society* (1973), and is fully elaborated in his later work (1976, especially pp. 54–84). An important contrasting analysis of such contradictions may be found in Stanley Aronowitz, *False Promises: The Shaping of American Working Class Consciousness* (1973, 51–133, 398–442).

during my fieldwork because the company had just implemented a new computer system. Rudi Ventura, a driver for three years, mentioned this as soon as I asked him how he liked his job:

> It stinks. It's the best paying job I've ever had, and that's the only reason I stay. That's the only reason people stay. If you paid 'em two dollars an hour less, 30 percent of the people would quit. . . . The company knows that by payin' these people high, one, it saves them money [because that way NDC] doesn't have a turnover rate; and, two, it forces [us] to work harder because they threaten you with your job. . . .
>
> They've got a computerized standard sheet now. You don't break standard this time, they pink-slip you if you don't break it again. If you do it again, you're fired. They can screw you around if you're not puttin' out, . . . kiss you with more work until you either quit or they find something they can fire you for. . . . Old-timers'll tell you. Like Buford Schmitt, they say, "Shit man, young drivers are gonna be bustin' their asses four or five hours a day more than I ever worked in a day." And I have a feeling NDC doesn't *want* drivers to last twenty or twenty-five years so they can get retirement. They want 'em in for five, six years and out.

Although Rudi "used to beat standard by an hour, hour and a half," under the new system he had to work extra hard, taking only "two quick breaks and a twenty-minute lunch . . . all I can afford," just to meet standard. He had complained to management but had seen no letup and feared that his file was becoming filled with "incriminating" information.

José Bustamante had a different attitude toward his job. He said it was the best he had had, although he too noted that something was wrong with the NDC organization and that the new computer system had made matters worse:

> OK, right now we're changing to a computer payroll. Before, the fifteen years I've been there, the guy would do the payroll here. . . . Now we're just turning in our time card, [and] you gotta make sure it's legible or they take it right back out . . . and you better have the right numbers on the amount of packages and stuff or else you're gonna lose out one way or the other. . . . That's why you see basically most of the guys hustling around quite a bit, because you know you've got ten hours or more in that truck almost every day, and who wants to stay out ten hours?

Greg Larson echoed these themes and claimed that he had heard similar complaints in the locker room. The incentive system, for Greg, "used to be great," but changes other than the computer system had turned a good thing bad:

> When I first started, we'd go like crazy, but we'd be through at three or four o'clock and we made good money. Now they've cut the incentive down.

. . . They gave us all time studies where these people from L.A. come and ride around with us and time [us] to figure standard. And they just turned around and told us, "OK, we're gonna cut your hours back one hour." No rhyme or reason for it, they just took away an hour from everybody. Oh, they had reasons, but you couldn't *understand* them, and *they* couldn't understand them if you pushed 'em hard enough. We were pretty much up in arms, . . . but you gotta realize that you're not going to get anywhere if you complain. That's the way the company is set up. . . . You can go in and argue with your supervisor, and nothin', or . . . your manager, and nothin'. And you never get any further than that. You know, they stick together because if this guy looks bad, it makes the [other guy] look bad, right on up the line.

Greg described what assembly-line workers might call a speedup. The blend of work load and pace that NDC workers had come to see as traditional, albeit heavy, had been accelerated a few notches. The number of stops and packages on a given route had increased, while the number of drivers had been held to "one or two less than they need to do the job right." The new, lower standard times were presented as faits accomplis by "the I-E guys," the industrial engineers. The drivers were "never consulted" about the design of the studies that were to define their work routines. Nor were the findings explained so that drivers got procedural suggestions on how to raise productivity to match the new times. Greg's phrase, "just took away an hour from everybody," seemed to have literal significance. Moreover, since everyone I spoke with at NDC felt that they already worked more than hard enough for their pay, it seemed likely that some of their resentment of the speedup stemmed from the implication that there was an hour of "fat" in their workdays. Whereas Greg Larson saw this acceleration as exploitation, Buford Schmitt's critique centered on the erosion of the quality of NDC service:

[Management] ought to consult with [drivers] more. It used to be they'd work with the drivers . . . working the routes out. Now, they just had some changes [where] they got a map—and they don't know the difference between Highway 405 and a cow path—and they have you goin' down the cow path at sixty miles an hour. . . . That's what they're basing their decision on. . . . A map doesn't show them what the traffic flow is at the time of day. The *drivers* pick that up from experience.

Businessmen, they expect something a certain time of day so they can process it that day. And if they get it [delivered] at 4:00 P.M., quitting time, why it's like getting it the next morning. Now what used to be nice about [the job] compared to what it is now is that you were more sure of what you were doin'. I [used to know] what I had in my truck and where I was going.

And now they have somebody else load them. . . . [Packages are] supposed to be in order, but they never are. . . . You don't have that relaxed feeling of knowin' what you're doin'. Used to be, before, you could really go like a house-a-fire, but now you can't do it. They claimed [the changes] would give them more profit. That's basically what motivates them, the profit motive. And I think they're sacrificing service for it, which is sad. Used to be we'd emphasize our service . . . the epitome of our job was our service. But now it seems to be profit. . . . If the truth was out, I don't think we deserve [our] reputation [for service] any more.

Thus, the computerized speedup, according to Buford and the others, may have boosted company profits, but in the bargain it had lowered the quality of service, the workers' sense of craft, and their pride.[7]

The importance these men placed on providing a high-quality service largely escaped me until the later depth interviews. A humility ran through their talk about their jobs; the work was demanding and well paying, but seemed to require few skills and offer little status. Yet each struggled shyly to convey the notion that although the work was neither glamorous nor complex, it was well done. They enjoyed the daily contact with their customers in part because they felt their service was appreciated as safe and reliable. This idea came across, for example, when I asked Greg what was most important to him in a job: "I guess my self-respect while I'm doin' it; actually doin' somethin' in a good way, providing a service." This theme also seemed clear in Buford's lament that the speedup entailed a trade-off of service for profits, which he felt had tarnished both his sense of craft and NDC's reputation. Such remarks suggest that labor, even if alienated, has dignity, and that those who provide it, even if they feel exploited, draw a sense of integrity from so doing.

The recent changes had disrupted work routines, increased work loads, and shook their belief in the quality of their service. The "I-E guys" whose work was the science of speedups were people to "watch out" for. With every move being scrutinized for inefficiency, NDC workers feared that the tricks of the trade they had culled from experience were at risk. The sub rosa science of knowing the alleys, knowing when to avoid downtown and the freeway, where one could double park and get away with it—nuggets of knowledge that had allowed them to beat standard *and* provide quality service—was vulnerable. Time studies and

7. On the erosion of the "instinct of workmanship" under the market system, see Veblen (1904), Braverman (1974), and Edwards (1979). The latter two works make compelling arguments that scientific management under large corporations has rendered strategies for profitability fundamentally dependent upon the power to reorganize the labor process so as to minimize skill requirements. Cf. Michael Burawoy (1979).

computerized routes threatened the tactics these workers had developed to manage their tasks. They feared that such unofficial efficiencies, if discovered, would be used against them as black marks in their files or as grounds for lower standard times.

What does all this have to do with political beliefs and behavior? According to sociological theory, one's work role, market position, relationship to the means of production, and relative powerlessness and alienation all influence political consciousness. Surely one's work experience has some bearing upon how one understands and acts upon the world. At NDC, complaints about the system and the speedup were voiced by virtually every worker I met. Yet, aside from the little surreptitious steps taken to conceal shortcuts and the locker room banter about the evils of management, I could discern few signs of worker opposition. Leaving aside for the moment questions about politics in general and focusing solely on the workplace, I still had to wonder: if there was such widespread discontent and if pressures were worsening, what prevented the workers from staging *some* form of organized protest? If human actions are caused, then what appears to be *inaction* also must have its causes.

There were at least three factors found in NDC workers' accounts that help explain this absence of overt opposition. The first concerns what I will call the NDC work ethic. Everyone who worked at NDC had it tough. Amid their list of dissatisfactions, both Greg and Buford noted that even supervisors had more work than they could do. "Management's hours are longer than mine," Greg said, one reason he had never sought a promotion. On all levels NDC was so organized that there was always a shortage of workers and an abundance of work, so everyone knew that if they did not pull their weight someone else would have an extra load. There was just "no leeway," as Joe Demski put it when explaining why his conscience prevented him from taking sick days even when he was sick. Almost everyone felt empathy and loyalty to coworkers, which they knew worked against them; to resist the work facing them was to burden others unfairly.

In addition to the machismo often characteristic of blue-collar jobs requiring strength and hustle, the NDC system engendered an ethic that minimized complaints. Just as the convict code in prisons contains moral rules like "do your own time" and "never snivel,"[8] so NDC workers abided by a code: "only pussies complain" and "hold up your end." These values could not be attributed to male bravado alone because women workers also held them and because they were drawn as much from cooperative impulses as competitive ones. Demski captured a related element of this ethic when describing how NDC workers' mere perseverance under such working conditions was something of an accomplishment:

8. See Irwin and Cressey (1962), and Irwin (1970).

I'm sort of thinking about men in society, how they're oppressed, you know? Women are certainly oppressed, but men are oppressed too. . . . Maybe in my lifetime we're gonna see men deal with their oppression, but we won't see it happen [soon] because what oppresses them ultimately supports them also, gives them some sort of reason for living. So if you're pressured, man, you're out there running your ass off, high pressure, to come back, well, you draw some strength from that. You tend to say, "Gee, I'm back. I worked my ass off today and I did a good job. I'm the breadwinner, I'm the man." But at the same time it's oppressing these people, you know? They're having heart problems; they're useless at the end of the day, you know?

Demski's insight suggests and shades into a second factor militating against protest, the often opaque gratifications NDC drivers wrested from their work. That they could take the pressure without complaining and devise ways of doing eleven hours' work in nine hours was a source of self-esteem. They claimed they were never praised by management and had only an empty truck and a sore back to show for their labor at day's end. But their "I can handle it" stance afforded them at least a dignified edge over what they saw as plodding postal workers, their competition. (Several drivers volunteered the idea that postal workers tended to be indifferent to either the quality or the quantity of their work because, in contrast to the market in which NDC had to compete, "if they don't make it, they just get another subsidy.")

Beyond the satisfactions stemming from what they endured, there were aspects of the work they enjoyed. Buford Schmitt liked "coming into contact with the people, being outside, and, to a certain extent, you're your own boss when you're out there deliverin'." Other drivers sounded the same themes. José Bustamante liked "just being out, especially around here . . . and I make a good living at it. I don't think I could handle a job being inside." Rudi Ventura, whose first words about his job were "it stinks," thoroughly enjoyed

dealing with the public, my customers. . . . Ninety-nine percent of them are just really neat people, and I like the fact that I am basically my own company when I get out there. There's no boss over my shoulder. I'm out there on my own, you know? I see the boss in the morning for fifteen minutes and I see him for fifteen, twenty minutes when I get in, and that's it. That's what I like about it. And I like outdoor work. Can't stand desk jobs, inside jobs.

Being outdoors amid beautiful scenery, freedom from scrutiny by supervisors, and the brisk variety of human contact and repartee afforded by two hundred stops seemed to provide significant counterweight to their discontents. To have gotten through a day at NDC was success; to have found things to enjoy en route was something of a victory.

A third feature of work life at NDC that augered against organized discontent was the individualized character of social relations. All drivers and most other workers carried out their tasks independently. The extent to which drivers could beat standard was not dependent upon others. The system gave them every incentive to rush through their routes and leave their work problems at work.[9] Such individualization was reinforced by the nonparticipatory nature of their relations with union and management. Work procedures were dictated by management, despite the fact that everyone seemed to have specific and strongly held ideas on how matters might be both more productive and fairer. Although there appeared to be many problems and little hesitance to speak up about them, this always took the form of a brief encounter between a given driver and his or her supervisor—encounters that, I was told repeatedly, led "nowhere."

The principal role of the union at NDC was to negotiate the high wages and benefits that would ensure comfortable private lives; thus, workers' only institutional power served as a collective means to individual ends. Any union consciousness regarding rights to breaks or maximum work loads was tempered by the incentive system in which the drivers earned enough to make the accumulation of leisure capital their top priority. The union presence, then, did not alter the atomized adversarial relations between workers and management. Union issues were rarely even part of shop talk. Workers often credited the union for their "excellent" wages but were quick to point out that the national contract that made them possible also precluded the union's usefulness for other issues. Grievance procedures, for example, were cumbersome and circumscribed at the local level, and the power of management was absolute on all issues concerning working conditions. Union meetings were rare and sparsely attended. According to Margaret, the "money clerk," only a few old-timers went, "mostly to get out of the house" and "have a beer." At one of the few meetings she attended, her naive request for a vote on a minor contract issue brought gales of laughter from the veterans, who understood that the purpose of local union meetings was to hear the officers report on what had already been done. Not even strikes were voted on. Buford Schmitt recalled a strike in the early 1970s: "We didn't have any choice in the matter. I would've voted not to strike [but it] didn't matter. All of a sudden they called down from L.A. and said, 'Hey we're on strike, go outside and picket.'"

Even if their relations with the union and the company *did* offer some democratic participation and control at the local level, I doubt that many would

9. For an empirical analysis of how many production systems manufacture workers' consent along with consumer commodities, see Burawoy (1979). This study focuses on industrial work organization in manufacturing, but his logic is useful for service industries as well. For a broader theoretical synthesis of these processes, see O'Connor (1984, 149–87).

have embraced the opportunity. Most seemed to agree with Rudi Ventura that "you can't fight the company" and expressed similar futility about a union they saw as huge, distant, and corrupt. Their perceived powerlessness seemed well founded. Moreover, workers who "busted ass" for nine or ten hours a day to make "real good money" were unlikely to spend their remaining energy and time searching for ways to alter that perception.[10]

Resistant Allegiance

Watching a driver make a delivery, the unit of production at NDC, I was struck by the grace and economy of movement that, to the unschooled eye, are camouflaged by the rapidity of the routine. The truck pulls abruptly to a spot on the curb. In what appears a single motion, the driver sets the emergency brake, shuts off the engine, grabs clipboard with one hand, parcel with the other, and with a minimum number of steps reaches the door. His greeting is warm but designed to get a scribbled signature on the right line in a short time. Climbing back into the truck, keys at the ready, he starts the engine and shifts into first with right hand while the left releases the brake. He is off again in a total of eighty seconds, already scheming (I thought) to make the next stop shorter still. These were a few of the intricacies composing the choreography these workers masked with shorthand phrases like "hustle" and "bustin' ass."

What was ironic about the physical and mental creativity entailed here was that it was both part of the pressured pace they bemoaned and a mode of resistance to it. By such hustle, they avoided the stick of management's pink slips and garnered the carrots of bonus pay and free time. Through the managerial magic of this incentive system, the contradiction between the workers' goals of pay and leisure and the company's goal of productivity ostensibly disappeared. Yet, to judge by the workers' descriptions, such coincidence of interests was illusory. The scent of resentment and resistance permeated their tales. José made it a point to *begin* his route with a *full* coffee break, his way of letting management know how much they could and could not expect. During a late-night visit to the center I watched a pre-loader named Ned throwing dozens of packages onto or near the belt. None looked much like a "guest of honor." Tori, the nearby send-again clerk, explained that Ned had much more work since management eliminated an off-loader:

> The I-E guys just come in here and look around, and they have to report *something* to justify their jobs, so they say, "eliminate him." It's so short-

10. I am grateful to Professor Bennett M. Berger for this point among others; personal communication, February 28, 1984.

sighted because sometimes Ned will just smash a package with his fist or against the wall out of frustration. So it costs them more in morale and damages than it would have to keep the other guy.

Each of the workers I met had ways of circumventing the system. Once supervisors left for the night, truck washers sometimes only rinsed the less dirty trucks. Buford not only sent long letters to management complaining of his load but sometimes deliberately brought back twenty or so send-agains as a way of telling NDC that his route standard did not allow enough time for the requisite second attempts at neighboring homes. In the same vein, one of the first nuggets of native lore I learned was a subtle system of winks and nods by which workers at one end of the belt communicated to their coworkers at the other when the coast was clear—no supervisors were on the loose. It was a subterranean etiquette not unlike that perennially invented by classroom cut-ups to plan pranks behind teachers' backs or that of commuters blinking their headlights to warn freeway comrades of speed traps ahead.[11]

To depict such undercurrents of resistance in this way, however, risks distortion. For descriptive purposes I have presented a sampling of comments and behaviors that are only drops siphoned from their larger flow. Although these workers were very critical of their company, they nonetheless arrived faithfully every morning and did their jobs. They did not strike or otherwise rebel after having worked at NDC an average of ten years. They were, despite their discontents and acts of resistance, *allegiant workers*; year after year, most of them just worked their routes and joyfully drank as much "free booze" as they could hold at the company Christmas party.

Resistance *and* allegiance—how was this done? As noted, they gained no small satisfaction from doing a tough job well. But this was not the primary basis of their allegiance. Nor were incidental gratifications like public contact and beautiful scenery. Sally Jones, the most satisfied of anyone I met, offered a clue when she explained why she was reluctant to explore other lines of work: "The money makes it hard to say, 'well, I don't want to do that work anymore.' You have to give up a certain amount of something [in any job]." Joe Demski, perhaps the least satisfied, gave another hint when he claimed that turnover at NDC

11. In their article, "The Ordeal of Consciousness" (1980), Matza and Wellman are instructive on the significance of such forms of resistance in a context of political subordination at the workplace: "Control of communication, ranging from the imposition of complete silence during work, to the invention of self-protective etiquettes of interaction with superiors, is part of the ordeal [of consciousness]. . . . Thus it is in the nature of working class consciousness that it frequently has to be whispered or winked; a certain subtlety is involved." For a useful critique of the tendency in discourse theory to assume working-class passivity—for example, to neglect as a matter of theory the oppositional meanings in practices of this sort—see Willis and Corrigan (1983).

occurred only among young part-timers because full-timers "all have mortgages and kids." Joe stayed on because he had seen no other job that came close to NDC financially. His family was "better off" with him there, although he hastened to add, "if it were me alone things would be different." For José, similarly, the security was important: "I don't think I could find anything, unless I had more education, that I could make as good money at."

I inferred from such reasoning that a simple phrase like "good money" tended to conceal the important ends to which wages were put. Joe lived up in the mountains with his wife and new baby. Sally drove her new British sports coupe to the beach every weekend. Rudi Ventura played golf, rode his motorcycle, and skied. The three veteran drivers all had "mortgages and kids." Along with most of the others at NDC, they had a stake in "split-levels and speedboats," a stake, that is, in a secure everyday life underwritten by work. As I began the individual interviews I had come to suspect that their allegiance-despite-resistance had to do with what the wages of alienating work could buy: *satisfying private lives.* Greg Larson expressed this clearly:

> The way I'm living now is just a thousand times better than where I lived when I was a kid. So I feel like I'm doin' really well. . . . I feel like I been bought. They pay me real good, can't hardly get away from it. Who's gonna hire a guy forty years old, one year of college? Nah, I haven't thought about changing jobs. . . . I'll probably stay here till I retire. . . . You have to be dumb to be fired, and I don't think I'd quit no matter how bad it gets.

These workers earned about fourteen dollars per hour plus Christmas overtime and bonus pay—over thirty thousand dollars a year for most. There was a pension plan and their families received full medical and dental coverage. As they looked around sunny Santa Teresa few of them perceived alternative opportunities that rivaled NDC. Under what they saw as their circumstances, it was only "common sense" to trade always exhausting often alienating labor for the dignities and pleasures of middle-class lives.

3

A Private-Sector Cast of Characters: Six Political Biographies from National Delivery Corporation

THE thirty or so mostly male workers at the NDC center included a devoted family man seen by many as a "religious nut," a muscle man notorious for "chasin' skirts," a twenty-year-old neophyte worker who had "missed the sixties," and a sixty-year-old veteran driver who vividly recalled the 1930s. Despite identical uniforms and shared work space, they were a heterogeneous bunch. Although such variety promised to make my work interesting, it presented the problem of how to select a few for individual case studies. I had no wish to try to generalize from a handful, however selected, to any larger population, but I still sought a combination of subjects who would roughly approximate the demographic makeup of the center's work force as a whole. On the other hand, selecting subjects so as to maximize ideological variation was essential to my exploratory ends. My procedure, then, was to play these two criteria off against each other until I had a half-dozen NDC workers who together offered an optimal balance.

The six case studies below are best thought of as biographical-political sketches. Qualitative methods such as ethnography and unstructured interviews have many advantages; they afford felicity to subjects' worlds and words, sensitivity to nuances, the chance to see the texture of experience and the structure of beliefs as they interact in the everyday lives of whole individuals. It is worth remembering, however, that my sketches are attempts to summarize in a few pages interview transcripts of about one hundred pages each, which were themselves attempts by my subjects to summarize their biographies and beliefs in a few hours. So, although I have sought to preserve the particularity of these people, I cannot claim to have avoided reductionism and oversimplification. I can only claim that I made every effort to summarize faithfully the unique configurations of concerns, values, and opinions expressed to me.

SALLY JONES, an occasionally boisterous blue-eyed blonde, appeared younger than her thirty-three years and taller than her sixty-three inches. She grew up in Sacramento, California, and attended public schools. Although raised as a Catholic, Sally had not been at all religious since high school. Her father was a college science professor whom she characterized as "very conservative, at times downright racist." Her mother raised Sally and her two older sisters, both of whom earned Ph.D.s and now worked in professional careers. Sally did not "get along" with her parents as a teenager, and she let years go by without seeing them.

She moved to Santa Teresa in the late 1960s to attend the university; she majored in art but dropped out after three years. Those years were turbulent ones around that campus as they were at many other colleges. Sally was involved with the student movement, but more from her links to a network of friends that included many radical leaders than from her own activism. Her boyfriend during much of this period was a principal in the Alliance of Black Students, and several other close friends were also activists who became enmeshed in conflict with both university and law enforcement authorities. At the time, 1969, most of these friends believed that revolution was imminent and that "struggle" rather than scholarship was the appropriate agenda. Although Sally took part in numerous protests and was certainly no supporter of the establishment, her commitment to student movements for radical social change was always tenuous. She recalled her outrage, for example, when an activist friend one night walked matter-of-factly into her apartment "with an armload of guns" he assumed he could hide in her closet. Sally angrily rejected his "for the good of the revolution" justification and threw him and his weaponry out. Weapons of any sort were extremely rare in movement circles, according to Sally, but, to her lasting chagrin, such uncomradely presumptuousness, "sexism," and "serious ego problems" were not.

After working for a summer as a secretary in a public interest law office in Berkeley and, later, spending a year with her lover in British Columbia, Sally returned to sunny Santa Teresa in 1976 and took a job at NDC. The job's title was clerk, but her work entailed tracing undeliverables and solving other production problems that demanded "a lot of creativity." The others respected Sally as skilled and diligent; to some, she was diligent to a fault. Most of her coworkers felt overburdened, but Sally enjoyed "the challenge" of the NDC system. The others tended to feel exploited and ignored by management, but she felt properly appreciated and "listened to." She told me she would feel that she was "cheating the company" if she ever "just stood around," and she had been openly critical of those who did.

Outside of work Sally relaxed and read but had few regular hobbies and no civic involvements. Although she was attractive and single, the fact that she had to be in bed by 9:00 P.M. to get to work by 4:30 A.M. put a crimp in her social life. Nonetheless, at least on weekends, she had her share of suitors, enjoyed driving her MGB roadster along nearby mountain roads, and lounged for hours on her favorite beaches "getting tan" and "drinkin' a few beers."

When I began the first interview, Sally made a point of telling me that she had no knowledge of or interest in matters political and therefore failed to see how her thoughts would be of value to me. She was actively inactive in political life. She never voted and refused to discuss politics. She eschewed newspapers in favor of historical novels and mysteries. My planned opening question on recent news having been ruled out, I asked what she saw as the major problems facing the nation. Sally saw only one:

> Greed. People's want of money stands in the way of a lot of progress. The people with the big bucks and the people in government are all mixed up together. The power is in the hands of those with money . . . and [they] want to continue to have the money and the power. . . . So the government and the people with money end up being one and the same.

Sally returned again and again to this model of power in America, whether explaining social problems or what she saw as government's failure to solve them. The most pressing problem facing the United States, according to her, was the lack of affordable medical care. She characterized the current system as "ridiculous" and attributed it to physicians' "exorbitant fees." Canada's national health care system seemed to Sally "great" in comparison: "They have socialized medicine there and I'm sure the doctors are still well-off. You pay five dollars a month and a dollar for an office visit. That's outrageous, yet it works. And people have good medical care. It isn't that the doctors are lousy or the offices are unclean or anything."

Sally believed that alternative forms of energy would help curb inflation but that they were being "stifled" because those in power "wouldn't rake in as many bucks." She attributed the severe housing shortage in her community to "people with money and power" wanting "the best life has to offer." When asked whether government might do something about such problems, her response was consistent: "The Mafia people, the big-business people all scratch each others' backs, do each other favors to make more money and have more power, and . . . I believe government is all mixed up in that. I'm not saying *all* politicians are crooked, but I would definitely say a majority [are]."

But don't we live in a democracy, I asked in various ways, where we can vote such people out of office? Again Sally responded, "We don't vote for the people with money and power," and "one rascal's as good as another; what can you do?" The more I played devil's advocate with probes about political pluralism the more incredulous her glances became. She seemed to take it for granted that anyone who could read must know that the distinction between economic power and political power is a fiction behind which the ruling class rules. Democrat or Republican, local or national—in Sally's view those with money get power and those with power get money until the two groups blend indistinguishably into a more or less permanently privileged class of the fortunate few. This uncomplicated conception of the power elite had a decidedly leftish tone, yet Sally's insistent extension of it across party lines made her beliefs difficult to categorize neatly in traditional left-right or liberal-conservative terms. Moreover, while the bipartisan character of her beliefs may have offered her a subjective sense of ideological coherence, the same quality would tend to make them objectively incoherent relative to formal ideologies and party platforms. The more she told me of her worldview, the clearer and more consistent it seemed, yet the more difficult it became to imagine how she would derive specific policy preferences from it.

Although Sally's cynicism extended equally to the "big shots" of both market and state spheres, it did not unambiguously constrict her vision of the social charter. True, she was offended by "bureaucrats" who "make more than I do for doing nothing" and by some who "lay back" and collect unemployment benefits rather than "trying to better themselves." But when I asked her a series of opinion poll questions on her spending preferences for some sixteen public programs,[1] Sally seemed less a conservative critic of the welfare state than a generous, albeit reluctant, liberal supporter of it. For example, she favored more spending for seven welfare state programs, supported the maintenance of current spending on another seven, and would reduce public funding only for police, county administration, and the military. Although Sally had virtually no trust in government as she had experienced it, she expressed no qualms about the positive potential of state programs designed to circumvent or intervene in the market to meet human needs.

Sally scoffed at the conservative notion that government spending per se deprives us of freedoms. She argued that, to the contrary, tax dollars *could* be well

1. These questions were drawn from a Field poll on public spending preferences taken just prior to the June 1978 election in California, at the height of the so-called tax revolt of Proposition 13. They were designed to measure voters' concrete opposition to or support for an array of specific welfare state programs then proclaimed to be losing legitimacy. See Mervin Field, *California Poll, Codebook* (Berkeley: University of California, Survey Research Center, 1978).

spent to achieve a more just and rational society—for example, in health care and public transportation, which she saw as basic necessities inadequately provided by the marketplace. In her view, the "giant profits" that motivate private business are simply incompatible with affordable medical and transportation services. If governments don't provide such things, she asked rhetorically, "how would [they] get taken care of?" These beliefs in particular seemed noteworthy because they were not self-serving in any financial sense; Sally always used her own car and had her health care needs covered by company-union insurance. Similarly, although her housing situation at the time of my interviews was quite agreeable (a modestly priced, charming Victorian flat in a tree-lined downtown neighborhood), she expressed clear support for more public housing and rent control. For Sally such policy preferences implied nothing particularly ideological. Her point was a practical one: the production of, say, housing was necessary, whether profitable or not. Thus, if her complaints about the state had a right-wing ring, they coexisted with strong support for state services that sounded left wing—a puzzling blend of political beliefs.

A strain of American individualism ran through Sally's ideas, but this did not appear linked to any reverence for the free market. It is arguable that this stemmed from her socialization—from her parents' conservative values which she had never fully rejected. But I came to suspect that a form of feminism was at work as well, albeit one unlike that of the early consciousness-raising groups many of her friends had formed. Sally had achieved success in a "man's job" through hard work. Moreover, perhaps because she was small and, in the argot of traditional gender culture, "cute," she had made it a point of pride to "never take any shit." She had earned a good income, personal independence, and the respect of her peers. This sort of individual responsibility was implicit in her criticisms of others she saw as less demanding of themselves. Yet, to judge from her rather broad vision of the social charter, Sally's sense of individual responsibility had not constrained her belief in collective or social responsibility.

If, however, despite this individualism and her conservative-sounding complaints about the state, Sally still believed social change was needed and favored public programs that promised greater social justice, then why her adamant refusal to participate in politics? Even those of her coworkers who shared her cynicism voted, seeing the ballot as at least a small way for the individual citizen to have a say. But Sally's stance was closer to that of a bumper sticker often seen in election years—"Don't vote, it only encourages them." Chronically low voter turnout in post–World War II America has been variously interpreted as a sign of basic satisfaction with the status quo, as a symbol of broad consensus, or as the sort of functionally conservative apathy that comes with economic security. But Sally construed her acts of nonvoting as protests against a political system offering only nonchoices. She seemed to feel more moral by abstaining so as to not lend legitimacy to the process than she would have felt casting a lesser-of-two-evils vote she felt certain would have no impact. Nor were extraelectoral politics like protests any more effective, according to her. Most of her student activist friends had been spied upon, clubbed, shot at, and jailed "on bogus charges" by police and the FBI. Families, relationships, and careers had been damaged. Skeptical of the movement from the start, Sally had drawn lessons from the heady days of the 1960s that buttressed her belief in the futility of virtually all forms of political participation.

JOE DEMSKI, twenty-nine years old and small of stature but ruggedly built, had curly blond hair and piercing blue eyes. He lived with his wife of six years and their three-year-old son in a small home twenty-five miles outside Santa Teresa. They lived out of town because, after looking for six months, they could not find an affordable house for rent that would allow small children and a dog. Joe grew up in the suburbs of Los Angeles in a large Polish-American family. He attended Catholic schools for twelve years, "the last four by choice," thinking that Catholic high school would be "better preparation for college." He "washed dishes for the brothers" to earn tuition. After his fourth summer of lifeguarding, Joe spent a year at a state university studying "the usual stuff, you know, general ed, surfing, pot smoking, how to get laid."

After a couple of short-term jobs to make money, he traveled for a year in Europe and Asia. Upon his return he moved to Santa Teresa where his long-time lover lived and got a job in a cerebral palsy center. Joe entered the nursing program at the local city college. After winning the "most promising nursing student award," he was expelled from the program for what he called "a couple of petty rule infractions." He still resented this expulsion and wanted very much to get back into nursing. Joe got married and took a job at NDC because it offered a pay scale twice that of his other job, even at the bottom level. At NDC Joe worked nights as a truck washer/gaser and spare driver. He liked the money, the benefits, and the hours that let him spend days with his infant son, but he had no love for the job or the company. "They care only about productivity," he said, not about how good a job he did or even his safety. If not for his family's financial needs, he would have left NDC long ago.

Joe identified neither with the working class he was now in nor with the middle class from which he came; instead he saw himself as part of "the living class, the surviving class." He was no more at ease with political party labels. He recalled supporting the farm-worker struggle in high school and gained some sense of class awareness from his father who "constantly" pointed out class differences "in gas stations and restaurants." His father had what Joe saw as "an almost inherent dislike for anybody with money" and had instructed his children, "There's you and there's them, and the reason you are you is because them is them."

Such socialization notwithstanding, Joe said politics was "not a major topic" in the family home when he was growing up. One exception was when his older brother, a Vietnam vet, "made the front page of the L.A. *Times*" for stopping traffic on the freeway in an antiwar protest. His parents were embarrassed at the time, but had since "mellowed" on the war and the brother. Joe's life was little different now in that he did not as a rule "get into [political] discussions unless it's something I know about, half-way well versed about."

He did think that U.S. involvement in El Salvador was a major national problem. In his view we were supporting a "fascist regime" there in the interests of "big business"; he did not at all trust what Reagan had said to justify this policy. Joe also noted that jobs were "so hard to get" that this too was a national problem. On this issue he offered more detail and kept bringing the discussion back to his own experience. It disturbed him that he could not "explore" what he wanted to do. In America, "the so-called land of opportunity," there should be more options for training. As for solutions, Joe thought that massive public demonstrations might "get us out of El Salvador," but that for more jobs and training the answers lay in making community institutions more responsive. When pressed for the cause of the lack of jobs and in his comments on the nature of poverty, Joe took pains to point out that "it's definitely the system," a system in which the powerful show an "unwillingness to share what is there."

For Joe, the government of the United States was not "really" a democracy in that most of what it did was not what the majority wanted. When I countered that Reagan could say that voters who elected him were saying they wanted intervention in El Salvador, Joe was overtly cynical. He simply did not believe that most Americans knew or cared much about politics but rather were very "frustrated." He explained popular support for Reagan's policies in terms of that frustration:

> I think America is frustrated now; they'll jump on any bandwagon that's offered them. . . . Somebody'll come in and say, "Well, goddamn it, these oil companies are fucking us up," and everybody will rally behind. Then they'll give this label of "big government." Well, big government is sort of a cloudy term and I don't think in our day-to-day dealings with government we see [it] as being big. But they can talk about "big government" and people can use this to get their frustrations out, as sort of an invisible punching bag you can yell at and say, "Well, goddamn it, you know it's big government that's doing this to us."

Asked about the sources of such frustration, Joe cited inflation and what it had done to the American dream of home ownership:

I think they're frustrated because they can make good money but they can't really do anything with it. They can't buy houses. Young people today can't buy houses. You know, we're brought up to [believe], "Now you be a good boy and study in school and you marry young and you get a good job and then you can buy a house," and, well, this just doesn't work out. People *aren't* able to buy a house once they've followed through with that plan. . . . And, I don't know, you're talking about a whole country; there's a lot of pressures. I think it was seen, you could sort of see it come to a head during the Iranian crisis. "We're this great country," I think the general mood said, "[and] we're being held hostage by a bunch of punks over there and here we are! Don't I believe in America? Before the Dodger games I stand up and sing the national anthem. What's going on here?" We can't do anything; our hands are tied not only politically but also economically during infla-tion.

Joe believed such frustrations were real, perhaps even rational, but that they were manipulated by political elites. Like Sally, he was more than a little skeptical of all politicians, but unlike Sally, he made distinctions between Democrats and Republicans. Joe's father brought up his children "to see Re-publicans as assholes," one reason Joe cited for being a registered Democrat. More serious was his impression that Democrats were "more socially concerned" and more aware of "the people" with respect to budget cuts, whereas he saw Republicans as apt to be "militarily concerned." This preference, however, implied little partisan passion. Joe noted that he did not follow politics very closely; in fact he rarely missed a chance to tell me that he was "not political." He could not think of a president he admired. Although he defined *liberal, left wing,* and *socialist* as positive terms because each meant being "more concerned with people as a whole than as individuals," he did not think any of them adequately described his beliefs. When I pressed him for a fitting label, he shrugged and said "kind of left." Although he felt little political efficacy or trust in government,[2] he always voted and often tried to persuade friends how to vote. On the other hand, he denied that voting is a meaningful form of political participation and saw elections as "political placebos" because "big corporations" are the predominant influence on what government does. For Joe, the vote in America is "like a popcorn fart," which I took to mean technically existent but without conse-quence.

2. The concepts of political efficacy, trust in government, and political participation as used in this book refer to the now standard scales used in national studies of poltical beliefs and behavior by the Survey Research Center at the University of Michigan. See Wright (1976, 89–110) for a description of their component questions and a good methodological discussion of their validity and reliability.

Despite such cynicism and his consistent criticism of government as it seemed to him to function, Joe remained committed to the idea that government does have an essential role to play. He repeatedly voiced support for a wide range of public services. Government should manage the economy and provide unemployment compensation, environmental protection, and other public goods and services the market does not provide. Joe felt his city government should be more aware of housing problems and pass some form of rent control because "the people who live here . . . are getting shafted by the rents charged by all these big folks who are making it hard for us little folks to get by." When I countered with the argument that such controls are said to impede economic development, Joe agreed this was "partially true" and added, "But it's also necessary, I think, to have these government controls. And if something dies along the way, if it's not 100 percent foolproof, then that's OK, these things are necessary." He made a similar point when discussing Reagan's plans for deregulation:

> I think [these controls] are necessary. See, I don't trust these guys, Craig, and I don't trust that if we lift controls there's going to be an ultimate good out of it, . . . [that] there will be cheaper energy, that there'll be affordable housing. . . . There was a reason these controls were put on, and I don't see that, economically, situations have changed that would demand the lifting of [them].

I tried to confront Joe with conservative objections to such an active state. If we were to have government programs like national health care, wouldn't people come to rely on government for everything? He strongly rejected this notion, calling it an attempt to conjure up an "invisible enemy." For Joe, the possibility of some dependence paled next to the certainty of human need:

> Whenever you talk about welfare, people never say, "Gee, it's doing a lot of people a lot of good." They always talk about this woman who's in court, you know, convicted of twenty-six counts of bummin' the government. No, it doesn't bother me at all. I would hope something like [national health insurance] would happen.

When I asked about the federal loans to Chrysler, Joe expressed an ambivalence that seemed consistent with his other beliefs:

> I have real mixed feelings about that. My feelings go to the workers who will lose their jobs and that aren't skilled in any other profession. . . . But I don't see that they would help the corner grocer. . . . I think they would say, "Well, that's capitalism; you play the game, sometimes you lose." So I feel for the workers, but I don't feel for the corporation. They should have seen the writing on the wall long ago. If they would have started building smaller cars, they would be in the plus billions by now [1980].

The fact that the federal government rejected a similar loan request from a worker-community group trying to keep a Youngstown steel plant open did not surprise him. Joe felt that government is generally more well disposed toward requests from big business than from workers. Although not in principle opposed to government aid to business, he would like to see such aid "create jobs" rather than "just profits." I offered the Reagan administration argument that more profits are what create more jobs. Joe was more than suspicious: "Yeah, that's what they said about deregulation and the oil industry, too, and all I know is that my gas jumped ten cents." He did not believe that if Exxon were allowed higher profits, more oil and jobs and lower prices would result. If the market's vaunted law of supply and demand could be considered a law at all, Joe was convinced it was one no longer enforced. He wavered little from this view across an array of questions about deregulation. He admitted that some regulations could be a nuisance, but he was sure that things would be much worse for everyone if state regulations on business were removed.

Without exception, Joe was against the Reagan cuts in public services and in favor of increasing or maintaining public programs. His voting behavior followed these beliefs. He voted against two statewide tax cuts, one of which would have benefited him directly, and he supported both the local rent control measures and the proposed state tax on oil. Joe was angry that programs that served the poor were being slashed while the military budget grew. He thought that jobs and training programs like CETA were the best investments for tax dollars and that defense was the worst. When I asked about government waste, he immediately mentioned military spending. Military spending "is wasteful because it's trying to pursue something, trying to keep shooting adrenalin into something that I just, you know, I don't see why it has to be. I don't believe in a 'strong defense.' I'm not paranoid of anybody coming to beat me up, you know?"

Joe's position on taxes was somewhat less clear than his positions on spending. He did not believe that the tax system was fair. He believed he paid much too high a proportion of his income in taxes and that this took away "all incentive" to earn more. Joe thought the wealthy take advantage of loopholes that allow them to pay less than their "fair share" while working people end up paying more. After answering that he would like to see spending increased for most public services, he asked, "Am I going to have any money left after this?" I asked if he would change his mind on increased spending if he knew this would increase his taxes:

> I am concerned definitely with these social institutions, but at the same time I'm concerned with my rent payment at the end of the month and mouths to feed and a car that needs gas and brakes now and then. . . . I'll pay my

taxes, but I want to see something out of it. [The tax burden] should be rearranged so that, I mean it always sounds good when somebody says, "We're going to pass a law that's going to cut 50 percent off your taxes." Well, that sounds OK, but who benefits from that? Fifty percent off my taxes might be four hundred dollars, where 50 percent off IBM's taxes can be four billion. So don't take 50 percent from me and 50 percent from the big guy over there. I'd like to see some rearrangement there.

Joe presented himself as a person who cared deeply about people less fortunate than himself, who supported the whole array of public services they need, and who would not mind paying even more taxes to support this. But make no mistake, he did not like paying what he saw as high taxes, and he resented what he saw as rampant waste in the Pentagon—waste for consultants and for junkets on which he believed congressmen "fly to Tahiti with their secretaries" when he could not "afford to fly to Idaho" to visit his brother. Joe professed to have no formal political identity, but he seemed to me the skeptical social democrat. He wanted very much to see government doing more for "the little guys" but held little hope for this because "big business" circumscribed what government agencies could accomplish. And he was certain that what is good for business is *not* what is good for America.

From such beliefs one can glean a glimpse of Joe's sense of the social charter. He had done his share of "shit work," labored long and hard for his income, paid his taxes, did not rely on government himself, but did not mind those who did. He had never collected unemployment or welfare, although he once got food stamps. Joe said he sometimes bought beer with them at his neighborhood market along with an occasional steak, a practice he half-jokingly called "abuse." I asked him what the person behind him in the checkout line might have thought about this:

> Well, I don't care much about what he thinks, you know? He's probably got a big steak, too, you know? It's only 'cause he's got a job and that's his choice what to do with his money. He has to eat the way he wants. But just because I need food stamps doesn't mean I can't have some fun, too, you know, or that I have to subscribe to lima beans four times a day.

The social charter seemed to Joe to become perverted for people like him. For example, he felt he was bounced out of the nursing program he loved for breaking rules designed for students whose "mom and pop send a check every month," rather than for students like him who had to work, raise a family, *and* go to school. He had "played by the rules" as he was taught them, yet he could not afford to buy a house per the American dream. He saw real estate speculators as the cause of this problem. He believed government should do something about it but that it would not because officials are influenced by "the big guys" who contribute to their campaigns, by the elite with whom they "drink cocktails."

Just as he held out for the ideal of a fairer government that would provide for the basic needs of its people, Joe was holding out for a better future for himself. He was dissatisfied with a job he found "emotionally suffocating" and hated to think of himself staying at NDC "just for the money." Self-fulfillment in work was important to him; he hoped to avoid the trap of the old-timers who stayed "because they had mortgages and kids." How he would build a more fulfilling future was not at all clear to Joe in 1983. He had little faith not only in the current political system but also in a union he considered corrupt, an NDC management he refused to join because of the way it treated workers, and even in the religion his parents wanted for him. Not even the working class for whose members he felt such empathy was home for him. Although Joe saw himself as on their side, his coworkers often appeared to him narrowly self-interested on political matters and, as such, too conservative for his tastes.

On all fronts, then, Joe found it hard—hard to wring coherent and moral meaning from his world and even harder to envision a means of change in either the system or his life within it. So, he was "hangin' in there," cynical but still hopeful, resentful but not bitter. Though put off by a political system he said he knew to be controlled by "big business" and "the rich," he always voted, hoping perhaps that his ballot might just help preserve the good things government did for "the little guys." Joe Demski also showed up every afternoon at NDC to plug away at a job he hated in order to support his family until he could get "a better shot." When he was not working, he did what he loved to do: played with his baby son, drank beer with his buddies, and spent a day at the racetrack whenever he could get away.

Although Joe never said so, I could not help feeling that his passion for betting the horses was cousin to his hope for a way to beat the system a little, to have a decent life without so much awful work. That the track odds made it likely that he would end up with less money, his working-class niche more permanent, did not alter the meaning of his quest.

BUFORD SCHMITT was sixty-two years old and had been an NDC driver for well over twenty years. He was tall, balding, bespectacled, and spoke with a slight lisp which seemed to accentuate his earnestness. Buford had been committed to evangelical, fundamentalist Christianity since he was "born again" at the age of fourteen. He proudly called himself a right winger.

Buford grew up in Salinas, California, during the depression, Steinbeck country both geographically and historically. Salinas was then a small agri-cultural community one hundred miles south of San Francisco, although farther in cultural distance. His father worked for the post office for thirty years and was the local Scoutmaster. When his father was in that role, Buford had to call him Mr. Schmitt. With some pride, he noted that his father was "quite strict"; he got "a lickin'" whenever he was "sassy." Buford's first political memory was hearing his grandmother decry the evils of "that Englishman" Roosevelt and profess her support for "Villkie" in her German accent. After high school and a summer job on a farm, he went into the navy where he served as a ship's librarian. Upon discharge, Buford married, went to work at a southern California post office, and entered a small Bible college, which he had to give up when his two daughters were born.

He now lived with his wife and youngest daughter in an immaculately kept tract home in a suburb about ten minutes from NDC. Nothing was out of place. If the American flag was not flying, it was folded regulation style on the living room cabinet next to a Bible, National Rifle Association magazines, and cassette tapes of Mozart, German marching songs, and hymns. The Schmitts owned a well-preserved Plymouth and a pickup truck (which he converted himself to propane during the 1973 oil embargo) used to travel to work and to tow their camper-trailer on vacations. Buford and his wife were active in their small church and spent weekends working around their home, but they did little else. He avoided "going downtown" because he disliked both the traffic and "the politics." He had not seen a movie since 1948 "because they are all trash"; he did not drink, smoke, or watch television.

The modern world just does not work as it should, according to Buford. "Slipping morality" is *the* major problem facing the nation today: women "using foul language openly, unashamedly," the "breakdown of the home," and "too much leisure time." Because "recreation has been on the increase," kids nowadays "would rather go out and have fun than do something worthwhile." These circumstances had allowed crime and violence to grow, aided and abetted by "liberal judges" who failed to punish. Buford was certain that if kids were "taught not to steal, why then they wouldn't steal." His two-year-old grandson, for instance, could not be left to "get into things," but had to be periodically slapped so as to "learn right from wrong." The cause of "slipping morality," in turn, was "rejection of the Bible." Buford saw this even in churches that now too often stressed "a loving God who winks at sin." He believed that these were "surely the 'last days.'"

If his view of human nature found people innately sinful, his view of free enterprise was the opposite. The market was moral perfection, offering freedom for all to succeed or fail solely on their own initiative. Poverty, therefore, was caused by the moral imperfections of the poor, who lack drive and discipline, "indulge in vices" rather than hard work, and are encouraged in their profligacy by government "bureaucrats" who lobby for welfare programs to "ensure their own jobs." Unemployment, similarly, was caused exclusively by people "choosing seasonal occupations" and "working just long enough to collect a government-paid vacation" (unemployment). As for racial discrimination and inequality, Buford cited Los Angeles's black mayor, Tom Bradley, and a local Latino physician as proof that minorities "have as much opportunity as anyone else." He was "irritated" by attempts to preserve ethnic cultures and by talk of discrimination: "I'd like to see nothing but red, white, and blue Americans around this nation. . . . If you tell a minority long enough that he's been stepped on, that he hasn't had a good deal, he starts to believe it. He'll get a gang of others together and they'll riot and start causing problems."

According to Buford, all problems not traceable to the moral flaws of individuals were caused by "government getting its hands into too many things," a phrase he used nine times in the interviews. He steadfastly denied that local government should do anything about the local housing crisis except "teach the next generation that it's not the government's job to provide that which they can provide for themselves." When I asked about Joe Demski, who had played by the rules and still could not afford a house, Buford said, "OK, so it's not his fault. But it's not my fault either, so why should I pay?" He explained his opposition to recent rent control initiatives by saying that *any* interference with the profit motive would "cause investors not to invest." To Buford this was a self-evident wrong; nothing else needed to be said in condemnation. In short, the domestic problems facing America—lack of medical care, unemployment, poverty, housing shortages—were all the progeny of an unholy alliance between immoral slackards and government bureaucrats who coddle them with social services and other "socialistic interventions" in the market.

Internationally, the United States faced a related threat. The "sovereignty" of America, Buford volunteered, is constantly in danger from "godless communists" who, if America lacked a strong military defense, would "come in and take us over in a flash." Indeed, for him the one good thing government offers is "protection." The communists' objective is "to destroy Christianity." We are increasingly vulnerable to this threat because of "one-worlders" such as the members of the Rockefeller-financed Trilateral Commission.[3] With a few exceptions like Ronald Reagan and Senator Jesse Helms (R–N.C.), our govern-

---

3. The Trilateral Commission comprises major corporate officers, a few labor leaders, and a variety of political elites from the United States, Europe, and Japan. Presidents Ford and Carter, Secretaries of State Kissinger and Haig, as well as the chief executives of several Fortune 500 companies were members. Its mission is to preserve the governability of politically democratic societies which sustain economic growth in the international capitalist system (see Crozier et al. 1975, and Domhoff 1978).

ment is dominated by "international bankers" who, in Buford's view, control the world in their own interests rather than "for the good of the country." These bankers, Trilateralists, and other "one-worlders" who would defile the United States by uniting it with Europe were linked in Buford's mind with the biblical prophecy about "the last days." At that point, he believed, there will be a "world government" run by "Anti-Christ" whose purpose will be to "destroy Christianity." The emphasis Buford placed on "protection"—from godless communists, foreign imports, criminals—suggests that he saw his world under siege, saved only by a powerful military, "the only thing our enemies respect."

Buford held the most restricted vision of the American social charter of any of the twelve subjects. He objected to most social services and government regulations, unless they "serve the whole," like employment training programs that "give a man skills so he can produce more" and thereby benefit everyone, air pollution controls, and highway maintenance. He felt it an injustice that he was forced to pay taxes "for welfare mothers who keep on having babies." Buford believed such women should be "sterilized after their second" child: "We only had two daughters; that's all we could afford. Why should I pay for someone else's kids?" He was also upset that public schools were not "instilling discipline," that they did not "clamp down on sexual immorality" (like "girls running around half naked" in southern California high schools), and that they taught "dessert subjects, not meat-and-potato subjects. . . . It's not the government's job to teach a kid a hobby. . . . I'm even beginning to wonder about athletic programs that don't pay [for themselves]."

He was offended as well by the government bailout of Chrysler because the free market "means freedom to fail as well as to succeed . . . and when you've taken away the freedom to fail you've taken away freedom. . . . They did it for Lockheed, Chrysler, and now [1980] Ford's been having problems. To me it's just not fair, it's not fair." Yet, although Buford applauded Reagan administration attempts at deregulation, he also thought the oil industry should be "demonopolized."

Among my twelve subjects, he was the most consistently conservative. He voted for Reagan because a more conservative candidate like Jesse Helms did not run. He favored more spending cuts and a far narrower terrain of state legitimacy than did any of the other subjects. In many ways Buford epitomized what Converse (1964) called an ideologue, one whose beliefs are constrained to fit with one another in a consistent ideological mold with voting behavior to match. In some instances he showed a cultivated incapacity to alter his ideology to fit even his own experience. For example, despite his knowledge of a local plant closure and having both a daughter and a son-in-law laid off when we spoke, he persisted in his conviction that unemployment results from individuals "goofing off." I was reminded of Sennett and Cobb's *The Hidden Injuries of Class*: perhaps such a conviction gave dignity to his own sacrifices and reaffirmed the value he placed on hard work. After decades at a difficult job, perhaps Buford invested his efforts with a certain sanctity or elevated his devotion to duty in a way that set him apart.

Although he would remain a consistent ideologue by any measure, there were intriguing exceptions in Buford's belief system. He defended the post office—that favorite of public-sector whipping boys that embarrasses even most liberals—because he knew that, as a technical matter, not even NDC could do better if required to handle several classes of mail. His reverence for free-market capitalism would make Milton Friedman blush, but Buford believed that NDC's zeal for the "profit motive" had damaged his sense of craft, the quality of the firm's service, and, owing to the mandatory overtime, the family lives of workers. In part because of this, he supported the concepts of employee ownership and workplace democracy, but he would wince if he thought such views could be considered left wing. Although Buford held that "the love of money is the root of all evil" and located the source of his discontents as a worker in NDC's hunger for profit, he continued to insist that the profit motive is the only moral means of justice in social life and that America's troubles are caused by either individual failures to adhere to the profit motive or "government interference" with it.

How was this seeming feat of intellectual acrobatics accomplished? With a little ideological work, the ostensible inconsistency vanishes. Buford grounded his support for employee ownership in conservative values; it would eliminate "overpaid union middlemen" and spur workers' productivity by making them capitalists. The infringement upon family life by NDC's version of the profit motive was wrong only because "it takes a man away from his family" when the *purpose* of the profit motive is to sustain family independence. Thus, rather than insulating him from the ideological appeal of the Right, Buford's frustrations with the logic of capitalism were transformed into raw material for its defense.

Over and above ideological work, the privatism that characterized Buford's life seemed to sustain his beliefs. In his years at NDC, he had been alone, distanced from his coworkers by both the solitary structure of the work and his discomfort with their "foul language" and "immorality" (for example, "adultery" and "alcohol"). Aside from teaching Sunday school and his "evangelical work," Buford had little social life and few ties to any larger collectivity. Thus, he was rarely confronted by experiences that might cause him to question or revise his beliefs. His exposure to political culture was similarly selective. Aside from the Bible, Buford's reading was limited to *Reader's Digest*, National Rifle Association magazines, and the *Lighthouse*, a tabloid put out by the extremely right-wing Liberty Lobby. He also subscribed to a Christian Law Association magazine called the *Defender*, which takes as its raison d'être the struggle against "secular humanism" in schools, evolutionism in textbooks, and the taxation of fundamentalist church schools. This self-confirming media matrix provided a narrow perceptual aperture through which flowed only ideologically homogenous information. Although Buford clearly did more systematic political reading than most of the others in either group, he was plugged in to a ready-made rightist subculture, whereas the media used by most others were markedly more diverse.

If, as Lane (1962, 1969) has argued persuasively, we must understand political beliefs as serving social-psychological purposes for their holders, then the content and coherence of Buford's ideology become still more understandable. Sally Jones seemed to get a certain psychic comfort from being apolitical—that is, by distancing herself from politics, she could avoid the anguish of the 1960s and the guilt she might have had about her current privatism. And Joe Demski, by juggling political cynicism and personal hopefulness, seemed able to make sense of class resentments without being overwhelmed by bitterness and despair. In my attempt to make sense of Buford's views, I was particularly drawn to this sensibility.

For example, I found his reverence for the ethic of individual achievement difficult to understand in purely cognitive terms. Lane found meritocratic ideology to be rooted in the experience of social mobility; despite their working-class status, his subjects were living "better than their parents" and felt sure their children would do better still. Like Lane's workers, Buford entered the work force after World War II, arguably the period of greatest economic growth and social mobility any society has experienced. Yet he retained the same socioeconomic status as his parents and had little reason to believe his children would surpass him. He expressed various insecurities about his own achievement: that he "lost promotions" by choosing a librarian's job in the navy; that he could not afford to finish college and support his family and ended up driving a delivery truck; that he was "not motivated that much by money," tended to be "kinda lazy," and had to "fight" himself to "get out and do something." How did he construct a dignified identity from such biographical facts if, as he claimed, mobility and achievement were "available to all who will work for them"? I came to suspect that the stridency with which he preached a creed according to which he had not succeeded might help him heal "hidden injuries."

Similar purposes may be seen too in Buford's zealous invocation of "the old days," the amorphous historical benchmark against which he seemed to measure all things. He admitted to being wedded to his own real or imagined ancien régime in most spheres of life. Male dominion, for instance, was for him part of the natural order. Buford marked his wife's ballot each election day. When I asked if it were possible that she might disagree, he dismissed the idea by noting that if they ever did talk over the issues "she would see things" his way, and so "she just leaves it up to me." All the other spouses were introduced during one of the interviews, but Buford's wife stayed in another room for the entire six hours we spoke. When explaining later why he admired Reagan most of all the presidents, the same patriarchal values were invoked:

> Well, his wife seems like the best First Lady we've had over the years. She's very ladylike and very loyal to her husband, a helpmate. And I don't think she's as dominant [as] President Carter's. . . . I think Mrs. Reagan is very passive and supportive. I thought President Ford's wife was the most unladylike one I've ever seen from a picture they had of her in the paper. . . . In fact I [clipped the picture and] wrote him a letter and I said I wouldn't vote for him because of his wife.

That a man who follows politics vigorously would base his vote on such reasoning, that he would in 1981 use the word passive as a complimentary adjective describing how women ought to act, seemed to me striking. Perhaps a man who sees modern trends eroding the values and social relations he believes undergird civilization will attach extra significance to order and stability in gender roles.

Buford's sense of traditional mores figured prominently in his reasoning on other issues as well. He argued for the Reagan cuts in funding for public broadcasting by saying, "We got along fine without TV when I was a boy." His railings against a mélange of immoralities were often followed by the statement, ". . . never would have been permitted when I was a boy." It was as if the remembered norms governing social life a half century ago were scripture, transhistorically *right*, as if American culture should not have had the impudence and temerity to *change*. Little wonder the nostalgic appeals of Reagan and the New Right were music to Buford's ears.

Little wonder, too, that *I* should have been struck by what seemed to me his obsession with "the old days." I am of the generation whose values seemed to Buford to be at the heart of what is wrong with the world. There is always the danger that my curiosity about a man so different from me (yet so willing to explain his opinions) led me to roam too speculatively into the realm of his psyche, a realm to which only psychoanalysts are privy. Readers and reviewers will properly chastise me if I have roamed farther than facts allow. In the meantime, however, I will risk sharing a hunch. If political beliefs serve purposes, then for Buford his may have served as so many pieces of personal armor—defenses of his sacrifices, bandages on a wounded dignity, shields for values as cherished by him as they were besieged by the new and different values of others. They seemed to me to constitute a support system for the increasingly precarious personal identity and social status he had built in his life. For him, and no doubt to some extent for most of us, ideology could be understood as a fortress for the preservation of a sense of self.

GREG LARSON was a handsome, affable forty-year-old white man, married for the second time. He had three children, two of whom now lived with him in a new split-level suburban home. He had worked as a driver at NDC for the last eighteen years.

Greg came from a large working-class Appalachian family who lived in the hills of West Virginia without plumbing or electricity. Although life was hard and morally strict, he never was aware of other ways of life so he "didn't miss anything." From age twelve on, Greg had to earn his own money for everything, even haircuts. He baled hay and picked ginseng until his last year in high school when he dropped out to enlist in the U.S. Marines. His family took little notice of politics other than occasional comments by his father about "damn Republicans" and winning the Korean War. His only sense of political "good guys" and "bad guys" came from John Wayne movies and cold war rhetoric about communists.

Greg visited Santa Teresa while stationed in southern California; he settled there when his hitch was up because "there wasn't anything [opportunities] back home; I would've wound up settin' around the general stores like the rest of 'em." He took various truck-driving jobs until he landed one at NDC in 1965. The most important thing in a job for him was the "self-respect" he derived from working hard and providing a good service. He hated the hours his job demanded, however, especially because his children were often in bed when he got home. Greg resented NDC management for this but felt he had "been bought" by high wages and good benefits which afforded his family a good life—a better life, in fact, than he felt someone of his background had a right to expect.

Greg became a born-again Christian in 1972. He had been a swinging bachelor, "drinking and smoking pot every day, goin' out with different women every night." Then, one day on the freeway, it "hit" him: this was, he recalled feeling, "the wrong kind of life." He wept, talked to some Christians on his route, bought a Bible, and was born again. "Now," Greg said, "God is the most important thing in my life." He attended the same small fundamentalist church as Buford, but unlike Buford he rarely invoked religion when speaking of politics. When he did draw upon his religious values for guidance on political issues, his sense of Christian charity tended to push his policy preferences to the left instead of the right.

Greg identified himself as a "conservative" and held many beliefs in keeping with that identity. He described himself as "hard" on welfare issues, for instance. He offered the familiar anecdote about seeing well-dressed people in the supermarket who used food stamps and then drove off "in a new Oldsmobile." He had "heard" of a local matron who drove her Rolls-Royce to pick up her welfare check and knew of men who worked "under the table" while collecting unemployment. On his route he had witnessed CETA workers "loafing" rather than training and concluded that he'd rather see a new WPA where "you actually went out and did something." He added that, now, unlike in depression years, "if you're really hungry, you'd go to work, no doubt about it."

On the other hand, Greg offered many other qualifying opinions that belied his self-identification and suggested that terms like *conservative* and *liberal* are far more amorphous and ambiguous than common usage would indicate. For example, after admitting that the word *welfare* led him to envision the "stereotype of a black welfare mother with a lot of kids who just collects," he immediately added, "but that's not fair and I don't mean it," and "as a Christian, I can't really feel that." Similarly, although he was a Reagan voter in 1980 and supported a strong defense as one of the best things government does, he cited as a major problem the risk of global nuclear war in which there would be "no winners." Like Reagan, Greg volunteered that he was a "firm believer in free enterprise"; but unlike the president, he qualified his support with "only up to a certain size" and the statement, "big business is behind every evil in the world." More concretely, he adamantly opposed rent control as unwarranted government interference with private property, but remained an advocate of stronger pollution controls and regulations on oil companies and land developers.

Greg observed that he got "a little touchy" about people who were not "pulling their own weight" because he was "brought up to believe you take care of yourself." Given his background, lack of formal education, and subsequent success, he firmly believed that "if I did it, anybody could" (cf. Botsch 1980). He "started with nothin'" and had worked steadily and hard. He expected no less from others. When speaking of social services, Greg took pains to note that he would "hate" to receive "anything for nothin', even if I paid for it [with taxes]" and that he tended to be suspicious of those who did. He was incensed, for example, when his stepdaughter brought home from school a notice of her eligibility for reduced-price lunches; he knew her Latino surname must have been responsible for the school's assumption, since he was "perfectly capable" of paying full price. Aside from any dents in his pride as a provider, such incidents confirmed his fear that his taxes were too often wasted on the undeserving.

Some of Greg's tales of government waste might have been taken from a Reagan campaign speech. Like his school-lunch story, he spoke of driving past the courthouse and seeing one city worker watering the lawn while another stood "ten feet behind him holding the hose!" Other examples, however, seemed to make the waste issue a nonpartisan one. In the marines, Greg had to take part in "dumping perfectly good truck engines" into the ocean because "it was supposedly cheaper than filling out the paperwork" for storing them. He was a fan of strong defense, not necessarily a fan of Defense Department spending. If Greg was drawn to vote Republican in some way by his resentment of government waste, it was because that party articulated and colonized the issue and not necessarily because he supported higher military spending.

Greg described a variety of other experiences that constrained his sense of the social charter. He did not use directly any government services and saw his life as self-made, self-contained. What contact he had had with the state had been unsatisfying at best. In both his child custody cases he felt victimized by government in the form of the courts. He not only did not receive justice but had to fill out "more forms" and make "extra trips" downtown for seemingly pointless procedures. He had once been accused of cheating on his taxes only to be exonerated after protracted "hassles." It was as if government was an adversary which, as he put it, one had to "be well informed about" or be "bulldozed" by its bureaucracy. For Greg, government was surely less than the guardian of the lone citizen's interests.

Although he claimed to be a conservative, Greg was also a class-conscious worker, and his sense of the social charter and the role of government reflected this, too. His sense of justice was offended by those who relied on government when they could work, but it was also offended by poverty among the elderly, some of whom, he noted, had to "eat dogfood" and "live in cars." He preferred not to increase social spending in some areas, yet made a point of saying that no one "should have to go without medical care no matter what." Some unemployed people, he suspected, were "just lazy," but "then again," he knew of a local plant closure that "took away six hundred jobs." Thus, although he was "not crazy about government providing jobs," he saw it as "a necessary evil [that] does help society." He was dead set against redistribution of wealth, objecting even to taking money from millionaires who may not have worked for it, because then government "could take it away from someone who did earn it." Yet he was sure the tax system unfairly burdens working people while affording the rich "loopholes" he could not understand, much less use. Similarly, he thought Reagan's tax cuts were "cuckoo" because those who needed them most got the least and vice versa. Greg favored stricter elegibility for food stamps and *increased* allotments for those eligible. He favored the maintenance of public spending for medical care and public housing and increased spending on welfare, education, environmental protection, and public transportation.

If such reasoning and policy preferences were not those of a classic liberal, neither were they those of a consistent conservative. Alongside Greg's resentment of government waste and his commitment to "pulling his own weight" and a strong defense, there was his acute awareness of "corporate greed," human suffering, and the need for Christian charity. Although he supported Reagan's notion of deregulation because of a "typical government snafu" he saw in a "60 Minutes" exposé of the Occupational Safety and Health Administration, it was upsetting to him that under the banner of deregulation Reagan moved to loosen the Clean Air Act, ease safety standards for nuclear power plants, and give oil companies freer play. In addition to seeing himself as a conservative and a worker, Greg said he was an "environmentalist." He came from "the earth" in West Virginia, settling in Santa Theresa where he enjoyed the local beauty on camping trips with his kids and where he witnessed firsthand the devastation of beaches by oil spills. There was no doubt in his mind that he was a true-blue, procapitalist American, but he saw "disaster ahead" if business had its way with our ecology.

If there was a pattern in Greg's responses, it was to reach first for a conservative ideal or principle and then, more often than not, add liberal qualifications and specifics. He favored free enterprise, but then said what he "really meant" was small business. He attributed his troubles at NDC to corporate "greed" and had rejected promotions to management because he did not want to have to "stab other workers in the back." At first, he nodded clear approval when I asked him about Reagan's supply-side, or trickle-down economic policy, saying that it "sounds right." He remained very skeptical, however, of the idea that the wealthy would invest in ways that would benefit everyone.

Greg was satisfied with his life and fairly optimistic about his family's future. He was less satisfied and optimistic about the state of the nation. Government, in his view, was incapable of solving our economic problems. On top of being inefficient, wasteful, and often intrusive, government was generally run by and for the "big interests." Such beliefs did not, however, lead Greg to despair; the United States was still a "great" system. He had done all right, and he pointed to our "basic rights, freedoms, to just pack up the car and go. Some countries you can't even go to another state!" In an ideal world, "no government" would be best, but "there have to be some rules," so government is "a necessary evil." Moreover, he knew of other countries where people may not vote at all—"at least we have a choice."

Every election day Greg exercised that choice in ways that reflected the ambivalent and seemingly conflicting beliefs he laid out for me. As an aggrieved taxpayer, he joined the tax revolt and voted for Proposition 13. As a powerless, overcharged consumer, he also voted for Proposition 11, a measure to place a special tax on big oil companies, on the grounds of "revenge . . . to show them there's still something we can do to them even though they own half the world." But if he held such animosity toward big business, why then did he as a former

Democrat support a solidly probusiness administration? First, after voting for Carter in 1976 in the hope that his "honesty" would make a difference, Greg felt "disappointed" by what he saw as Carter's indecisiveness. Second, Greg saw no alternative party or candidate; thus, for him, Reagan became the lesser of two evils. So even as he voted for the nuclear weapons freeze and the bottle-recycling bill, which his presidential candidate vigorously opposed, he put a check in the Reagan column. Given Carter's ineffectiveness, Greg's sense of simple fairness meant that Reagan deserved "a chance."

In a follow-up interview in November 1982, Greg still generally approved of Reagan's performance because, "right or wrong, at least he's doin' *something*." But by 1983, and in spite of his lingering suspicions about welfare programs and the like, he had changed his mind:

> I've soured on Ronald Reagan. He's for the rich man, the wealthy. Every time I turn around he's telling everybody they've gotta tighten their belts, but this is his fourteenth trip to California. The working-class man is getting screwed by his policies. I've changed my mind completely on him. I've changed my mind on the military, too. I used to be hawkish. I used to say, "give more money to the Pentagon," but now there are just too many people out of work. Reagan is rattling sabers all over the place, but his Buck Rogers war technology leaves me cold. There's more need for jobs and social programs now.

Although Greg's about-face was striking, it seemed to me of a piece with his switch to the Republican camp in 1980. In the shadow of his disappointment with Carter, many of Reagan's campaign themes resonated with his experiences and conservative values. But, after four years of Reagan's policies, Greg's working-class sensibilities took center stage. Apparently his initial vote implied no depth of commitment, no mandate for the Right, just as his previous support for Carter did not stem from any consistent liberal ideology. A certain species of ambivalence ran through Greg's responses. He frequently hedged his opinions, expressed doubts, and claimed a lack of knowledge by saying, for example, "I really shouldn't say, I just don't know enough." What he did know was that the system just doesn't work as it should and that he had no political vocabulary, no coherent ideology that might allow him to say precisely why and what should be done about it.

More detailed knowledge and/or a more formal ideology could give some order to what now appear to be anomalies, but this would entail a good deal of effort. He would have to immerse himself, during precious free time, in the corrupt and confusing milieu of political elites whom he distrusted. Perhaps more salient, since he had a secure job and a rewarding private life, what incentives did he have for developing such knowledge or forging such an ideology? I recall thinking as I left his lovely home after my last interview, "This guy is an individualist conservative *and* a working-class liberal." Now, after several years and several readings of his transcripts, I have arrived at no more adequate characterization.

RUDI VENTURA was a native of Santa Teresa, as was his mother. His father now had a white-collar job at the college library, but he worked nights and went to school when Rudi was growing up. After the children began school, his mother worked as a silk-screen artist in a commercial plant. Although his parents never discussed politics, they always voted. Rudi also observed this civic duty: "I always vote no matter what." His folks were lifelong Democrats who voted for Carter in 1980. Rudi was a registered Democrat, but he reserved the right to "vote for the man" he thought best regardless of party.

Mexican culture was not a strong theme in Rudi's childhood, but he recalled identifying with other Chicanos "not because they were minorities but because they seemed like they always got the raw end of the deal" and because "I'm a very sympathetic type of person anyway; I have a very soft heart." He traced these sympathies to the regular visits his family made to poorer relatives who were farm workers in the Sacramento Valley. "They were working twelve or thirteen hours a day, leaning over, and ended up going back to a shack." Rudi recalled thinking this was "pathetic" and being surprised they could still "be happy and play with their kids outside in the dirt." At age six, he swore to himself he would "make sure it wasn't going to happen to me." Believing that one could choose any job, he asked his father why they didn't just leave, but he got no reply.

At fifteen, Rudi lied about his age to get a job in a local market. He worked there ten years, moving up from box boy to night-shift supervisor, but felt that he was under too much pressure the whole time. He studied police science at City College for a year and then joined the army. He enjoyed the service, recommending it for all young men as a route to maturity and education. Upon discharge, he got a job as a policeman. He still considered it his favorite job because he had felt he was "helping people." He thought it might "sound crazy, [but] every time I got a call, a 415, a family dispute, and I was able to find a solution and resolve the problem, it made me feel good." After transferring to a sheriff's department in northern California where he was assigned to less reward-ing jail duty, Rudi resigned and went to work at NDC for better pay.

Despite the fact that the most important feature of a job for Rudi was "security," he was certain in 1981 that he would leave NDC for a better job. He was exploring some business deals with a corporate lawyer friend who was in real estate. In "six months to a year," he said, "I'll be gone." His friend led a life with which Rudi was enthralled: "It's great money; he likes it. He deals with very, very elite-type people. He handles millions every day. . . . My goal is in the next ten years to be able to retire—not that I would." Rudi, then, was not satisfied with his station in life. Even though he made "real good money," NDC held little allure for him as a career:

> I can't see myself being fifty years old pumpin' out four hundred boxes a day. I've seen what it does to other people. You know Buford Schmitt? He's worked all his life, hard, hard worker; honest, very religious, and what does he have to show for it? A house that's two-thirds paid off, a body that won't go very far. All he looks forward to is his six weeks vacation and a little income. For what?! Thirty years hard labor? That's not for me.

This was Rudi Ventura at age thirty-three. He was on the tall side, athletic, and had dark curly hair and brown eyes that twinkled when he got excited, which was fairly often. Most of the time we spoke he wore a broad and infectious smile that belied his discontents. He lived in a modest rented apartment near the beach, sparsely furnished with the essential accoutrements of bachelor life: a bar, a Naugahyde couch, a large color television with a host of cable channels, and a lone painting of a nude woman over the fireplace. Rudi's active leisure life included trips to the mountains, various sports, and, more weekends than not, thirty-six holes of golf. He had worked hard without interruption for eighteen years and was now actively seeking greener pastures.

Rudi hoped for a future on Easy Street, but he was very critical of how "the system" times the traffic signals there. That system, he thought, is run by and for "big business," a term he used to explain many of the problems he saw in the United States. He held "the oil companies" responsible for inflation, for example, because they created an artificial gas shortage in order to "jack up" prices; then "everybody needed a wage increase." When I asked him if government should do something about this, he replied, "I think the oil companies *are* the government. Who do you think pays these people? Who grooms a president? It's definitely not me; I don't have the bucks." He also noted that big agricultural corporations pay lobbyists to win subsidies for not growing food, which he said resulted in higher prices—a situation he saw as absurd when "40 or 50 percent of the world is dying of hunger."

Rudi's critique of the corporate economy and its hold on politics extended to many spheres. He thought the tax system fundamentally unfair because corporations and the wealthy had loopholes while the rest of us were "soaked" for "five months [wages] out of the year" for taxes. He would like the good politicians ("there's a few . . . we can still believe in") to investigate "these large corporations who've done nothin' but take their money and run," but he doubted this was likely to happen:

> In essence, the government doesn't really care about what I say. You think they're gonna care if I wrote a letter? No.
>
> Q: But what if they got a flood of letters?
>
> Yeah, I was gonna say, now you get yourself a hundred thousand people, . . . then they're gonna start listening. But you, as an individual, they don't care. You gotta form a posse. . . . Then they are forced to do something about it. But as an individual, they don't give a goddamn, you're a number on a computer.

Although Rudi never missed an election, he had no illusion that his vote really counted; he believed that the electoral college and the media time bought by big campaign contributions dilute the influence of citizens. Regardless of party, "people with money," he said, control government.

To judge from Rudi's folk theory of American capitalist society, he was a liberal, if not a leftist. In fact, he was neither. His beliefs about foreign policy were quite hawkish and would surely be interpreted as conservative if viewed as discrete survey responses. For example, when I asked what in the news lately had struck him, good or bad, he spoke enthusiastically about the space shuttle:

> I like [the shuttle]. I don't know, it sounds kinda phony to a lot of people, but statistics show recently that Russia has surpassed, as far as power over America. They have so many percent more jets, . . . more rockets, . . . more battleships, . . . nuclear weapons, and so on. And then yet to see America still continue on with the space program . . . shows that we're trying to keep up with the Russians.

Rudi got most of his statistics from the mass-mailings of the American Security Council, a conservative, promilitary political action group. He was sure they were right about our dwindling military might because their mailings listed "hundreds of senators, mayors, high political people" who "all can't be wrong," and because "a little island like Vietnam can push us around." Rudi did not serve in Vietnam, but he was certain that the U.S. error there lay in not heeding the likes of General Westmoreland, whom Rudi quoted approvingly as having said, "Goddamn it, I'll just bomb it all, blacktop it, and put parking meters there." Instead, we listened "to the goddamn politicians who get in the way all the time." Rudi felt we should have followed General Patton "when he said, 'The war isn't over, let's go to Russia now.'" For Rudi, our failure was one of political will to use force to stop the falling dominoes: "You see, in the last twenty years communism's been stretching their fingers out farther and farther."

Clearly there were cultural supports for such views. Rudi grew up believing the Russians were the villians, and certainly neither media reports on Soviet policy nor American Security Council newsletters contradicted him. But the same childhood and media influences were shared by Jones, Demski, and Larson, for whom the spread of communism was simply not a pressing matter. "Winning" and not being "pushed around" were also much higher on Rudi's list of concerns than on the lists of most of the others.

The simultaneous holding of rightist and leftist views may be a campaign pollster's nightmare, but for Rudi, as for Greg Larson, it was no problem at all. His conservative foreign policy stance seemed to coexist easily with his liberal-left criticisms of the domestic political economy. The same was true of his beliefs about public services and state regulation of the economy. On one hand, he was very critical of what government does and how. Catalytic converters robbed his car of power and made it hard to tune properly, thus "*adding* to pollution." "Government should get out of Detroit's ass" was Rudi's unmistakable point. His hassles as a car consumer rendered him sympathetic to the Republican deregulation theme. He cited a story about "four guys standing around a manhole" while one did all the work as the leitmotif of public-sector inefficiency. Though not a property owner, he championed Proposition 13 as a means of cutting such waste and insisted that critics who claimed public services would be damaged were wrong. Cuts in public television and food stamp funding proposed by the Reagan administration were all right by him. He justified his cynicism toward welfare programs in terms of his knowledge of several people who collected unemployment and worked under the counter. This in particular angered Rudi because he had sent back the last of only three unemployment checks he had ever received and once overheard someone trying to decide "whether to buy jeans or grass" with his unemployment money. Rudi walked away shocked: "I about died."

On the other hand, Rudi advocated policies that were liberal if not socialistic in their implications. When I pressed him on what might be done about under-the-counter workers, his first thought was to make unemployment recipients work in public jobs four hours a day for their benefits. But when I asked about the lack of jobs, he insisted that government should guarantee jobs for all who cannot find them: "It's not impossible, it can be done." Rudi thought the proposed cuts in black-lung benefits to miners were "a disgrace," that Social Security should remain sacrosanct even if current workers had to pay a bit more, and that government spending on public housing, welfare, and education should all be increased rather than decreased. He mentioned in several contexts the "incredible" poverty that remains in the United States, "the richest, most beautiful country in the world." His solution to this was more education, although he was quick to note that "you have to pay for education, [and] the person who hasn't got the money doesn't get the education." Thus, for him America remains a nation in which "the rich get richer and the poor get poorer." Rudi showed no discomfort when expressing his desire to strike it rich one moment and to put a ceiling on all incomes over $100,000 per year the next. He criticized Soviet "restrictions," which meant that a Russian "can't become a millionaire," but in the next breath he advocated extensive state planning and welfare programs to ensure that all U.S. citizens have the basic necessities. Indeed, he favored maintaining or increasing all but two of seventeen areas of public spending.

Although he bristled at some forms of regulation and endorsed Reagan's concept of deregulation as a "good idea," he rejected four specific deregulation proposals. Moreover, he voted for the "tax big oil" initiative and for rent control because he felt oil companies and big landlords were "screwing the public." He had some doubts about land-use regulations but favored state controls in the coastal zone. If government "just lets it go, these realty people and these big-business people will just put skyscrapers all along the beach front so they can make a killing. Just like Miami and Malibu."

When all was said and done, Rudi's criticisms of the state amounted to just that—criticisms. Although he expressed some very conservative opinions, again and again he resorted to a general sense of justice in which the welfare state retained essential legitimacy, even when it infringed upon the free market. His sense of the social charter was a broad one. This is not to categorize Rudi as a fan of what government *actually* does, but only to note his support for what government *attempts* to do:

> I'm poor, too. I mean, I don't like seeing my paycheck, you know, gettin' cut off a third and having it go to the federal government. But, like I say, they must need it. And I would rather live here than anywhere else. I mean, this is [the] price we pay, so I just can't complain really.

Rudi's childhood experiences with his poverty-stricken farm-worker relatives, his continued awareness of suffering amid affluence in America, and his feelings of daily exploitation at NDC all seemed to be ingredients in his support for the welfare state. But his support of the idea of individual self-sufficiency led me to ask him if all the public assistance programs he favored eroded the work ethic:

> Do you think a garbage worker or a street sweeper is thinking of that? He's dreading that he has to get up at six in the morning just to do his job for eight or nine hours and hoping he has enough money to pay his bills. Don't you think he'd be a lot happier and his family would be a lot happier, his marriage would be a lot happier if he knew he had the money, so he could go to work and *know* he's still gonna have that house?

My question seemed to elicit his frustrations as a worker rather than his pride and to highlight his support for a nonmarket principle making basic human needs primary. He saw little work ethic left to erode for most workers.

There was, of course, another facet of Rudi's experience that emerged in response to related questions. People who cheat on unemployment, get more food stamps than they are entitled to, or take undue advantage of public medical care, as he felt some do in England, all symbolized for him what is wrong with the welfare state. Because he had worked at mostly unpleasant jobs for nearly twenty years, he felt that people who don't "pull their weight" are an affront, an injustice, as surely as the exploitative rich. When I asked how such people could pull their own weight without sufficient job opportunities, all the evidence on the structural nature of unemployment went out the window. Despite his support for government-guaranteed jobs for all, Rudi did not object to Reagan's plan to cut unemployment eligibility by thirteen weeks:

> I think any able-bodied man who can walk into that building and collect his unemployment should be able to find a job. I can do it, anybody else can, too. I'm not a smart man. I'm not that intelligent at all compared to a lot of people. I can find a job anytime.

Rudi "knew" that the inequities of the market system are neither natural nor legitimate. He tended to assume, however, that they are inevitable—an assumption that seemed to be rooted in both his understanding of the structure of power and his sense of his own powerlessness. His solitary efforts had given him whatever status and leisure he enjoyed. He had never relied on the state and had little reason to believe government would improve his situation. As he saw it, the road to a better life wound through the marketplace and could be traveled successfully only with the aid of his own cunning. When I asked him how he reconciled his feelings for the poor and for workers with his desire to enter the privileged class, Rudi said simply, "I told you I made up my mind at age six I'd never be like them." It struck me then that the experiences that accounted for his empathy for the have-nots and his support for the welfare state also accounted for his aspirations and support for a market system in which he had a chance of becoming one of the haves. The system may be an unjust plutocracy, but if this was inevitable, if Rudi could not imagine it differently, then he was determined to make himself its beneficiary rather than its victim.

His support for a broad social charter, then, was not an indelible aspect of his character or ideology, but only one facet of a dialectic of ambivalence in which his beliefs remained both malleable for his own purposes and vulnerable to the ideological framing of political elites. Politics had little day-to-day salience for Rudi, and he had no group ties that might push him toward a consistent ideology. Indeed, I came to suspect that the *lack* of a formal ideology—the capacity simultaneously to hold what might appear to be contradictory opinions, to juggle working-class consciousness and visions of upper-class membership— was well suited to his experience and purposes. Thus he felt no subjective inconsistency in voting for Reagan and for other candidates and measures anathema to Reagan. When I asked him how he could vote for a probusiness president given his antipathy toward big business, Rudi shrugged and said, "You can't beat these guys, so we have to pick the one who would be the best of the four or five, even though they're all polished up anyway. The big companies don't care; [they say] 'Whoever you want, you take, and then we'll take care of things from there.'"

Despite his identification with the poor, his surprisingly broad vision of the social charter, and his registration as a Democrat, Rudi remained open to Reagan and the Right and to their claim that a renewed laissez-faire capitalism would help everyone. His union, seen by Rudi as corrupt and in bed with management ("They don't get those nice homes and Cadillacs on their salaries"), had backed Reagan, but he would not have accepted an alternative endorsement anyway. Democrats had long since squandered whatever party loyalty Rudi may have had since they too were under the control of big business. Thus, Rudi was free to "vote for the man."

If he succeeds in his plan to become well-to-do, Rudi's beliefs may congeal into something like a consistent conservative ideology. If he comes to see himself stuck at NDC, a driver-worker for life, then his working-class consciousness may become more coherent and predominant. But then again, like so many of his older, married coworkers, he may just drift along and not think too much about politics. Bereft of ideological moorings, he may continue to drift into whatever political channels he finds appealing, feeling little need to chart a consistent course.

JOSÉ BUSTAMANTE was a forty-four-year-old Chicano, short, rugged, with dark hair and deep brown eyes that seemed shy and warm at the same time. He was born in southern California and had lived nearly all his life in Santa Teresa. His parents came to California from "the old country" to find steady work and a better life for their children. José's dad worked on a ranch at first, moving to a baking company as a truck loader and then as a baker. His mother spent most of her time raising José and his seven siblings, working occasionally in a meat packinghouse. Neither parent became a citizen until José joined the U.S. Air Force and won a job requiring high security clearance.

José attended a Catholic high school where he earned his tuition by cleaning the local Mexican-American theater in the early morning; this left his afternoons free for varsity football and basketball. He told me that the priest got him that job so he could attend on his own "rather than through charity." He was a good student. Upon graduation he enlisted in the air force because it was "not quite as gung ho as the army or marines, more of a nine-to-five type thing." As a teletype operator, José was privy to top secret messages:

> I saw the whole Vietnam thing going in front of me. You could see what they [pilots] were going over there for . . . supposedly as advisers, but after a year or so you knew what was going on. I knew I didn't want to go. Basically that's why I got out. . . . I was ready to stay in, make it a career, but I was no hero and there was no way I was going over there.

After discharge, José collected unemployment for eight weeks, but "I couldn't stand to hang around for too long; I had to get a job." He worked for a time at the post office, but he "couldn't afford to stay" at the wages they paid then because he planned to get married and have a family. On his way home he would often walk past the NDC office to ask about openings. He eventually started as a pre-loader on the 4 A.M. shift while earning an A.A. degree in business at night at City College.

Politics were not central in his family life. When his folks came to the United States, they learned that Democrats "look out for the working man," so they had voted solidly Democratic ever since. "It's kinda sad," José commented, "but they didn't have no education at all, so it's hard for them. I'm not making any excuse, but that's probably the reason." He, on the other hand, took some pride in voting for "good" candidates regardless of party, viewing this as more sophisticated. José recalled no awareness of ethnic or class distinctions during his school years. Although he knew he "wasn't wealthy," he "didn't feel poor either." Peer groups at his high school did not form along racial lines, and he could not remember ever feeling any ill-will in that regard. Besides, José noted that "it takes a lot to really get me going on something like that." He did not discuss politics in the air force either because "I couldn't vote, so why bother?" The events of the civil rights movement in the 1960s, however, had made him aware of politics: "The people who were trying to suppress black people and stuff, I thought they were the bad guys. . . . I guess it was the big marches we had. . . . I never focused on [politics] until those things happened."

José was a quiet man in all senses, satisfied with his life. Perhaps because he was living the American dream—acquiring more income and education than his folks and expecting the same for his two daughters—he could say, "I'm content where I'm at." Both he and his wife worked hard, enjoyed their standard of living, and aspired to little more. They owned a comfortable, well-kept, four-bedroom tract home in a quiet, tree-lined suburb. José now hoped only to keep his health so he could "continue to provide" for his family, put in his years for retirement, and "go fishin' once in a while."

This is not to say, however, that he was satisfied with the state of the world. The news he tried to keep up on was "almost all bad." He worried that "all the little wars" will end up causing nations to "choose sides in one big war. . . . What's to stop them? The United States used the bomb the last time, and supposedly the United States was the good guy." More concrete and immediately pressing was what José saw as our biggest problem:

> America doesn't take care of their own people. Like all this foreign aid. Those people need it, but we got people starving to death right here, too. . . . [And] it doesn't seem like our government, you know, America or whatever you want to call it, does enough about it. They've got their priorities mixed. They buy friendships with other countries, [but] 80 or 90 percent of it doesn't get to the poor people.

When I asked about other major problems, José homed in on a dilemma that is central to debates over the social charter:

> We are taxed too much. I like some of these new ideas like the Reagan administration is bringing out, but I realize that if they do [cut taxes and services] they're gonna have to take money away from somebody else, and some people need help. So I'd like to see it come, but I really . . . hope it doesn't happen, you know what I mean? It's like a dream, you know; God, cut my taxes 'cause I sure would like to see that; but I really don't want to see anybody get hurt.

Indeed, José voted against Proposition 13—despite his high taxes and the fact that he stood to gain hundreds of dollars per year in property tax relief—because he felt "education would be hurt." Interestingly, both his daughters were in a Catholic school. "I voted the way I felt right," he said.

Like many of the others, this tension between the tax squeeze and the desire for human services was a theme running through his comments. He did not resolve it by recourse to the waste/fraud arguments used by many to justify cuts, although he agreed waste and fraud were problems. When I asked what government ought to do about poverty, he expressed a similar ambivalence:

> That's very hard to answer. You can't ask government to initiate more welfare programs 'cause that doesn't solve the problems. Some of the people on welfare, quite a few of them really, took advantage of the situation where they could get this money, and they were able to work at some kind of job— might not be the best job—but they figured if they could get the money here, why not? . . .
>
> Some programs waste too much money, hire too many people. Not

enough gets down to where it's really needed. Too many bureaucrats. I really couldn't say how it could be solved. I wish I knew. There's fraud, there's waste, it's just so screwed up, the whole system. Basically it's a good idea to help people that need help, but it just doesn't seem to work out right. . . . There's waste, yes, but you *need* some of these [programs], 'cause otherwise, what would people do? . . . But on the other hand, there are a few who just like to get things the easy way.

José came closer to a clear resolution to this issue when he described the one time in twenty years of working life when he personally experienced the welfare state. Following a back injury at work,

I had to go on disability and I got kind of pissed at them because you know, . . . I drew disability one time in my life and they treat you like it's *their* money! I've been puttin' into that darn thing for . . . if I get disabled, and they just treat you like it's theirs and they don't want to give it to you. And that really got me upset because I felt horrible. I been workin' [at NDC] fifteen years and for a lousy $150 you gotta fill out all these damn forms that probably cost $30 to print! It's ridiculous, but that's the way the government does things.

Q: But you said you didn't want them to make it "too free." Shouldn't they make it hard to get?

OK, but only for abusers. There's people that abuse it and you're gonna have people like that in everything. . . . Some that'll take advantage no matter what. But that's human nature, and basically, I think the problem is not there. I think they're wasting more money [detecting fraud] than is actually being wasted by fraud. . . .

They're so far in now they can't get out. It's so messed up. Reagan's supposed to be trying to cut down on all this, and I hope he can. But he *should've started at the top!* And I don't think he is. It seems like the only people getting scared are the people on Social Security, the ones with pensions. And he shouldn't take that away from our old people. They should start at the top; that's where all the big salaries are. Things like that really burn me up.

José's desire for cuts that would "start at the top" was shared by all six of the public-service workers. Like them, he wanted to end the fraud he considered inevitable and the waste he saw as not so inevitable. This did not mean that he supported cuts in welfare programs. José favored increased spending in six areas of social spending and maintaining current spending in eleven others. He would decrease none. In fact, he noted several times that he would raise spending for the needy by cutting funds for high-level administrators. Although he liked

Reagan's ideas on tightening the belt of the welfare state, he opposed each of the specific cuts I asked about. As a squeezed middle-income taxpayer the *principle* of cuts had some appeal; but as a worker the *manner* proposed for doing so offended him. For José there was "no justice" when he had to pay six thousand dollars a year in taxes to support the needy while the rich avoided "paying their fair share" by using loopholes. In his comments on such issues, he hit upon an irony stressed by his public-sector counterparts:

> Shoot, everybody likes the idea of lower taxes. Like I said though, you're paying the taxes and eventually you could benefit from it. They're high and everything, and people complain that government doesn't do this or that, but then they don't want to give 'em the funds to do it with. *So they're either gonna complain because they're talking too much or not doing enough.* And we're so damn used to the government doin' all these things for us that they gotta get the money somehow. No, I don't like paying taxes, you know, but I'll live with it. (emphasis added)

José's vision of the social charter was broad. His resentments about taxes and waste at the top notwithstanding, he granted the state a wide sphere of legitimacy to meet human needs. As a practical matter, however, he placed little trust in the political system. He firmly believed in democracy but doubted that the United States really is one:

> There are too many special interest groups. The people who get things done are the ones with the money to have somebody lobby for them. That's the way our government is run. That's the way I feel. *It's run for big business.* I've just had that feeling for a long time now. It just seems like, like I say, I'm content, right? But I see these things going on around me. These people with money are getting bigger and poor people are getting poorer, I think. I think big business runs the government and I think they are just greedy.

When I countered with a question about the value of leaving decisions to the free market, José dismissed the idea. For him, the free market was but a euphemism for big business as usual. He shared with Rudi, Greg, and Sally a folk theory: the United States is a corporate plutocracy in which "politicians are basically all the same":

> You hear that they're gonna help you. They're gonna cut your taxes, they're gonna help the working man, they're gonna do this or that. And to me, OK, it's my opinion that once they get into office—whoever it is—the only guy they're helping is themselves and big business which helped them get there. They tell you, OK, "I'm a conservative," or "I'm a Republican" or "a Democrat," whatever. But once they get to the top, it's all the same.

It was puzzling to listen to a man say such things—and support all manner of public spending despite his material interests in lower taxes and his clear awareness of welfare state flaws—and then mention that he voted for Ronald Reagan in 1980. José was a registered Democrat who saw himself as "on the liberal side," one who would very much "like to see government take care of people." By many standards he was a class-conscious worker. Yet, despite Reagan's reputation as a fan of business and an opponent of social services, José made up his mind early and easily.

An explanation at the level of political culture might show that Reagan's campaign themes of cutting taxes, red tape, and regulations appealed to José as a burdened middle-income taxpayer and unjustly hassled seeker of disability payments. But José voted against two tax-cutting initiatives, and although he liked Reagan's notion of deregulation, he opposed each of the specific deregulation proposals I asked about. He was dissatisfied with Carter: "naive," "always backing down," and took "no initiative of his own," so "how could things get worse?" José offered such judgments without affect; they were the words neither of an impassioned opponent of Carter nor of an ardent supporter of Reagan. Even if Carter's catastrophes and Reagan's rhetoric left him without firm partisan allegiance, it is still difficult to imagine how a registered Democrat could have put aside his long held professedly "liberal" beliefs about social justice and government's domination by big business. After all, Reagan rode the coattails of Proposition 13, which José rejected, and Reagan preached repeal of the windfall profits tax on oil companies and pledged to hasten deregulation. José, on the other hand, strongly favored Proposition 11, an *added* state tax on oil companies: "Every time I see [oil companies] print their profits I get upset. I just think big business is too greedy. They should share [their wealth] with all the people who are helpin' 'em get there."

Explanations of voting behavior that center on political culture beg the question of how campaigns, say, interact with the particular voter. Why was José so *open* to switching parties? I would hypothesize that this vote simply was not all that significant to him. First, his general dissatisfaction with the political economic system—lack of trust in government, low sense of political efficacy, conviction that politicians are "all the same"—is a common mode of political alienation. If that was how he felt, and I believe it was, then it would have been irrational for him to invest his vote with much significance—the probability for disappointment was great. If we may understand alienation as a *practice*, then it is possible to see how it insulated him from frustration by minimizing the gravity of any given voting decision.

Further, the social organization of José's daily life militated against his seeing significance in national politics. He often did not get home until the 6 o'clock news was over and he rarely could stay up for the 11 o'clock edition. He found the *Los Angeles Times* intimidating in depth, and besides, "The only part of the paper I read is usually the sports section because basically that's *people*—things they're doing, accomplishments, you know? Some of these people are great; individual things. And I feel any news or newspaper—basically all they tell you is bad news." In light of his other remarks, I took this to mean that compared to the often depressing, opaque, and tainted complexity of hard news, the clarity and inspirational comprehensibility of, say, a brilliant double play or last-second touchdown was far more rewarding.

Even if José had had the background and the time to follow politics, why would he have done so? What salience would elections have when he earned a good living week in and week out regardless of the state of the economy and throughout the Vietnam and Watergate debacles? For him, politics neither changed nor affected much and he believed the future would be "pretty much the same" as the present. Salience aside, José did not like to talk about political issues for what were very good reasons, given the exigencies of his everyday world:

It's hard. It may be a copout, but I hate to talk with people about politics and stuff because it can get pretty heavy, you know? I don't want to do that with people at work because I have to work with them. And religion is another thing. There's too many people that feel strongly about some things. I don't want to offend anybody. . . . I have feelings all right, [but] I want to be able to work with these people. . . .

And, well, maybe I don't feel that I'm that knowledgeable about things. If I knew, if I felt I knew a lot more actual facts and everything, then I might be able to do it, you know, strike up a conversation with somebody about politics. But I'm not going to talk about anything that I really don't know anything about 'cause first of all, I don't want to sound like a fool. And the other reason is that, like I said, I want to keep the friends I have. I don't know how they feel about politics, and you could say something, all it would take is a statement or so and boom! That's it.

To get along, to be liked, to not appear the fool—those are omnipresent objectives in social interaction. And if in José's case politics were seen as corrupt and lacking salience, then to invest energy in political discussion—to say nothing of involvement—entailed high risks for low rewards. If such beliefs were measured in a survey, surely José would be cast as an alienated voter, and perhaps he was. But such an interpretation would fail to measure the extent to which he was employing a *strategy*, actively dissociating himself from a world of politics he found alienating.

I cannot deny the irony in José's vote for Reagan in 1980, but there was less inconsistency here than meets the eye. His belief that independence from party was a necessary form of sophistication did not necessarily contradict his solidly liberal values and policy preferences. If, for example, politicians of both parties are seen as controlled by big business, and if the search for political knowledge with which to distinguish between them is seen as frustrating at best, then there is an odd form of consistency in José's matter-of-fact assertion: "you gotta give the other guy a chance, you gotta see what he's gonna do." He perceived an impoverished choice between a known and an unknown evil. Perhaps a simple sense of fairness, rather than a critical shift in basic beliefs, was all it took to tip José's electoral scales rightward. Indeed, I would argue that it was the very continuities in his values and discontents that led to his decision. Certainly there was not a word in his eighty-page transcript to suggest that he *intended* his vote as a contribution to what Reagan and the Right quickly called their mandate.

For me, the paradox here is that José's strategies for living with his discontents helped make him an unwitting accomplice in the subversion of his own political values. It is unlikely, however, that this will disturb him much as long as his family life remains undisturbed by politics. José was justifiably proud of his accomplishments, satisfied with *his* world if not *the* world.

Six individuals, each with a unique blend of beliefs, each belief a relic of a unique life history. All were in some ways critical of both state and market. Like conservatives, most believed in the opportunities of the market. But, like liberals, most knew that just as the market giveth, so the market can taketh away. All expressed anger at some facet of the state—bureaucracy, regulatory red tape, waste, or welfare fraud—yet five of the six held out for a stronger state that could better meet human needs. How are both types of beliefs juggled? How can one be suspicious of the poor and support more funding for poverty programs? Surely these sketches raise more questions than they answer.

If there are themes running through the rather divergent beliefs of these six subjects, then one of them must be ambivalence—about the state *and* the market, and about the nature of the American social charter. This chapter has focused upon the particularities of individual belief systems; the next attempts to discern dimensions of ideology that were shared by the group.

4

Reluctant Liberalism, Residual Conservatism: Visions of the Social Charter among NDC Workers

RUDI VENTURA proclaimed America the greatest and the richest country in the world, a country he gladly served in the army and on the police force. Moments later, however, he decried as "absurd" the fact that the United States lets some of its citizens "starve" while lobbyists fight for subsidies that pay farmers not to grow food. José Bustamante told of his pride in America's strength, saying that it could and should help poorer nations. But he quickly added in anger that such aid "doesn't get to the people," that too many Americans need help too, and that he suspected our leaders of simply "buying" allies abroad.

Each of the others expressed similarly conflicting feelings about the United States. Were they patriots or dissidents? Probably, like most of us, they were both. Each of the six sets of transcripts had a subtext: a rather large gap exists between the ideal of America—what each imagined it once was, could be, should be—and the reality of America. Their complaints about this gap took various forms. Buford Schmitt worried constantly about the "slipping morality" he saw as the cause of our national ills, about "communists" coming "to take us over," and about a host of other trends conspiring to push America away from the traditions that he believed it once lived by. Joe Demski said he shared with most Americans a maddening frustration that stemmed from belonging to a "great country," the world's leading power, which was nonetheless impotent before Iranian "punks" and systematically unable or unwilling to provide work and housing for millions of its citizens.

Like the others, Joe felt that if America stands for something, it is oppor- tunity—in the United States one should be able to enter whatever line of work one desires if one is willing to work at it and become qualified. He had not found this to be true in his case, although he continued to hope. Although Joe supported more public services than the other five, he still believed in meritocracy. In fact, part of the reason for his broad sense of the social charter was his conviction that "the system" *blocks* opportunity, prevents people like him from forging livelihoods. He identified himself as "kind of left" and would be classified as a social democrat in most Western democracies. It is noteworthy that such a stance derived from his desire for more opportunity; the meritocracy of the market seemed to him stifled, so he looked, a little reluctantly perhaps, to the state for solutions.

Greg Larson too thought that America means opportunity. He was actually living the American dream rather than just looking for it. He believed he was "doing really well" for a barefoot boy from Appalachia with little education. His family was secure. A new Volvo wagon sat in the driveway of a new split-level home set against a backdrop of lush mountains. He had worked very hard for twenty years, but compared to friends he left behind "sitting around the general store," he was living proof of the viability of American meritocracy. Although Greg supported a wide range of welfare state services and delivered scathing criticisms of big business and the tax dodges of the rich, he did not like the principle behind redistributionist policies. To take from even the undeserving rich would be to deny a freedom he took as a defining feature of U.S. society.

Both the current successes and the future hopes of these people seemed to me hinged to meritocracy, to the belief that more than any other country they knew anything about, in America there are opportunities (however too few) and effort matters (even if not enough). Perhaps the one ideological strand that connected Joe on the Left, Buford on the Right, and the other four in between was that democracy in America ought to stand for this. It is important to note in this context, however, that with the partial exception of Rudi Ventura, the word *opportunity* did not signify anything resembling the ritual rags-to-riches Horatio Alger model of mobility. On the contrary, like the workers described by Rubin in *Worlds of Pain* (1976)—who expect opportunity in America to mean only the ability of one's children to go to college, to live better than they, the parents, do; who, if they were to inherit suddenly a million dollars, would likely just "pay off bills" (205) and go on working—the NDC workers desired the modest serenity that comes from economic security. For them, the opportunity to achieve meant simply a steady livelihood and a "decent life for my family."

Opportunity, effort, individual achievement, democratic ends—all six NDC workers shared the basic vision embodied in that equation. But all six via rather different logics dismissed as hopelessly naive the idea that American society actually works that way. For Buford, state intervention had nearly ruined an otherwise perfect market; the notion that market failures had engendered the welfare state was just short of communist propaganda. The others had a different view. Sally Jones argued, less subtly than Joe Demski, that U.S. capitalism has a ruling class that dominates both market and state to the detriment of the many. Even Greg Larson, a self-identified conservative and friend of free enterprise, said that "big business" is "behind every evil." His support for capitalism was limited to small business: a local roofing contractor should not be encumbered by the state, but Exxon and giant agribusiness are another story. José Bustamante believed that the market fails to provide sufficient opportunities for the poor, that state aid is also inadequate, and that politicians are simply too beholden to corporate interests to change things. Only Buford expressed even the residue of belief that the market mechanisms that lead to wealth at the top will somehow allow enough wealth to trickle down into opportunities for those at the bottom.

Aside from Buford, the other five granted legitimacy to American capitalism on the condition that the market really must be meritocratic, that it must indeed lead to democratic ends. The legitimacy they granted to the state was also contingent, although, again, only Buford insisted that "it's not the government's business" to do anything beyond provide for defense and law enforcement. All the others claimed to want the state to provide for the basic human needs of the disadvantaged—in fact, they wanted the state to do a better job of this. What struck me most about their discourse was not that government was seen as wrongfully intervening in the market but rather that its interventions were seen as failing to make the market *work*—that is, provide adequate opportunities for ordinary people to sustain their lives.

The disparity between ideal and real pervaded their understanding of both capitalism and democracy, market and state.[1] Yet their talk of this gap implied a crucial distinction. For all six, the world as they experienced it was a *market world*; that the word capitalism was never used suggests that it was taken for granted, like water to fish who inhabit it. In their experience, control by what they saw obliquely as "big-money interests" was inevitable if unjust. A reasonable niche within this world or perhaps a shot at a scam for a slightly better one was all they felt they could expect. The state, on the other hand, was not seen as the product of some invisible hand but as a visible, less than inevitable human construction. Thus, they tended to hold "government" responsible not only for its own flaws but for the failures of the market as well. Ironically, this tendency seemed to be both the source of their support for state programs and the reason for their reluctance about such support.

1. Samuel P. Huntington (1981) argues that this disparity between the ideal and the real in political life has always existed in the United States and always will, probably for the better.

Private Workers on Public Spending

It is relatively easy to express support or opposition in the abstract for, say "the welfare state." It is more difficult to specify whether one would vote to increase, maintain, or decrease public spending on particular programs. Spending preferences, when elicited in the context of an interview, have the advantage of concreteness; responses are less likely to be drawn in the broad brushstrokes of ideology and worldview. I asked my six NDC subjects about ten areas of welfare state spending: public schools, higher education, welfare benefits, medical care, mental health services, environmental protection, public transportation, public housing, job safety, and employment and training programs. These items were borrowed from the Field Poll (1978) as indicators of the sort of social charter my subjects envisioned.

To my surprise and, I suspect, to theirs, the NDC workers expressed rather solid support for the vast bulk of welfare state programs. Although I questioned them during my first round of interviews when the tax revolt was at its peak, clear majorities favored maintaining or increasing public spending in all ten areas. Recall that they complained frequently about unfairly high taxes, wasteful red tape, and abuses in the public sector. Moreover, their utilization of public services was minimal. None even knew of anyone living in public housing; none had ever been on welfare; none used public transportation; and out of a group total of one hundred years of adult work only about twenty weeks of unemployment benefits had been paid to the six in the past. All were hard pressed to list any direct benefits they had received from government in general.

Yet when I asked the six their preferences on the ten areas of public spending, only twelve out of sixty "votes" were cast in favor of decreased spending. Buford Schmitt as a matter of principle favored less spending on public schools, welfare benefits, and public housing. The other exceptions were more difficult to interpret. Joe Demski, the most consistently liberal of the six, favored a decrease in spending for job safety. As a bit of aggregate survey data, Joe's response could be interpreted as a conservative, antistate answer and an inconsistency. It takes on a very different and more consistent political hue, however, when his reasoning is considered:

> I'd like to see [job safety programs] put into the business spectrum. Big business seems responsible for that. . . . I don't think I should spend my money to go for a safety program for J. B. Construction Co. I think J. B. Construction Co. should be held responsible for their own [workers'] safety.

Greg Larson was the only one who even considered a decrease in spending for employment and training programs. When I asked why, he cited his observations of a local program in which there seemed to him much make-work and little real work going on. In isolation, this preference would be taken as support for the position of President Reagan and other conservatives who often invoke the word make-work to justify cutting spending for public employment and training. The political valence of Greg's choice is less clear, however, when it is viewed in conjunction with his prescription for joblessness—more *rigorous* training and *guaranteed* jobs—the latter, at least, anathema to conservatives. Greg was no closet socialist, but his policy preferences seemed always to reflect both the laissez-faire lore by which he lived ("a dog-eat-dog kind of thing") and a strongly felt sense of social justice and Christian charity.

With the exception of Demski, the respondents were somewhat suspicious of "people on welfare" in the abstract; each seemed to harbor a hunch that many such people could not have tried as hard as they had to make it on their own. Moreover, they were suspicious of a state about which they knew little save its reputation for waste at the lower levels and its domination by a corporate plutocracy at the top. Such suspicions seemed behind their reluctance to support more spending even when they talked of pressing needs. There was much equivocation in their responses to spending questions, and they chose mainte-nance of spending levels as often as increases. Such choices, however, amid suspicion and equivocation, highlighted the surprisingly broad sphere of legit-imacy these people granted to the state. Their spending preferences and the reasoning behind them offered scant evidence (Buford excepted) of support for a contracted social charter.

I also asked about spending cuts proposed by the Reagan administration at the time of my second interviews. The general idea of cutting government programs to aid economic recovery appealed to Schmitt, Larson, Bustamante, and Ventura. Although neither Greg nor José located the major source of waste in welfare programs (the military being the worst offender in their experience), the Republican campaign theory that excessive government spending was the cause of our economic woes made sense to them. Joe Demski opposed the idea because he felt sure that those most in need rather than those who wasted the most money would suffer the brunt of the Reagan cuts. Sally Jones could not decide because, although she agreed with Joe, she felt certain there were abusers and "fat cats" who were wasting her tax dollars by not pulling their own weight.

The appeal of spending cuts dropped off sharply, however, when I asked about *specific* programs. Buford alone favored cuts in funding for public televi-sion. He watched no television, feeling that most programming was "immoral" or "junk" and that news was controlled by "liberals" and "one-worlders." "We got along fine without television when I was a boy," he said, and public television was just one more thing that was none of "the government's business." The other five supported continued federal funding of public television. Buford also approved of proposed cuts in the number of weeks of eligibility for unemployment, arguing in the precise parlance of Reagan's stump speeches that there were "too many government-paid vacations." Rudi Ventura also supported this proposal; the Reagan cutback to twenty-six weeks of eligibility would "only put us back where we were." He added that further cuts would be unacceptable because he would "hate to be out of a job and have nothin' to back me up." All the others opposed the idea of reduced eligibility.

The proposal for cuts in food stamps and reduced-price school lunches received the most support; half favored it. Again, Buford's position was the most extreme:

> Once again, it's not the government's job to provide that for which a person can get out and earn himself.
>
> Q: Well, a lot of the people who advocate school lunch programs say that a child whose parents for one reason or another, good or bad, don't have much money, that that may be the one nutritious meal they get during the day.
>
> I think as often as not it's because the parents have not put nutrition as a priority. I'd say they put their vices and habits above that. Try and find a man what would go without his beer to sacrifice [for] a nutritious meal for his kid. . . . Or would they go without a pack of cigarettes a day to have a better meal for their kids? No, they wouldn't. . . . I don't think that, ah, [such children] should be taken care of unless the parents are willing to sacrifice.

Whereas Buford's account of his position contained both the far-right principle of opposition to government food aid and a rather severe personal judgment of the morals of people who need it, Greg's account offered only his anecdote about his stepdaughter's eligibility being erroneously based on her Latino surname. Although Greg would tighten eligibility, he would recoil at the thought of children not receiving food, no matter how he might feel about their parent's morals. Similarly, Rudi Ventura approved of food stamp cuts on eligibility grounds, citing Reagan's statements, which he took to mean that *each* member of an eligible family could now get a full allotment. When I countered that food stamp rules did not allow this, Rudi concluded that perhaps the administration was merely looking for a "happy medium" and that tighter rules would leave *more* food stamps for families who "really need it."

The only other instance of support for specific spending cuts concerned federal benefits for miners who contract black-lung disease. Buford opposed this on the grounds that mining was "like defense" in that energy independence benefited "the whole country," but José Bustamante supported the idea. Did this preference constitute a contradictory conservative strand in José's otherwise largely liberal belief system? Only if the raw response is severed from his explanation. José strongly believed that all miners with black lung should get full benefits, but *in keeping* with his other beliefs he thought that this is the responsibility of the mining companies who profit from the miners' labor.

What does it mean that on this issue the conservative free marketeer Schmitt broke his pattern of opposition to nearly all forms of government spending and supported public benefits for private workers, and the more liberal Bustamante broke his pattern of support for most welfare state programs and opposed such benefits? At a substantive level, it may mean merely that Schmitt saw miners, as he said, contributing to the whole of society and thus deserving support when they contract the dread disease; and that Bustamante the liberal was tired of what are in effect subsidies to a powerful industry, with taxpayers footing the bill for suffering through which corporations reap profits. But at another level it is possible to catch a glimpse of an often elusive quality of beliefs. Neither Buford nor José saw anything inconsistent in their policy preferences here. And if these issue positions are examined in the context of the basic values and procedures of political reasoning from which they were derived, then apparent inconsistencies are rendered consistent. This suggests that for their holders the meaning of beliefs is *relational*, that the ideological valence of a given molecule of opinion is not an intrinsic feature of its structure as a solitary unit of political thought but instead a feature of its relation to other opinions, sets of opinions, and the broader systems of values that underlie them. If so, then surveys and polls that attempt to assess the political significance of beliefs or policy preferences as if these were discrete may be manufacturing what they purport to measure.

To return to the story line, the more general inference about these subjects' beliefs about the social charter was the strength of support they showed for the welfare state. Buford opposed most forms of social spending and favored proposed cuts because most such programs were simply "not the government's business." For Joe, Greg, José, and usually Sally and Rudi, however, these were legitimate functions of the state. Although each of the five offered complaints about waste, abuse, or maladministration—that is, about illegitimate state *practices*—none of them expressed any *principle* against the idea that the state should serve such myriad functions. Even sympathetic critics have worried that the distinction I have inferred here is tantamount to hairsplitting in search of liberalism—a fair question. Surely some conservative, antistate ideological principles may lie concealed in this or that complaint about particular state practices. I believe, however, that the broad patterns of belief articulated by five of these six across a wide range of topics and the consistent differences in their discourse about state and market compared to Buford's suggest a critical ideological boundary: "the state has no right" versus "the state has a right but is doing it wrong." Moreover, if what I have said about the relational nature of beliefs and the importance of context has merit, then this hypothesized boundary and its meaning may be made less visible by polls, surveys, and other tools that infer shifts in political opinion from discrete units of belief.

The State as Regulator

I also asked about the related issue of government regulation, another dimension of the social charter. Debate over state regulation is as old as the United States itself (see, for example, Wolfe 1977). But with the decline in economic growth and the onset of stagflation and fiscal crisis in the 1970s, and particularly in the 1980 presidential campaign, it has become central to political conflict. President Reagan claimed as part of his "mandate" the elimination of the "regulatory nightmare" that "unnecessarily" hampers American business, reducing its productivity, profitability, and thus its competitiveness in the world market.

All six NDC subjects had bemoaned in one way or another the red tape involved when government touched their lives. Three of them—Buford, Greg, and José—stated their support for the general idea of deregulation. Rudi initially exclaimed, "Without the government, the oil companies could jack up [gas prices] to three dollars a gallon. They don't care about us. I think the government should regulate them." Then, after reflecting on the "farce" of the catalytic converter, he settled on wanting at least the needlessly bothersome regulations "cut back a bit." Sally trusted neither regulation as then practiced nor Reagan's claim that deregulation would be a boon to the economy. Joe Demski felt the whole concept of deregulation was a ruse for big business to further fleece the public. Although he agreed with the others that some regulations were a nuisance, he believed most were "necessary."

Although all six had complaints and half supported Reagan's general deregulatory thrust, inferences based upon this alone would be misleading. Just as they favored spending reductions in the abstract while opposing concrete cuts, so their support for Reagan administration deregulation proposals was decidedly weak. Buford agreed that the oil industry and land development should be deregulated, but opposed any relaxation of environmental protection. Greg Larson thought deregulation was a "great idea" because there were "too many regulations," but on specifics he favored only the *easing* of occupational health and safety rules. When he expressed his general enthusiasm, I asked if there were any aspects of business that he felt should remain regulated. An emphatic no was his reply. Next I asked him about the proposed relaxation of pollution controls:

> No! We *have* to [regulate that]. It's not a matter of we should or shouldn't. Who's gonna have a car to drive if you can't breathe? . . . The world's not a factory and it can't take this kind of abuse. I think business, and I [am] probably contradicting myself, what I said a little while ago, but businesses—there *should* be regulations on businesses, even though I do believe in free enterprise. You've got to have some kind of rules or the game just doesn't work, you know?[2]

Thus, while the idea of deregulation appealed to most of them, only Buford would leave the "public interest" in the hands of the market alone. The others, whether seeing themselves as conservative or liberal, were no fans of deregulation in practice. On specifics they consistently granted government's regulatory functions broad legitimacy, the public benefits apparently seeming worth their costs in inefficiency.

A Dialectic of Ambivalence: Affinities, Estrangements, and Experience

I have pulled from these six interviews some fairly conflicting themes. Five of the subjects seemed to hold that "the system" is a plutocracy run by and for the powerful, yet they held out for the principle of achievement based on merit. Their support for meritocracy, however, had little to do with protecting capitalism and much to do with democratic ends like opportunities for self-sufficiency. Most held that government is not only flawed in its own right but a failure at making the market a better mechanism for democratizing opportunities. Yet despite their criticisms of the abstraction "government," most favored continued and often expanded public spending on most specific programs and supported government regulation. In short, their accounts of their policy preferences and

---

2. Public sentiments on environmental issues, at least as measured in polls in the late 1970s and early 1980s, mirror those of Greg Larson in showing a strong majoritarian support for environmental protection across party lines. In opposition to Reagan administration arguments that such protections raise unemployment and prices, a 1983 Harris poll reported in *Business Week* (January 24, 1983) found 89 percent of a national sample believed it is possible to reduce pollution *and* unemployment simultaneously. Moreover, *Business Week* noted that "1983 is the year the Reagan Administration has [planned] less stringent regulation of polluting industries. Unfortunately for the deregulators . . . the American public is dramatically renewing its commitment to keeping anti-pollution laws intact—and even to strengthening them." This conclusion is supported by political action as well as polled attitudes. In the first two years of Reagan's first term, membership in the Sierra Club grew 81 percent, from 188,000 to 341,000 (*San Francisco Chronicle*, April 5, 1983).

political beliefs frequently borrowed bits of lore from the Left and the Right simultaneously.

Cognitive theories of beliefs suggest a basic human drive for symmetry and consistency among beliefs, arguing that both logical and psychological constraints push people to iron out their contradictions so as to relieve dissonance. The accounts of my subjects have led me to a different approach, one that assumes that because human beings have contradictory experiences and interests that impose constraints of their own, their beliefs will necessarily contain asymmetries and inconsistencies. The issue then becomes the sorts of circumstances that underlie and constrain what appear to be, in the formal sense, inconsistent beliefs. Because my respondents showed few signs of the angst predicted by cognitive models, I propose a different question: through what experiential prisms do ostensibly contradictory beliefs "make sense"?

I began my initial interviews by asking what they had seen in the news lately that gave them satisfaction or worried them. Three immediately mentioned poverty-related issues as worrisome. Recall that José was disturbed that the United States did not "take care of its own people," that Rudi was outraged that a nation as affluent as America would tolerate "people starving, right here," and that Greg lamented news of elderly couples "living in cars." Demski countered my probes about the faults of the welfare state by insisting that for all the exposés of welfare cheats, one never sees how much legitimate need there is nor how much important aid is given. Rudi Ventura's longing to join the ranks of the rich did not seem to fog his childhood memories of farm-worker relatives who wore rags and lived in shacks. And although Sally's health care was covered in her union contract, she immediately cited the poverty of a health care system based on "greed" as our number one problem. Four noted plant closings and budget cuts as disheartening developments.

True, some offered anecdotes about food stamp recipients with new cars and others insisted that there are jobs for all who really look for them. Policy preferences that can be seen as liberal-left did coexist, sometimes in the same sentence, with the rhetoric of the Right. But most held the system *as well as* the individual to blame for poverty and its attendant troubles. That five of the six consistently invoked first one, then the other, and then both sorts of explanation says much about their folk theories of how the world works. Rather than understanding this as cognitive confusion, I will argue that juggling multiple frameworks, like being liberal and conservative simultaneously, was a functional if less than fully self-conscious strategy for making sense of their experience and allowing them to get on with their lives.

All six thought of themselves as fair and generous folk. All took pains to demonstrate that they would not allow their personal interests to override their concern for the larger public interest. Indeed, they seemed to hold that some sense of the public interest is *intrinsic* to their personal interests. For example, despite their complaints about high taxes, both Demski and Bustamante voted against tax reduction measures that would have put money in their pockets, and they did so, they said, on grounds of the larger good. Of course, in Buford's case, the end of state controls and the granting of free reign to the market was not only the best but the only real route to the greater good. But even if his sense of the public interest might have been less developed, his commitment to *private* Christian charity was strong. Each of the six, then, in his or her own way expressed concern for less fortunate others, and this concern was a point of personal pride just as their sense of the United States as a generous society was cause for national pride.

Rubbing against these public-spirited selves, however, were *self-made selves*. All six saw themselves as individuals who, despite generally humble beginnings and a fair share of difficulties, had achieved self-sufficiency without assistance. This too was a point of pride for them, as it has been found to be in other studies like this one. Botsch, for example, speaks of southern, rural, blue-collar workers in terms that apply equally well to my southern California suburbanites: "Time and again they talked about the satisfaction they get from knowing that they earn what they have and from feeling relatively independent of others" (1980, 64; see also Lane 1962; Sennett and Cobb 1973).

Their own histories and hopes seemed to tie them to meritocratic ideas. Each had achieved some measure of success via private individual effort, and none felt that he or she had received any breaks or help along the way. Though most were quite sure the structure of opportunities in America is limited, they were also sure that they had tried and succeeded anyway. They had for years done work they had not freely chosen and did not enjoy in order to provide "decent" lives for themselves and their families. That they had something to show for it helped convince them that such success was, at least in principle, possible for all who "really" try. What does the qualifier "really" really mean? For Buford, the structure of opportunities within American capitalism was wide open to individual initiative. Joe Demski saw plenty of obstacles strewn in the paths of all who were not already well off or well connected. The other four clustered around a midpoint, holding out for the principle of merit until they had proof of blocked opportunity. Although they had seen such proof, they had also seen themselves succeed according to that principle. They had had to try, against the odds, and in order to try one was obliged to hope that one could succeed; that they had done so allowed them to entertain the belief that success was still possible despite the obstacles.

For me the irony in this subsystem of belief inheres in the fact that their achievements came *despite* the obstacles in the market system, not merely *because* of its opportunities. By some blend of cunning and courage, diligence and discipline, they had hurdled the obstacles. Yet, the notion that achievement is available to all seemed to blind them to the view that their success might be seen as an achievement and not just the minimum to be expected of everyone. Perhaps as they gazed out to the gorgeous green mountains speckled with the mansions of movie stars and millionaires, or into their television screens displaying scenes from lives of greater consequence, their tract homes and family rounds paled into something more mundane than achievements. While proud in the certainty that they had earned all they now enjoyed, they were also humbled by the uncertainty engendered by the thought that a meritocratic culture tacitly took this as the measure of their worth. The individualist frame through which they viewed their lives gave them dignity and identity—which it simultaneously demeaned.

The lessons they seemed to draw from their work histories—for example, that if they had made it, then America does offer opportunites and that, therefore, success is a matter of individual initiative—tended to raise the moral ante for others and to hold in check both their critique of the injustices of the market and the charitable and public-spirited inclinations that flowed from it. This was one source of their affinity (though still equivocal) for the laissez-faire code and their estrangement (though incomplete) from the needs-based code of the welfare state.

In addition to their high self-reliance and low utilization of public services, their own insulation from the hardships of market fluctuations also tended to restrict their visions of the social charter. Their union contract with NDC provided a full range of benefits, and despite bitter complaints about productivity pressures and management insensitivity, union-negotiated rules on firing ensured strong job security. For this the workers paid steep union dues and worked ten-hour days. The benefits were not perceived as "fringe" in nature. Such elements of their economic security were seen as *earned*, part of the work-for-life trade that for them was central to the social charter.

This experience of earned economic security did not, however, lead them to believe that all workers had the opportunity to make the same trade. Despite the fiscal problems of the Social Security system and the skyrocketing costs of public health care that were in the news in 1980, all except Buford Schmitt held that these benefits were sacrosanct, rights not to be handed out according to market criteria. Their complaints about those who worked under the table while collecting unemployment or food stamps suggested that other income-support programs were less apt to be considered universal entitlements. Yet, the modal opinion was that anyone "legitimately" in need was *entitled* to public assistance.

Even though none of the six expected ever to need such help, they took as given (albeit sometimes reluctantly) the basic elements of the welfare state as part of America's social infrastructure.

They would all *reform* it, certainly. Each would like to see fraud, waste, and abuse eliminated, and they were not unaffected by the appeals of Reagan and the Right on these issues. But unlike the administration's policies, they would begin budget cuts with top-level bureaucrats and the Pentagon rather than with benefit levels. In fact, only Buford questioned the premise that Americans have a right to a livelihood which, *in the absence of market opportunities*, should be guaranteed by the state. The work histories that seemed to be the source of their resentments and reservations with regard to the welfare state also seemed to be the reason subsistence rights were not really at issue. For me there is a concealed consistency here: these were hard-working people who expected no less from others, but in the same way they believed that others must have the opportunity to work hard. The longer I talked with them the more I came to see coherence rather than contradiction when tales of welfare cheats were followed by expressions of support for state-guaranteed jobs for all. Whether they would be coded as liberals or conservatives in a poll would depend largely on the question asked.

What was and is at issue for these workers is the meaning of qualifying terms like *legitimately* in need or *in the absence of market opportunities*. The notion of entitlement existed but in restricted form. For five of them, government should be the employer of last resort, but each individual is obligated to take almost any job opportunity offered. Yes, Americans have the right to work; no, publicly supported jobs need not be interesting or rewarding since none of the NDC subjects had ever had that luxury. The meaning of what they had given up everyday in time and sweat, and the contributions they had made as workers to various economic security programs would have been demeaned if everyone was entitled to them regardless of effort. Thus, their support for programs like unemployment, Social Security, and disability to which they contributed was stronger than for more general entitlements given on the basis of need alone.

A final facet of the tension between earned benefits and need-based entitlements deserves mention. The union was important and unimportant in their talk of such issues. All noted that the union got them high wages and good benefits, but none dwelled upon this. It struck me that they had played no role in negotiating for such mechanisms of economic security; a national union worked out a national contract with a national corporation which covered all fifty thousand NDC workers. As lived experience then, their benefits were earned and at the same time handed down from on high. My suspicion here is that this process tended to mitigate their awareness that any union's ability to extract such benefits has been won historically through the struggles of the labor movement.

In one sense this may mean that the NDC workers were more likely to *expect* benefits as part of the basic social charter. But in another sense it may well have made them less aware that other, nonunionized, competitive-sector[3] workers— to say nothing of nonworkers—did not enjoy and could not expect the sort of economic security afforded by such benefits. The welfare state logic of entitlements was not part of their experience, whereas the laissez-faire logic of earned benefits was.[4]

Market and State as Lived Experience

There were additional dimensions of my subjects' lives as workers and citizens that helped make sense of how their beliefs made sense of and in their world. As workers in a market milieu, they knew something about powerlessness. Sally Jones was the one NDC worker who approved of the way the company was run. All five of her coworkers chafed under company policies, repeatedly criticizing what they saw as deliberate underhiring and arbitrary increases in productivity pressures. The union that got them good wages and benefits was also perceived as being "in bed with management" when it came to working conditions. The result was a feeling that the company had organized their jobs in ways that had robbed them of the private time with their families which they saw as the raison d'être for those jobs.

Five of the six expressed support for workplace democracy. This was more true for Buford the archconservative than for Sally, whose views on most other issues leaned leftward. The efficiency/profitability system at NDC was rational according to Sally, but the others saw it as exploitative and illegitimate. They were critical not only of the ways NDC's work organization cut into their free time but of how this eroded their sense of craft and, as Buford put it, affected "the quality of our service." Although few had any concrete idea what the term *workplace democracy* meant, most wholeheartedly endorsed ideas like electing

3. See O'Connor (1973) on the characteristics of monopoly-sector workers like those at NDC versus workers in competitive and state sectors.

4. The extensive private benefits allocated at the level of the firm in more industrialized, unionized sectors of the U.S. economy contrast sharply with the analogous public benefits allocated more broadly by the state in European industrial democracies. The political and ideological implications of this difference are significant. For example, because the American labor movement has won substantial benefits *for its members* (just under 20 percent of the labor force in 1984), neither that movement nor those members have as much of a stake in pressuring the state for universal benefits covering all workers. This both helps create and reinforces the stratification within the U.S. working class that has historically impeded the development of the labor movement (see Aronowitz 1973; O'Connor 1973). The extent of such private benefits and their politicoideological implications have contributed to the relatively anemic development of the U.S. welfare state (Wilensky 1975; Stephens 1979; Mosley 1981).

supervisors and having a say over the organization and pace of work. Moreover, they felt sure this would improve not only their work lives but the company as a whole.

Is it self-serving to cast complaints about having to work harder in terms of lost craft and lowered quality of service? A convenient coupling perhaps, but if this is ideological work, it is not merely that. Recall that these workers drew pride and part of their identities from the fact that they could "take it," that they worked long and hard and in so doing provided a service of such quality that NDC remained atop an increasingly competitive industry. Note too that the recent speedup had palpably added to their work loads, infringed on customary work practices, and necessitated the relaxation of NDC's traditional policy about trying neighbors' homes if consignees were not in. Further, their expressed concerns for craft and quality were not used to conceal objections to more work. They all felt they worked more than hard enough already, so the lower standard times were openly resented as intensified exploitation rooted in the corporation's obsession with profits.

This resentment of powerlessness and exploitation in their corner of the market world seemed to lead in two contending directions. On one hand, all but Joe Demski seemed to worry that too many people loafed on welfare and unemployment when they should be working; and most seemed parenthetically to harbor the suspicion that public-sector workers, postal workers in particular, were less constrained, thanks to *their* taxes, by productivity and profitability pressures. (Paradoxically, it may be that much of what they struggled against in their own work led them not toward the view that those who "live off the government" are *also* struggling implicity against alienating and exploitative work but instead toward a backlash against the welfare state and its perceived beneficiaries.)

On the other hand, in their humanistic concern for the less fortunate and their surprising support for welfare state programs, I sensed a tacit desire for a way of life or at least a sphere in which neither they nor others were at the mercy of the market's visibly impersonal invisible hand. Their work lives aside, five spoke of being "ripped off" by "big business"—utilities, oil companies, landlords, and price inflation against which even their wages offered no protection. Such experiences helped me understand why, despite some distinctly social-Darwinist, antistate beliefs, most retained some affinity for a strong social charter, for the idea that a good government ought to insulate its citizens from the raw play of market forces.

Yet part of their residual affinity for the laissez-faire moral economy and their estrangement from a new moral economy in which all citizens are so insulated appeared to stem from their experience of the state's failure to provide such insulation. For example, Rudi Ventura, Greg Larson, and José Bustamante all switched from Carter to Reagan in 1980 in part because with Carter at the helm, the ship of state had failed to halt the rising inflation that was eating into their hard-won ability to consume in private life. Aside from schooling for their children, these men never used public services, yet their already high taxes were creeping upward with every cost-of-living raise. All save Buford supported a broad social charter in principle, but because the state as a whole had not worked for them in practice, this support remained reluctant.

What little contact the NDC workers had with government was alienating if not degrading. They did not move often or comfortably in the world of public bureaucracies. Their occupational relation to the state was not only distant but in some sense competitive (the post office), and their experiences as citizens were nearly always unrewarding. When forced to deal with a state agency, they encountered not an institutional safety net that insulated them from the economic insecurities of the marketplace but a regulatory maze that more often than not took them away from work and thus from wages (for example, Greg's custody and tax battles, and Rudi's hassles with the catalytic converter on his car). Although their incomes gave them a certain efficacy in a market that often exploited them, their taxes offered no corollary power in the state sphere.

Their complaints about such state practices could be read as raw materials for antistate, capitalist conservatism. I believe, however, that a more textured reading would see all except Buford as not so much ardent free enterprisers as *private* citizens whose lives had been infringed upon but not improved upon by government. Still, it is not difficult to see why such inadequately insulated worker-consumers and underserved taxpayer-citizens are at least an attentive audience for conservatives who slander the welfare state and advocate a constriction of the social charter.

Corporate Plutocracy and Tweedledum and Tweedledee

"Big business" was the typical response to my questions about what was wrong with the American economic system. Even a fervent believer in capitalism like Buford had grave doubts about "big banks," energy "monopolies," multinational corporations, and his own NDC. All six supported the idea that our economy should be open enough to allow individuals to accumulate wealth *because* only with such openness could ordinary folks like them have opportunities for "a decent life." In any just world, individual effort should lead to individual rewards. Rudi seemed to feel this most strongly perhaps because, unlike the others, he was still planning to get rich. Yet, although they shared a certain support for such a system, they held few illusions about it; all but Buford resented the poverty of the many that seemed to them somehow to accompany the ability of the few to accumulate wealth.

Although none of them used the term, each took it for granted that power in the United States is held by a corporate plutocracy, that the economy is controlled, inevitably if unjustly, by the Fortune 500. None expressed approval of this, but none imagined either that anything could be done about it. It was a fact of life to which they seemed resigned. I asked them what the term *economic democracy* meant to them. Only Buford even attempted a definition and he described it in free-enterprise terms. However, when I then asked if, for example, workers, consumers, and communities should have a say over corporate investment decisions, five strongly favored the idea. On specifics, their grievances as workers and consumers coupled with the impotence they felt in the face of corporate power left them at least open to forms of democratic control over the freedom of capital—Buford excepted. Certainly these five did not see themselves as socialists of any sort, but they were nonetheless estranged from the laissez-faire moral economy.

But if most of them favored a government that protects citizens from at least the worst blows of the market system and if indeed they supported democratic checks on the power of the corporate plutocracy, then why their reluctance about state aid and regulation? In my search for an answer I encountered more questions. To whom, to what institutions could they turn in any hope that such power *could* be checked? Given their experience, what precedent might be cited for, say, economic democracy? By and large the political world was a dirty one, its leaders corrupted by the very powers they might otherwise constrain. Part and parcel of the resentment these workers felt toward corporations who exploit workers and raise prices at will and toward the rich who use loopholes to gain tax rates lower than their own was a contempt for the political fat cats who made such injustices possible. No fine distinctions were drawn between elites of the business world and their brothers who run government; the ruling class stands in shadows where it is hard to discern a line between economic and political systems. For at least five of the NDC subjects, there was a "them" atop both worlds and an "us," period.

Politicians who had seemed to have fresh faces and new ideas usually turned out, sometimes sooner, sometimes later, to be one of "them." José juggled hope and cynicism; he voted in every election but was fairly sure that Republicans and Democrats were "all the same" once in power. Sally's view that "one rascal's as good as another" was still less sanguine. Rudi found me naive in suggesting that perhaps corporate lobbyists do not simply purchase the politicians and policies they want with big campaign contributions. In the context of such views they would have felt foolish having faith that one segment of the dominant "them" would or could exercise political control over another segment. With little time, energy, or intellectual proclivity for the kind of critical search it would take to find shades of moral distinction in the electoral arena—and without much incentive to do so given the steady joys of their private lives—politics became a choice between Tweedledum and Tweedledee.

In my attempt to cull this theme from my subjects' words I have again risked lapsing into caricature. I am confident that this Tweedledum and Tweedledee sensibility was shared by most of the six, but there were exceptions and variations. Buford found meaning in selecting the most conservative candidates possible from a field he thought was dominated by "liberals" of both parties; his was the right-wing version of the phenomenon. He hoped the candidates of the Right would get elected and dismantle the welfare state, erase "secular humanism," and reassert the morality of days past. For Sally Jones, both parties were so dominated by big-money interests that voting was pointless. Demski would agree with her premise but not her inference. He did his best to find the lesser of evils, usually voting for liberal Democrats in the hope that they would be able to press progressive reforms that would serve the have-nots. Joe and Sally may be seen as holding the left-wing version. José Bustamante, Greg Larson, and Rudi Ventura shared with Joe and Sally the idea that big money basically controls elections, but unlike Sally they always voted and unlike Joe it was not always for Democrats. None of the four voters, however, expected much even if a chosen candidate won. For them the idea of a state able or inclined to humanize a capitalist economy was exceedingly utopian, although each hoped things would not, as José and Greg put it, "get any worse."

For Buford the market, if only it could avoid defilement by the welfare and regulatory apparatuses of the state, was a morally perfect social universe, and government as currently constituted verged on the opposite. For the other five, however, *both* market and state institutions had a legitimacy in principle, which by virtue of their practices had been delegitimated. To the significant extent to which the market did not lead to democratic ends, these people retained both an affinity for a democratic moral economy and a broad social charter and an estrangement from the laissez-faire moral economy of unfettered capitalism. On the other hand, this ideological sensibility coexisted with a counterbalancing one in which the state and politics in general were seen as a corrupt arena where both parties remained more or less subservient to corporate power, and where rare contacts with public institutions were uniformly frustrating. The public sector was a realm of costly hassle rather than a repository of cautious hope. On this side of the ideological ledger, then, there was a net estrangement from the state and, at least with respect to individuals and small business, a net affinity for the market.

This web of affinities and estrangements, taken together, constitutes a *dialectic of ambivalence*. I brooded a bit over each of those words. The *Oxford English Dictionary* draws on Kant and Hegel to define *dialectic* as a "process of thought" in which "contradictions are seen to merge themselves in a higher truth that comprehends them," a process that develops "by a continuous unification of opposites" (1971, 310). *Ambivalence*, in *Webster's New Collegiate Dictionary*, is defined as the "simultaneous attraction toward and repulsion from an object, person, or action," a "continual fluctuation (as between one thing and its opposite)," and as "an uncertainty as to which approach to follow" (1981, 35). Thus, at the risk of adding to the already mind-numbing jargon of social science, I will stand by "dialectic of ambivalence" as capturing at least the sense *I* have made of the sense my subjects made of U.S. society.

Similarly, I chose the words *affinities* and *estrangements* to distance my analysis of my subjects' patterns of belief from conventional analyses of ideology. The ideas about the social charter I encountered were almost always protean, like those described by Lane (1962) a generation ago. Indeed, the very concept of social charter is an abstraction chosen by me for its analytic utility rather by my subjects for its descriptive accuracy. Aside from Buford Schmitt's largely but not totally consistent formal ideology, what I heard were fluid tendencies in attitude and opinion, qualified and hesitantly rendered. It therefore seemed important to avoid both what Clifford Geertz astutely sees as the ethnographer's equivalent of a statistician's type-one error, namely, overinterpretation or "reading more into things than reason permits" (1983, 16), and what Bennett Berger wisely worries is the possibility that ethnographic analysis will reify into culture and ideology ideas that are only "tentative, exploratory, and improvisational" (1981, 74). Thus, a "web" of "affinities" and "estrangements" seems a fair characterization.

Within such a web the state got mixed reviews from the six citizens discussed here, their visions of the social charter both surprisingly broad and unsurprisingly constricted. I have argued that for most of them the state was often seen as a double villain—ineffective both in its own sphere and in making market processes lead to democratic ends. It is surely true that Americans have long been ambivalent about income-maintenance programs and that the size of those programs expanded substantially beginning in the 1960s (see, for example, Piven and Cloward 1982). But it is also true that this ambivalence has not always been successfully mobilized or used by the Right to effect cuts in spending. And, while total expenditures of social welfare have grown from about 10 percent of GNP in 1960 to about 18 percent in the early 1980s, this growth was in large part driven by an expansion of the range of benefits to the nonpoor and the middle class. Gilbert (1983) calls this a movement toward "universalism," which there is good reason to suppose might have *broadened* support for the welfare state (cf. Wilensky 1975; Esping-Andersen 1982).

If such spending has increasingly benefited the working and middle classes, then their resentments either have been mobilized on ideological grounds alone or have been exaggerated. Perhaps both are true. Certainly the slackard's long history as scapegoat in our culture would give a nostalgic resonance to attacks on welfare chiselers even if the proportion of welfare state spending going to the poor has declined. But is is also true that such attacks have been overemphasized. For example, a *New York Times*/CBS news poll taken in January of 1984 found that 48 percent of those sampled preferred *increased* spending on "programs for the poor," 39 percent would maintain current spending, and only 8 percent chose less spending. In fact, neither during the tax revolt of the late 1970s nor in 1980 when Reagan's first victory was interpreted as a mandate for shrinking the welfare state was public opinion unequivocally opposed to programs for the poor (see Katznelson 1981; Piven and Cloward 1982).

For the NDC workers discussed in these chapters, the state, despite their strong if reluctant support for it, seemed the more visible villain; their criticisms of it were more easily and often articulated than their equally harsh criticisms of the market. Why? I offer a three-part hypothesis. First, the ideological frames, vocabularies, and modes of discourse required for state bashing that historically have been readily available in U.S. capitalist society were given renewed currency by the boldness of Reagan and the New Right and the timidity of the Democratic Left. Second, in a capitalist culture, the market is not often or clearly conceptualized as a humanly constructed and maintained set of social institutions. It is closer to an all-encompassing, taken-for-granted habitus in which ordinary perceptual schemes do not include the cognitive means for recognizing or naming the social order that constitutes them (Bourdieu 1977; Douglas 1984). For such private-sector workers, the market, unlike public policies and programs, appears to have no authors (Smith 1974). Finally and most concretely, in the lived experience of private-sector workers who neither rely upon nor have competence or efficacy within the state sphere, that world is never in short supply of the red tape, waste, and bureaucratic bungling that seem to confirm in real life what available ideology leads them to expect.

If this hypothesis has validity, what is surprising is the extent to which these workers still afforded the state legitimacy. Their accounts of their values and beliefs seemed to me to try to sustain rather than resolve the classical tensions between capitalism and democracy, liberty and equality. Buford Schmitt leaned almost exclusively toward the liberty he believed inheres in the free market. The others remained more or less committed to both liberty and equality, perhaps even to some dimly perceived notion that each makes or should make possible the other.

Their ideal of equality, like many of their most basic values and assumptions, was almost never explicit in *their* words. What *I* inferred it to be was very much like what Homans (1961) sees as the essence of folk rules about distributive justice: "a curious mixture of equality within inequality."[5] Moore is instructive on the nature of the juggling act that such an ideal entails:

> In the course of searching for recurring forms of moral anger and what ordinary people regard as socially unfair, evidence repeatedly showed the existence of contradictory requirements that moral codes had to meet, along with signs of fundamental ambivalence toward social rules and regulations. There are perfectly good reasons why human beings cannot have their cake and eat it too. But there is no reason why human beings cannot *want* both. (1978, 47)

What my subjects seemed not to want was equality at the expense of liberty, but neither were they likely to give such license to liberty that serious inequality would become institutionalized. If they had used the word *equality*, what would they have intended it to mean? Walzer (1983) makes a useful distinction between "simple equality" and "complex equality," which helps make this question less speculative. Simple equality would yield the same income, work, and privileges for all and would, therefore, entail regularized intervention by the state in distribution processes that are now ostensibly grounded in relatively respected forms of merit, effort, or ability. If this is how the ideal of equality were drawn, I am sure all the NDC workers would join in Buford's conservative critique and reject it forthwith.

Walzer's notion of complex equality on the other hand can be summarized as a process by which there is much democratic participation in the determination of what social goods are to mean and how they should be distributed. Although there would be a strong welfare state and a regulated market, private life and most day-to-day distributive procedures would be relatively free of interference. With complex equality, the state would see to it that all citizens had livelihoods and that power in one sphere of life would not lead to power in another in such a way that domination was the result; rank, race, and gender, for example, would not translate into wealth. If the ideal of equality were defined in this way, I suspect that everyone except Buford would endorse it. Of course, such endorsements would be qualified. Rudi could well object if his opportunities for

---

5. Homans cited in Moore (1978, 43). See also Hochschild (1981) on the important insight that people apply very different conceptions of distributive justice in different spheres of life.

upward mobility would be thwarted, and Greg would be wary if such a system were called, as it well could be, democratic socialism. All five, however, would be likely to feel that such a form of equality offered real justice.

Such speculations lead us quickly back to the notion of a dialectic of ambivalence. Although most of the NDC subjects had more than enough complaints about the injustices of the capitalist market to entertain policies based on the ideal of complex equality, they also had many doubts about the state's ability to make that ideal real without resorting to an authoritarian simple equality that would encroach on the liberties and luxuries of private life. And, insofar as their private lives continued to offer such liberties and luxuries, and some prospects for improvement, I doubt very much they would feel any compulsion to push themselves in one political direction or another.

5

City Social Services: The Bureaucratic Belly of the Welfare State Beast

I F my NDC friends are any guide, many private-sector workers have difficulty feeling a bond with public employees. The suspicions and resentments described in previous chapters cannot be considered representative, but neither can they be seen as unique. In a nation whose culture is rooted in frontier individualism and the spirit of the independent entrepreneur, the public sector has long been stigmatized. "Government," a single word, is all that need be said in many circles to evoke an array of commonplace pejoratives: "inefficient," "bureaucratic," "red tape," "waste," and "welfare cheaters."

Certainly such caricatures have grown partly from the experiences of citizens, but their enshrinement in folklore does not stem from reality alone. The mass media routinely report and even relish government snafus, catch-22s, and cases of corruption and abuse. Conservatives and Republicans have played heavily on such tales for most of the twentieth century, and corporate editorial-advertisements began to stress them in major newspapers and magazines in the mid-1970s. By constructing a composite of complaints about big government, they have both drawn on and helped foster resentments toward people receiving public aid and those working in state bureaucracies. This helped them frame problems of economic stagnation in terms of state interference in the market and excessive taxes and public spending (see O'Connor 1973).

Such folkloric stereotypes and conservative frames often imply an image of civil servants as security-conscious paper pushers who produce nothing of value while collecting overly generous pay and pensions for enforcing incomprehensible regulations and/or coddling those dependent on public programs. They are depicted as incompetent at best, and at worst as empire builders who create client dependency to justify their own existence.[1] In this chapter and the next a welfare office and six of its inhabitants will be offered as a descriptive yardstick against which to measure this image. But first a word or two of background on the situation of public servants.

On top of the government institutions created during the New Deal and World War II, the War on Poverty programs of the 1960s and the consumer and environmental protection legislation of the early 1970s further enlarged the ranks of public employees. But as the social movements that engendered them waned and the economy began to inflate and stagnate in the 1970s, visible political support for such programs declined. By then, however, public employee unions had grown in size and strength. The American Federation of State, County, and Municipal Employees, for example, had become the fastest growing union in the nation by 1978. In the context of an economic crunch, these unions' success in winning collective bargaining rights for public workers and their increasing militance in a series of teacher and sanitation worker strikes helped make public workers more vulnerable to attack (DiTomaso 1978).

By 1975 the much publicized near-bankruptcy of New York City made "fiscal crisis" a household word. The eventual solution to that crisis—which became a model for other cities and states as well as for the 1980 Reagan campaign—was one proposed by the network of banks that held New York's bonds and, thus, its financial future: drastic cutbacks in public services, wages, and jobs.[2] The growth of the public sector and the gains of its unions helped fuel the "welfare backlash" (Wilensky 1975) and the subsequent tax revolts (Kuttner 1980) that Reagan and the New Right first helped shape and then capitalized upon.

In what ways do public employees accept the criticisms levied against them? In what ways do they defend their work and their clients against such criticisms?

1. Former Nixon administration treasury secretary and wealthy conservative leader William Simon offers this example of the caricature of "bureaucrats": "Bureaucrats should be assumed to be noxious, authoritarian parasites on society, with a tendency to augment their own size [sic] and power and to cultivate a parasitical clientele in all classes of society" (1978, 219). A far more sophisticated, insightful, and radically different although equally critical analysis of public service bureaucracies may be found in Ferguson (1984). Of particular relevance for this chapter is Ferguson's "Bureaucratic Discourse and the Production of Clients," pp. 136–48, which provides a masterful treatment of the constraints upon both workers and clients, although, in my judgment, it overemphasizes the powerlessness of workers vis-à-vis managerial constraints.

2. Space limitations prohibit adequate discussion of the origins of the urban fiscal crisis. But it is important to note that both suburbanization and capital flight had eroded the tax base of many cities, leaving a growing number of poor and unemployed in need of expanded public services at the very moment when the public sector's capacities for financing them were weakest. Two thorough and accessible sources on such issues are Alcaly and Mermelstein (1977) and Newfield and Dubrul (1977). The first and most powerful theoretical analysis of fiscal crisis is James O'Connor's (1973), whose final chapter traces the rise of both public-sector worker militancy and unionism.

Depending on one's location in the belly of the bureaucratic beast, one's views on the state can vary widely. I selected various welfare workers for my public-sector political biographies because they stand in the eye of the storm, if not at the helm then on the deck of the ship of state referred to so critically by the private-sector NDC workers, the Right, and the media. Individual case studies are presented in the next chapter. What follows here is a sketch of their agency as I encountered it and their work as they saw it.

City Social Services as Workplace

A block from the downtown banking district and fashionable tourist shops of Santa Teresa on a sunny boulevard lined with tall palm trees sits the City Social Services Department (CSS). It is situated, ironically, between prestigious law offices and chic antique stores on one side and the Gourmet Gastronomique, a fancy French luncheon spot, on the other. At least one new Mercedes-Benz was parked in front of CSS each time I visited there. The city rents two buildings for the department. One is a graceful Spanish-style stucco edifice that houses administrative offices and faces the street. It has no marked entrances, only signs directing clients to the building in the rear, a modern two-story complex where the intake and eligibility offices and social workers are housed.

At 8:00 A.M. on any given morning there is a line of fifteen to thirty clients and would-be clients outside the back building. Some are unkempt and asking passersby for spare cigarettes; most are neat and clean and asking nothing; all are waiting—a routine feature of the welfare experience, which they appear to bear both anxiously and listlessly. Behind a set of double glass doors (so often broken by those frustrated or denied they are now ordered in lots) there is a waiting room furnished with schoolroom-like rows of chairs and a bulletin board covered with instructions and announcements in English and Spanish.

On the left as one enters is a three-foot-square window of thick glass with a small hole in the center to speak through. Behind it sits a receptionist flanked by several clerks, all young women. The window protects them and regulates the number of people who can approach them at one time. The receptionist instructs applicants as to initial procedures, takes completed forms, makes appointments for eligibility interviews and social workers, and calls them when appointed clients arrive. A recently installed alarm system—necessitated by attacks on workers whose work in part is screening out the ineligible—connects the reception area to back offices in case help is needed in a hurry. On all sides of front-office desks are steel-gray file cabinets, a decor punctuated only by occasional travel posters and potted plants presumably brought in by the clerks to add personal touches of color to an otherwise impersonal and colorless space.

In his vividly ethnographic, Kafkaesque novel *The Case Worker,* Konrad captured the ethos of offices like CSS when he described his caseworker-protagonist reflecting upon the file cabinet and its contents:

> Every morning I reach with sickening pity into this ancient object, where three rows of case histories, filed according to date and category, await decisions. Now and then they are removed, stapled to sheets of background information, refiled under new reference numbers, sent for consideration to other offices, and returned dog-eared and covered with endless scribblings. And here they lie.
>
> I sometimes wonder what would happen if suddenly they were to start talking. What sounds would issue from that cabinet! Children's cries, women's moans, resounding blows, quarrels, obscenities, recriminations, hasty decisions, false testimony, administrative platitudes, jovial police slang, judges' verdicts, the vapid chatter of . . . supervisors, the incantations of psychologists, my colleagues' embittered humor, my own solitary invective, and so on and so on. It would be as if a powerful radio had picked up all the stations in the world at once; all these sounds, en masse, would become as neutral and indifferent as the yellowing documents in my drawers. (1969, 9–10)[3]

Between the reception window and the hallway leading to other offices stands a guard, a gray-haired bespectacled man in a powder blue uniform serving as a mild symbol of order to the waiting and a mild symbol of reassurance to the workers. He sees to it that only those with an appointment and a worker waiting are allowed down the maze of hallways to inner offices. "They're pretty paranoid about people just walking around the building," one worker explained. Yet, in each of my visits I walked directly past the window and the guard, at first out of ignorance, later as an experiment. Apparently my clean, albeit disheveled clothes and briefcase gave me the appearance and demeanor of one with legitimate business inside.

Along the main hall were four-by-six-foot interview rooms for screening new clients, each containing only identical chairs on either side of a small gray desk. The sameness of the chairs seemed to me deceptively democratic after I had watched, furtively, a few interviews done over those desks. Konrad's caseworker renders this, too:

> The standard desk is no more than a yard deep. But the two persons facing each other across it are as far apart as convict and jailer on opposite sides of

---

3. I am indebted to Professor James Baumohl of McGill University who, after reading an early draft of this chapter, said it reminded him of Konrad and implored me to read *The Case Worker.*

the bars. There is no way around this desk; it stands between two faces, two enigmas, inert, but apportioning the roles as unmistakably as a whipping post or a guillotine. (1969, 13)

In these small rooms the typically disorganized details of clients' daily lives and personal histories were as gently as possible shoved through the categorical sieves of federal, state, and county regulations and recorded in the appropriate boxes on the appropriate forms. There were separate rules and forms for Aid to Families with Dependent Children (AFDC, the largest welfare program), food stamps, Medical Assistance, and General Assistance (the smallest, most restrictive aid program). Past these rooms were a series of larger offices housing three to six workers each, and a staff lunchroom/lounge furnished with coffee urn and a motley collection of used chairs, sofas, and end tables covered with old magazines.

The building served as workplace for approximately ten clerks and typists, perhaps forty eligibility workers, about fifteen social workers, and a dozen managers and administrators. Most were young (thirty-five or under), college educated, and single. Several workers told me that only single people could "afford to work at these salaries." All but the social workers and managers made less than sixteen thousand dollars per year in 1982.

My first interview was with an eligibility worker who appeared to be catching his breath between cases. His only available time was at noon since the office closes then for half an hour. "I always brown-bag it here at my desk, try to read and relax a bit," he told me. He had spent the morning on two difficult cases. The first was an older woman who had been sleeping on the streets. He had noticed that her face was black-and-blue and that she had urinated on herself. This struck him because it was spring and "clients usually only smell bad during rainy season." He had taken her to the hospital where one doctor told him "she's OK," and another said she was indeed not OK. After his third trip to the hospital, he finally managed to get her admitted; she had had an unset broken arm. His other case was a suicidal man who had walked away from a hospital psychiatric unit. The hospital then claimed they had no authority to readmit him, "something about not enough beds," my informant explained. He had then driven the client around for about two hours "trying to find a place for him, to keep him alive."

The worker, Kurt Wilson, age thirty-one, later told me that such cases were not really typical but not at all unusual. Kurt gave an interesting description of his job when I asked about the conservative lament that public workers produce nothing:

The [CSS] director told me, "Your job is to keep things out of the newspaper." See, they don't want the old ladies starving along Main Street, so they have to trust us. What we do is what you *don't* see—the crime, the suicides, you don't see beggars. How many people want to see beggars or old ladies down in the street with no clothes on? We keep a lid on the volcano to a certain extent.

I asked several questions about who the clients were to find out if "volcano" was too strong a word. For most clients, it was not:

With the recession there are a lot more clients. They are more desperate. Many haven't worked since the last recession, so working to attain something is not part of their psychology. What is part of their psychology is "I'll take what I need to survive." They've gone through life with nothing, so everything out there is an enemy to them, or something to be taken. They are particularly vicious. It scares you. It worries me to see the look in their eyes. . . .

With the new [1981 budget] cuts, the mood of the clients is getting ugly; our job is getting a lot tougher. . . . There's a new breed of young, desperate, violent street person out there. They have no empathy, tremendous racism, glorification of violence, swastikas on their arms. I just get the feeling society is hemorrhaging from the bottom. The ghettos won't go fascist, but these guys could since the ideology of violence appeals to them. . . . People get pissed about the public dole, but they don't understand that some of these guys would go out and kill for a dinner.

This "new breed" is only a fraction of the General Assistance clientele, the smallest set of cases. When I asked about cheating, the focus of public criticism, Kurt said, "That does happen sometimes." He explained that some workers "take it personally" and get angry when clients lie to them, but others expect it because "the system sets up liars. You have to lie to get on welfare. They set ridiculous standards. Nobody in Santa Teresa lives on an AFDC grant; it's almost impossible to do. To survive, you get on AFDC and try to get a little work on the side." Another worker confided that "the system manufactures cheats by using so many regulations that clients can't understand," implying that not all cheating was an intentional survival tactic. A third elegibility worker explained that there was not as much cheating as people believe because most clients are obviously disabled. He added, however, that a few "don't look incapacitated to me at all. They usually have back problems and doctors' notes, often from the same doctor. That's why they call [the doctor] 'lower back so-and-so.' "[4]

All the workers I spoke with agreed that those who cheat to get a bit more public aid than they are entitled to constitute a small proportion of clients. One social worker stated that only four of his thirty-eight clients were employable at

4. For a brief discussion of "profiteering in the social welfare state," a widespread, costly, yet neglected form of fraud and abuse, see Piven and Cloward (1982), pp. 4–7.

all. The rest were clearly disabled or infirm. Miguel White, a senior eligibility worker, estimated that "chiselers may amount to 10 percent, but they get 90 percent of the news. The 90 percent are the quiet ones. And sometimes there are marginal cheaters. You realize the system creates them. It's hard to get by on $408 a month for two people."

None of the workers I met made any attempt to conceal the fact that some clients abused the system. None approved of this; in fact all workers spent much of their time collecting information useful only for detecting potential abuse. It was simply an unfortunate fact of life in their line of work. What galled them more than the few clients who managed to chisel a few extra resources out of the system was the amount of system resources devoted to detecting this. One eligibility worker who dealt with AFDC, food stamps, and MediCal told me he spent nearly 60 percent of his time on paperwork, most for the purpose of catching fraud. His supervisor confirmed his estimate, adding "Too damn much money is spent checking, interpreting, and applying crazy guidelines."

In one way or another each person I met at CSS spoke of a central irony: criticisms of welfare cheats have engendered such complex sets of rules designed to stop chiseling that much of the total funding is allocated to rigorous policing functions rather than to raising benefits to livable levels so that the *incentives* to chisel would decline. Thus, in the name of accountability there is tremendous waste: "All these changes to tighten regulations screw up our clients and our workers," a supervisor explained. "They make our tasks increasingly difficult and lower our efficiency." State government procedures create another layer of constraining contradictions between service and police functions. The state determines local funding levels partly on the basis of the rate of "client error"—the frequency with which clients understate their income as detected by state auditors. This presents welfare workers with a choice: either expend staff resources rigidly policing client reports, thereby diverting the resources from needed services, or be more lax about policing so staff time is spent on services, in which case state auditors will detect higher rates of client error and reduce the agency's funding accordingly. Needless to say, this accountability procedure works in only one direction; errors by which eligible clients are *denied* services or benefits to which they are legally entitled are not tallied.

A few visits to CSS taught me that such catch-22s were but one of the problems that have kindled what I will call an *insider's critique* of the welfare system—a critique that dwarfs the more familiar and less detailed complaints of citizens who have no contact with the system. Conservatives and others have long claimed that welfare programs erode the work ethic and create an unhealthy dependence on government. The CSS workers volunteered their own version of this criticism: "The economic system is producing poor people like it's some kind of factory, and welfare subsidizes poverty. It does not set out to get people up on their feet; it's not set up to give people jobs. It's set up to subsidize poverty at a particular level—just keep them alive."

Another worker noted that the very restrictions placed on aid programs as a spur to the work ethic—as a way of keeping welfare less attractive than low-wage work—actually function to *prevent* clients from ever "getting out from behind the eight ball." When I asked about getting clients jobs I was told repeatedly that this is precisely what most clients and all workers take as a goal, but "there's just not enough training around right now, and I guess there'll be even less [after the Reagan cuts], but you can't expect people to get jobs with no tools."

One social worker, Marc Driscoll, was particularly incensed about the "irrationality" of a system that simultaneously creates dependency and then blames the dependents for it. For him, common sense demanded a more comprehensive approach. More than the others he believed in free enterprise and insisted that there were jobs for those willing to look and work hard. However, the current system, Marc said, "never gets the job done." He believed that "conservatives," paradoxically, "are just afraid to get tough with people." Marc argued that keeping benefit levels so low perpetuates poverty. His approach would entail significant increases in benefits, job training, and guaranteed placement to be followed by cessation of all aid. He knew such a system was not in the offing because policymakers "never listen to the people who run the programs" and are "totally out of touch." Experience had convinced him that nearly all nondisabled people receiving aid want work and are quite capable of it "if they're given half a break." But such breaks are unlikely in the current system, Marc argued, because so many resources go to catching the few who cheat. He considered this to be the single greatest form of waste in the public sector (followed closely by "higher management people who make thirty thousand to forty thousand dollars a year and can't find their ass with both hands").

Each of the other welfare workers interviewed agreed that there is indeed waste in the welfare state. All were sure, however, that most of it stems both from paperwork designed *not* to help poor people get on their feet but to restrict eligibility and detect abuse, and from featherbedding in the management ranks. Is there featherbedding at the line level? Kurt Wilson's response typified the sentiments of the others: "I wish!" He explained that as president of his union local he had fought running battles with the county over caseload sizes and that it had taken all his negotiating skills merely to maintain work loads at the point where workers were only moderately overworked and clients only moderately underserved.

Karen Mullavey, the line supervisor for food stamps, gave a telling illustration of caseload-size problems. She had just received notice that the formula used by the state government to set her staff budget had changed so that caseloads were to rise from 175 to 235 clients per worker. It was her professional judgment that her staff was already working over capacity, well beyond what was required for competent supervision of cases. When she investigated she discovered that the new formula was predicated on the assumption that CSS had a computer for paperwork, which it did not in fact have. Her only recourse was to try to get management to live up to the union contract then in force, which specified maximum caseloads of 175.

Many of the problems these workers had with the welfare system took the form of labor-management conflict. Aside from political work done by their union's international and state bodies, there was little the local members could do at CSS to reform the system. Within these broad constraints, however, a constant battle raged between the workers and city officials over how CSS was to be run and the work organized. Labor contracts and department budgets were negotiated annually, a long and typically bitter process. Wages remained well below those of most other small cities in California, even though the union local representing CSS workers had an active and unified membership. As the workers told it, caseload-size issues were a struggle every year. They fought to keep caseloads at levels all agreed were too high for competent casework and then maintained a vigil against management's extracontractual efforts to undermine the Memorandum of Understanding (MOU) the rest of the year.

Santa Teresa was the seat of a notably affluent and conservative county marked by low levels of unionization and run by a Board of Supervisors dominated by conservatives for longer than anyone cared to remember. Few private-sector businesses were unionized, and workers in most local government agencies were represented by acquiescent staff associations rather than labor unions. A militant sanitation workers' strike in 1976—virtually the only recent labor struggle aside from those at CSS—was defeated. No representatives of lower-income communities or labor held elective office. "This is a bad county to deal with, laborwise," Miguel White told me. "Without the union, we'd probably be making 20 percent less."

He later noted, "It's not a big strong union as unions go, size or anything, but it's all we have." Whereas the NDC workers did not trust or participate in their union's decisions, the CSS workers were very active in and felt well represented by their union. The CSS members elected a president and four negotiators every year to represent them in contract talks. When talks broke down and a strike was called, the vast majority of members would go out and walk the picket line. When the county offered a zero percent wage increase in 1975 there was a seven-day strike, during which county officials found the wherewithal in the budget to offer a 5 percent increase. Again in 1978 during a one-day strike, over 90 percent of CSS workers went out. Each year since, there had been a close call in which a settlement was reached just prior to a strike vote.

Unlike the business unionism of NDC and the private sector in general, however, labor-management issues at CSS usually did not center on wage and benefit questions. According to the workers, county officials had always attempted to cut funding for client services, hold the line on salaries and fringes, and reduce the number of line positions while often expanding the ranks of management. The union historically had fought for maintenance of client services and line staffing levels and improved working conditions rather than for higher wages and benefits.

The 1982 negotiations, which took place during my later interviews, were a case in point. The local had surveyed its members to determine priorities. The union wanted formal management action to discourage sexual harassment and the establishment of procedures for handling complaints, a clear policy on layoffs before the Reagan budget cuts made them a fait accompli, and changes in county employment rules that would allow part-time work in lieu of layoffs. The workers maintained that all these changes were noneconomic, that they "wouldn't cost the county a penny," one negotiator said. In fact, even though the Proposition 13 tax cuts and the recession had reduced county revenues, management offered a 5 percent raise early on and later proposed to increase this to 6.5 percent if the union would drop its other demands. The union negotiators continued to press the members' top concerns. Management rejected all of them on operational grounds ("it can't be done") and on philosophical grounds ("the union can't dictate management prerogatives"). According to Kurt Wilson, local president and chief negotiator, the fight boiled down to "the issue of worker rights versus management power." He said that the climate of expectations created in Reagan's first term led all other bargaining units in the city to settle, giving management the power to impose a contract on CSS.

The 1984 negotiations were equally contentious. This time, however, the fight had more to do with money because CSS management had received a 16 percent pay increase in 1983 and another 9 to 20 percent in 1984 while sticking to its offer of 4 percent for line workers. Several staff members resigned in disgust, and their vacancies were used as a lever by management, which imposed a hiring freeze until the union signed. Morale, according to Wilson, was "at rock bottom." Moreover, Reagan administration "streamlining" in the food stamp program had imposed a requirement of monthly income reports, which had to be processed at a rate the workers claimed was simply impossible. They already had food stamp caseloads of two hundred and felt their treatment of clients suffered as a consequence.

Workers ranted bitterly about management's "elitism" and "arrogance."

When I pressed them for details I was told that management personnel had gotten hefty raises so as to achieve parity with other cities, whereas staff members—who on the basis of the same survey of other cities were further below parity—were offered raises equal only to the rate of inflation. Also, management had gotten a one-year contract while insisting upon a two-year contract for workers. One worker who sat in on the negotiations summarized the situation this way to a reporter:

> It's incredible that they can have this attitude. We work daily in highly stressful situations and it's emotionally draining on all of us. Some days we have to separate battered children from their parents. We hate to take them away, but we also hate to see them battered. We deal with alcoholics, . . . drug addicts, . . . and it's not always pleasant. The guys down here were really upset [about management's raises].

After listening to css workers' accounts of the most recent episode in a long history of labor-management conflict, I was struck by how inherently *political* their work was. Over and above the personal ideological proclivities of the individuals I interviewed, the everyday elements of the jobs themselves were shrouded in politics. Public debate over tax cuts and the tightening of eligibility rules and reduction of benefits by the Reagan administration were only the latest examples. Unlike the ostensibly nonpolitical work culture and labor-management conflict at NDC, the already contentious work context of welfare and social service agencies was exacerbated by its location at the vortex of political debate over the social charter.

The Fate of the Ideal of Service

In *Street-Level Bureaucracy: Dilemmas of the Individual in Public Services* (1981), Lipsky makes a persuasive case as to why the ideal of service presumably held by welfare workers tends to be converted—particularly under the sort of working conditions sketched above—into careerism and/or cynicism. This tendency helps account for the stereotypic criticisms of public service workers. He argues that a series of related conditions built into the structure of the welfare state produces a form of worker alienation that undermines not only their ability to meet the needs of their clients but also the very ideals that nurture careers in social service.

First, according to Lipsky (1980, 1981), resources are chronically short relative to the size of the potential client population and the obstacles to self-sufficiency most of them face. Occupying the tenuous terrain bounded by the political conflicts that shape all levels of social policy, welfare workers are confronted on one side with clients whose needs they are systematically prevented from meeting adequately and on the other by conservative critics who claim that even such aid as they are able to give is too much. One consequence of our societal ambivalence about poverty, Lipsky argues, is a drift toward mediocrity in the service sector, which demoralizes clients and workers alike (cf. Edelman 1977).

Second, the mission of helping the needy, therefore, is too often forced to take a back seat to the organizational imperatives of maintaining a minimally functioning agency in such a political milieu. Altruistic satisfactions from helping others can give way to what Lipsky calls a "client-processing mentality." Caseloads become things one must bureaucratically manage rather than groups of people in need whose lives one could help turn around if one had the time and resources. Finally, in the interests of cost reduction and productivity, public-sector managers have "Taylorized" social service work, that is, broken down tasks into many simple steps like the routinized specialization found on assembly lines after Frederick W. Taylor revolutionized manufacturing with scientific management (see Braverman 1974; Livingston and O'Donnell 1980). Thus, the client walks into places like CSS a whole if troubled person, but his or her problems are quickly parceled out into programmatically defined pieces, each handled by a different specialist who is obliged to use forms and rules different from the others. Intake is separated from casework, food needs from medical care, employment from housing. The result for workers is they lose control over the outcome of their labors and over their ability to help their clients.

Under such circumstances there can be little mystery regarding the origins of horror stories about the dehumanizing maze of rules, regulations, and referrals in public-service bureaucracies. It is ironic, however, that the workers ("paper pushers") who are cast as the living symbols of institutional villainy in such stories are themselves engaged in a constant struggle against the system responsible for them. Because they can so rarely effect change in that system, because their day-to-day jobs make them accomplices in its perpetuation, because they are "set up to fail" to achieve the humanistic objectives that could sustain their career commitments, the ideal of service takes a pummeling. Among the effects of this dynamic are increasingly unrewarding work, services that are neither comprehensive nor comprehensible, high rates of burnout and turnover, and greater client dependency and debilitation.

Like the private-sector NDC workers, alienation was a theme in the descriptions CSS workers gave of their labors. Their jobs too were demanding, yet unlike their NDC counterparts most CSS staff members were paid relatively little—and this in an expensive city. Their function was to do something for the parade of problem people who daily marched through their offices, but they felt perennially ill equipped for the job. All agreed that the worst part of their work was "giving people bad news." This was a routine difficulty under normal circumstances, but now they had to serve as the shock troops in an austerity drive and "discontinue" more clients. Several css workers used the phrase "caught in the middle" to describe their frustration. Chente Palacios, the newest eligibility worker, was learning that regulations and paperwork were a problem for clients as well as for him:

> Numerous clients fail to fill out the right forms . . . on time. Then they get cut off. They don't meet their responsibilities and right away they blame us. We're caught in the middle. There are lots of problems with Accounting, not getting checks out on time or sent to the right address. Accounting is swamped, and there's only a small percentage of errors, considering. But when you have to explain that to a client it's no fun.

Miguel White, a veteran eligibility worker and Chente's supervisor, used the same phrase in another context:

> You're always caught in the middle. The clients can't live on what you're giving them and the other side is saying, "you have to give them only this much." And now it's less, and how do you tell someone that? On the other hand, it's your job and you can't very well not do it. . . . You get callous after a point. No matter what [clients] call you it doesn't matter. Most of them say they realize *you're* not doing it, [but] you're the only one they have to yell at.

Workers at css may be said to have been "caught in the middle" in a broader sense. Not only did they have to navigate between clients and the federal and state bureaucracies, but they had to confront the increasingly hostile criticism of conservatives and overburdened taxpayers for whom they had become a favorite target. After Reagan's election in 1980, css workers more often had to "give clients bad news": discontinue them, reduce their benefits, apply stricter eligibility requirements.[5] All this inevitably raised the ire of those they had set out to

---

5. Reagan administration cuts fell disproportionately on the poor, especially the "working poor." Aid to Families with Dependent Children, for example, had provided partial grants to working mothers whose wages were very low and work-related expenses high. Such partial grants, designed to encourage recipients to work their way off welfare, were all but eliminated in 1981 (" 'Working Poor' to Feel Cuts," *Los Angeles Times*, November 11, 1981). Similarly, cuts in food-based aid (infant feeding programs, school lunch subsidies) hit the working poor hardest ("White House Mulls Further Reduction of $2.5 Billion in Food-Welfare Programs," *Wall Street Journal*, December 10, 1981). Even the disabled were summarily eliminated from disability programs until federal courts forced their reinstatement ("Disabled 'Devastated' by Reagan's Policies," *San Francisco Chronicle*, August 1, 1982). According to the Census Bureau, such cuts, particularly in the context of the 1981–82 recession, pushed the poverty rate to its highest level in nearly two decades ("House Democrats

serve. Moreover, their caseloads were heavier since there were fewer workers, and they were receiving less money and had less job security than previously. Of these developments Miguel White said:

> Every place you go you hear pro-Reagan sentiments. Sunday in the butcher shop all these people were saying how good it was to have someone doing something for a change in the White House, like, you know, stopping all this horrible welfare spending, bringing the county back to its feet and all that. . . . I just wish sometimes these conservatives could work in a welfare department for *one day*. I'd like to see that. They wouldn't see their stereotyped lazy bum welfare cheater. They'd see this mother and child who'd been abandoned by the father or beaten up and sent to the Violence in the Family home. I don't know—to just work there a couple of days would sure change some of the views they have.

Increasingly harsh attacks from conservative quarters, increasingly tepid support from liberal ones; greater need for public aid, yet fewer resources for it—these then were the circumstances, according to CSS workers, that accounted for their high rates of turnover and burnout. They used the term burnout for the loss of zeal, the lowered morale, and the lack of esprit de corps many welfare workers experience after a few years of casework. Konrad's cynical caseworker-protagonist begins his narrative with a reflection reeking of burnout:

> Go on, I say to my client. Out of habit, because I can guess what he's going to say, and doubt his truthfulness. He complains some more, justifies himself, puts the blame on others. From time to time he bursts into tears. Half of what he says is beside the point; he reels off platitudes, he unburdens himself. He thinks his situation is desperate; seems perfectly normal to me. He swears his cross is too heavy; seems quite bearable to me. He hints at suicide; I let it pass. He thinks I can save him; I can't tell him how wrong he is. (1969, 1)

For this fictional caseworker, "the client vanishes behind his case, the official behind his function," so that "on the whole, my interrogations make me think of a surgeon who sews up his incision without removing the tumor." After a dozen pages describing his malaise in grueling detail, the caseworker shrugs: "I do what the law and my fumbling judgment permit; then I look on, mesmerized, as the system crushes him" (13–15). He soon asks, "Why, then, have I chosen a job that obliges me, day after day, to put up with the stench of other people's

---

Ridicule Stockman on Poverty Statistics," *New York Times*, September 23, 1984). Another consequence was to make welfare workers more often the bearers of bad tidings. For a comprehensive review of the early Reagan cuts, see Palmer and Sawhill (1982), pp. 76–96, 308–28, 363–92, 468–84.

suffering? How could I possibly summon up enough smypathy to contend with the misery that is wearing out the chair on the other side of my desk?" (20). Several chapters and many clients later he is still asking, "What can I do in the face of this frenzied squirming? Nothing, or next to nothing. I observe it, I draw parables from disaster, and compile records of failure" (65). Yet just when I, as a reader, began to squirm under the weight of Konrad's existential despair and began to believe that the caseworker could only "regulate the traffic of suffering" (109), he takes leave of his job and his hundreds of clients to care for a lone abandoned idiot child in whom he finds answers to his questions.

Like the caseworker and their NDC counterparts, the CSS workers devised various strategies for avoiding burnout and for making their uphill battles meaningful if not always rewarding. Karen Mullavey, for example, found herself close to burnout after eight years of working directly with clients. She found new hope in a promotion that made her an adviser to line workers on the new food stamp regulations. This allowed her to offer concrete if indirect help to clients without becoming part of the management she so often opposed, thereby avoiding burnout. She also had to force herself to separate her work from her private life more sharply than before. Since the time of my interviews with her, Karen has enrolled in graduate school to improve her public administration skills. She says this gives her more career options and makes her feel less trapped. Do such moves constitute "careerism"? Not in the stereotypic sense of merely collecting paychecks and promotions while putting minimal energy into her job. Karen turned down promotions until she was offered a role in which she could use more of her skills and keep her hand in direct service; she remains an active advocate for both clients and other line workers against management efforts to trim services. Moreover, she seeks neither high salaries nor more power, but rather sees her recent moves as means of relief that will allow her to sustain her sense of self as a social service professional.

Kurt Wilson is a political activist in both the union and the community. He has no delusions that his day-to-day work will change the welfare system, much less the economic system that he believes creates the need for it. He is an activist outside of work in the hopes of doing something about the deeper sources of the suffering he sees inside it. Meanwhile he draws satisfaction when he is able to "help a few" with the skills and resources at his disposal. Whereas Karen maintains her morale in part by learning how to "leave it all behind" at 5:00, it is the continuity of commitment across life spheres that sustains Kurt.

Marc Driscoll shares most of the frustrations described by the others, but he avoids burnout by focusing on his sense of professional craft. His is "not a *job*," which he defined as work one does because "one needs the money," but rather "a profession one chooses and develops." He chose a career as a social worker because "the work itself is important." Mark derives gratification from his work when he feels "able to use whatever knowledge and skills I've acquired to an effective end." He keeps burnout at bay by creatively applying his skills to the great variety of particular people and problems he encounters:

> Having to deal with the same supervisors year after year, with the same repetition of problems, that burns me out. . . . [But] when you get involved in a case, no matter how discouraged you might be, you begin to see the people as individuals in their own unique circumstances.

The satisfaction derived from using one's professional skills are more of a luxury for eligibility workers, whose caseloads are usually three to five times those of social workers. Their contact with clients is apt to be more fleeting and bureaucratic, and their ability to creatively address multidimensional needs is constrained. Chente Palacios often feels "drained" by the task of collecting "tons" of data on clients just to determine eligibility for each of three types of aid. He rejuvenates himself by jogging every night after work and indulging his passion for science fiction novels. But what sustains him is the *chance* of perceptibly helping some of the many wounded who walk past his desk—"That's the most important thing to me." He told of a young woman torn up over what she saw as a futile future. Chente first warned her, "I'm no social worker, that's not my job," but then proceeded to bend the rules, work through her problems with her, and offer advice and options she found helpful. Such experiences make him feel good about his current work and kindle his interest in graduate training in counseling.

Miguel White, who has done eligibility work for a decade, made much the same point when I asked what he liked best about his job: "Once in a while you help people; once in a while you get a 'thank you.'" Miguel spoke for the others when he said that the most important thing about this work is "to *try* to help people. It doesn't always work out, but that's what keeps you there." Even though css workers are ceaselessly confronted by the inadequacy of their efforts relative to the needs of their clients, they seem to stretch the meager rewards gained from "helping a few." There did not seem to me to be one idealist among the twenty or so welfare workers I met. If they started out that way, the gritty reality of limitless poverty and limited power that constitutes their lived experience quickly disabused them of all but the most modest altruism.

Theirs is a *skeptical altruism.* With it they seem able to wring drops of self-esteem from the flow of their frustrations—self-esteem they somehow make serve in lieu of the higher salaries and respect people with their education might earn in the market. More intimately and comprehensively than either their clients or their conservative critics, the css workers know the red tape and irrationality of welfare programs. Yet each in his or her unique way is holding out for what the welfare state *can be* rather than burning out on what it *is*. In those rare but relished cases when they can seize opportunities to use their skills to make a difference in a troubled life, to move a client an inch or two closer to self-sufficiency, their work as a whole is given some meaning.

Armed with a modicum of such experiences, with a sense of gray/black humor tailored to suit the painful peculiarities of their bureaucratic subculture, and with a good deal of camaraderie and mutual support, the CSS workers continue to arrive at the department office just before 8:00 A.M. everyday. There they walk past the early-assembled, often-desperate, not yet "processed" poor. There, where the ideal of service always flickers but is never quite extinguished, they approach their desks, reach for the top file in the in box, and turn on for another day the relentless public-sector assembly line on which people in trouble are made into clients on welfare.

6

A Public-Sector
Cast of Characters:
Six Political Biographies of City
Social Services Workers

WHAT are they like, the people who inhabit such a workplace? How did they come to do this work? What sense of the American social charter did they bring to their jobs, and how have their experiences affected their political beliefs about state and market?

This chapter addresses these questions by presenting biographical-political sketches of the six CSS workers who were interviewed in depth. They were selected from among their many coworkers on two grounds. First, like the six selected at NDC, I wanted subjects who were ideologically diverse, whose backgrounds and beliefs varied significantly. Second, I attempted to enlist individuals who matched as closely as possible the basic demographic characteristics of the NDC subjects so as to afford myself some comparability across groups. Here I will describe these workers as discrete individuals, attempting to convey the unique and idiosyncratic features of their personal histories and ideas. An analysis of common themes in their worldviews and visions of the social charter follows in chapter 7.

KAREN MULLAVEY had worked at CSS for nine years, most of them as a food stamp eligibility worker. She was the oldest of three children who grew up in a "very political" Irish Catholic family in Los Angeles. By "very political" she meant that her father, a Republican real estate broker and member of the Chamber of Commerce, often debated with others in the family who were Democrats, social workers, and psychologists. Karen recalled feeling more affinity for the views of her aunts—for example, that human problems demand government action—than for her father's laissez-faire beliefs. Although no longer religious, she said,

"The Catholic church is still with me." Her vision of social justice was influenced by a priest she admired in her youth; he was the first to tell her of "the suffering masses." Her first real political beliefs developed in college in the 1960s (and clarified when she was arrested at a demonstration).

Karen was a tall, attractive, athletic woman with large earnest blue eyes, thirty-three years old at the time of our interviews in 1981, and single (although she had lived in a common-law marriage for the previous nine years). When I first talked with her, she lived alone in a sunny two-bedroom apartment full of plants, colorful fabrics, and wicker furniture, located in a comfortable middle-class neighborhood ten blocks from her downtown office. She jogged regularly and played tennis whenever she could.

She spent a week of her vacation at a tennis camp. This embarrassed her slightly because the camp was "real bourgie," and thus a little out of character for a left-liberal whose work was ministering to the poor. Despite her middle-class background, Karen now felt "closer to the working class." Her political identity, however, was "a real mixed thing because many of the moral majority types [whose views she adamantly opposed] are working class." She felt strong ties with the have-nots and the consumer and environmental movements.

Until she began taking graduate courses in public administration two nights a week, she was active in local politics. But her studies, and having to change apartments twice in 1980, had left her with less time and energy for politics. Perhaps more significant, her activism had added to the accumulated emotional toll of her work, so that she felt the need for "more personal space." The combination of direct service work and evening meetings made her feel that she was "martyring out, just spending all my time being unhappy, butting my head against the wall. . . . I have to worry about myself more and not so much the whole world. Now, when I leave work, I leave work."

Her years of dealing with thousands of clients had worn her down, made her feel "stuck" in her job, but her recent promotion to staff resource person for food stamps gave her back some enthusiasm. Karen had refused promotions into management because she opposed much of what they do and because she saw such jobs as "unchallenging" next to casework. Just prior to my interview, CSS had tried to eliminate her position, but rising caseloads robbed them of the necessary justification. Instead she was upgraded to a role above line workers yet below management. There she felt caught between her support for fellow workers and her opposition to the management of which she was now nominally part. She enjoyed the analysis entailed in explaining rule changes to line workers but was ill at ease about making decisions on budgets and the transition to a computerized record system. This bind, Karen said, was "just what management wanted"—a respected worker to take part of the blame for replacing workers and raising work loads. She hoped to turn this around enough to push for better service and working conditions. In any event, the new role would help her avoid burning out, while her graduate training would give her the "career flexibility" she felt she needed to sustain her commitment to social service work.

Karen's views on how the world works were rather consistently leftist. Consumers are powerless and victimized, she said, because "business has too much power, that's just my feeling." The local rent control initiative was defeated, according to her, because the landlord lobby spent over $100,000 on deceptive advertising: "Money talks, and it scared people by lying about what the repercussions would be." Skyrocketing rents were "forcing good people to leave Santa Teresa." When I offered the laissez-faire argument that a free market that allows maximum profits will ensure higher production and lower prices, Karen was unconvinced: "We have a *controlled* economy. Monopolistic enterprises, big corporations control 80 percent of the economy, so they can boost prices to whatever they want as long as they can brainwash us into believing we need these things. There isn't much real competition any more."

Interestingly, she did not attack free enterprise per se, but rather maintained that America no longer had it and that Americans suffered as a result. Her favorite example was the "monopolistic" oil industry, which she felt makes "an inordinate amount of profit" at the expense of consumers while alternative forms of energy and transportation do not get the government support the oil companies enjoy. Karen did not see herself as a socialist but as a small-*d* democrat who would like to see the state regulate in the interests of people rather than profits. When I offered oil industry arguments to the effect that regulations inhibit production, she disagreed:

> Regulations don't inhibit production, but the fact that oil is a finite resource does. Solar should get government support, not the oil companies. . . . There must be some criterion for who's going to get indirect subsidies and tax breaks—like, if it's not ecological, no money. . . . I think [oil companies] ought to be nationalized. Not that I trust the government to do something wonderful, but if not, tax the hell out of 'em.

If she did not trust the government, I asked, why did she favor regulation of oil, housing, and the environment? Karen never defended current regulatory practices because she was sure that regulated industries have a knack for turning regulations to their own ends. This logic became apparent, for example, when I asked her about the local housing shortage. Hadn't land-use controls helped make housing scarce and costly? "No. There's just not enough water, and even if there were, they've never built enough *affordable* housing anyway. They just speculate more and more. . . . The politicians would like to eliminate [land-use controls], but not for our benefit, for the developers."

One theme in this and many other comments was that big business had become a fetter on rather than a guarantor of the American dream. Karen wanted to see, instead of a society ordered by corporate priorities, a form of democracy in which "wealth was more evenly distributed" to better meet people's needs, and "the rape of the environment for profits" could be stopped. She spoke of "real democracy," the good society, in terms of "collective decisions," "planning," and—linking what capitalist wisdom holds apart as opposites—"shared wealth and individual freedom." She was at pains to point out, however, that "we don't have such a democracy now because we're ruled by special interests with big money." Doesn't democracy depend fundamentally on free enterprise? "The two have nothing to do with each other necessarily; you can have social democracy where individuals have rights and institutions are democratic."

In keeping with these beliefs about how the world is and how it might be, Karen held a very broad vision of the social charter. She wanted to increase public spending in all but three areas: the military ("the MX missile is a waste; . . . we can only blow up the earth so many times"), public administration ("administrators get paid for sitting on their asses; they're burned out and don't care"), and criminal justice ("crime is a serious problem, but more cops and prisons won't help unless we deal with the underlying causes"). She strongly opposed Reagan administration cuts in extended unemployment benefits ("What do they want people to do, starve?!"), and in job safety programs ("OSHA's hands are tied—four hundred inspectors for a million plants"). Karen had expected cuts in public assistance programs, but she maintained that such cuts, along with the rhetoric invoked to justify them, would lower public-sector morale, thereby actually helping create the negative stereotypes of public workers used in attacks against them.

As might be expected, she also stressed her opposition to cuts in food stamps, which affected her work directly. Karen agreed with the familiar charge of waste in the program, but offered an unfamiliar interpretation of it. Food stamps were originally designed to benefit agribusiness as much as the hungry, she claimed. The program had taken the form of a needlessly complex coupon system because "the government doesn't trust the poor. . . . They know what they need as well as anybody; just give 'em the money." Her point was that the state had *created* wasteful administrative headaches and a "political football" because biased, punitive attitudes toward people in poverty had been built into the structure of food aid. This irony, in Karen's view, was a typical by-product of the politics of public policy:

> You start out with good ideas like national health care, but they end up getting negotiated to death. Intentions don't get translated into workable

form. Special interests create legislation, and by the time the Republicans and Democrats and committees get done with them they come out shlocky and costly.

Like most of her coworkers, Karen was convinced that most of the waste in the welfare state is due not to fraud and abuse but to the attempts to prevent it with redundant and rigorous eligibility and screening procedures. This makes social service workers into inefficient and costly "cops" who, despite their intentions, must enforce rules that *presuppose* fraud and degrade recipients. Karen maintained that, yes, there is waste, but that this complaint overlooks many of its causes and is really serving another agenda:

> "Bureaucrat" is a real convenient scapegoat for a lot of our ills, [but it is] a cheap shot. . . . Top administrators are often politically expedient crooks, but there are so many people in social work in a service economy that [the stereotype] is unfair. Administrators get big bucks and do nothing. Better to spend the money on line workers to deal with the public. . . . Granted, government misspends money, spends it ineffectively. But we still need government, not anarchy, to provide public services. We're not doing that effectively, but there are ways of dealing with it without just giving corporations more money by lowering their taxes. They won't share it and problems won't get dealt with.

Karen believed that tax dollars are being wasted on "big business." The Chrysler bailout, she thought, had helped preserve an "outmoded, unecological" system rather than helping build better public transportation to reduce gasoline use and air pollution. "I don't support Chrysler," she said. "I support the people who would be out of work." Rather than prop up failing corporations, she would use public funds to retrain workers. Besides, "some corporations shouldn't exist anyway, they're not providing a service." But if people buy their products, don't sales legitimate their existence? "That doesn't legitimate anything to me." This was a key premise behind many of Karen's positions on state-market relations. She never repudiated free enterprise but maintained that it was more imagined than real. To use public funds to support private profits, to equate sales with votes while failing to consider broader public interests, made no sense to her—particularly when services she saw as essential were being assaulted.

But hadn't a majority of voters just elected a president who campaigned against such reasoning? Karen countered that "in difficult economic times people get scared. . . . We can deal with [our problems] by electing Reagan, but I don't think we meant to go that way." She implied that an electoral hoax had been played on U.S. taxpayers: the have-nots were being sacrificed to suit the needs of business. Voters' legitimate concerns had been manipulated; their perceptions about what was wrong and what was to be done about it had been distorted. Karen did not believe that they had really intended an attack on basic public services or that such services really eroded the work ethic by creating unhealthy dependence on the welfare state.

After spending several hours with this uniformly left-liberal Democrat, I was puzzled by her ability simultaneously to criticize and defend the welfare state. She had, after all, told of her detailed dissatisfactions with a host of public programs, yet she maintained a staunch support for virtually all of them. And her tone made it obvious that she saw no contradiction in this. I was puzzled, too, that she could not only vote religiously but participate in local politics believing that the United States was controlled by corporate power and Democrats were "only a little better" than Republicans.

She may have given me a clue to her thinking when early in the first interview she had discussed why her long-term relationship had just ended. Her lover was stridently critical of government from a leftist point of view. He saw no possibility that the state could overcome the influence of corporate wealth and really "meet human needs." Karen claimed he "saw government only as it *was*," and never "how it can be." As a result he "went around depressed all the time." Karen chose instead to see electoral distinctions as worth making (even though her candidates "never get elected"), perhaps because she felt that even half-hearted support for humanistic policies was better than no support at all. Perhaps, too, she had seen public services actually *work* for a few of the thousands of needy clients she had faced across her desk. And perhaps she *had* to hope, in the face of such need, that the welfare state might be made to work a bit better. At least it seemed to me that if she had let herself share her lover's depression she would have found it exceedingly difficult to get up and go to work everyday.

KURT WILSON described the neighborhood where he grew up in Orange County, California, as "the heart of Birch country." Many of his friends supported the John Birch Society, and the "public schools taught right-wing Republican conservatism as the way things were." His father was a machinist and his mother worked in a bank and a fabric store. Both had grown up poor and "struggled" to live in a community that was "a little more upper middle class than they could afford," one in which "everything had to be new or it was 'poverty.'"

Kurt was thirty-one years old in 1981, tall and lanky with an easy smile and a mustache matching his curly brown hair. His first political memory was "every-one shopping for war, loading the family van with food" during the Cuban missile crisis. His folks felt it indiscreet if not wrong to state one's party or how one had voted, but they often discussed politics—"mostly conservative, anticommu-nist foreign policy talk," he recalled. Kurt attributed their conservatism to several sources: "not wanting to go back" to the poverty from which they had come; his father's "compensating" with patriotism for being 4F during World War II; and their being "in over their heads" in a posh suburb populated by Republicans. His folks also had a "humanitarian strain," however, which he thought came from their experience of the depression. His mother "worshiped Roosevelt," and both parents were registered Democrats who "had a soft spot for the underdog, as long as the underdog wasn't labeled communist."

They taught him that service to country was a duty and an honor, a lesson Kurt took to heart both then and later, although in radically different ways. As a junior high school student, he had worked for both the Rockefeller and Goldwater presidential campaigns because these men "would stand up to communism." Kurt laughed bemusedly when describing his beliefs then. He had held "the devil idea of communism. I mean, who knew what 'communism' was? I could equate it with fascism, just that it was barbaric and cruel and mean and they just wanted to take everything away . . . almost a religious conception of evil." Such political ideas persisted through his high school years, although the 1960s took a toll on them. Kurt became one of a small minority of hippies at his high school who took drugs and rebelled against both authority and the "sterility" of clean, wholesome suburban life. Yet his right-wing beliefs persisted, coexisting somehow with those of the other half of his hippie clique who supported Robert Kennedy. After high school Kurt enlisted in the marines so that he could go to Vietnam and "fight communism." This turned out to be a transforming experience:

> It was just sort of, you know, a religious conversion. We were six miles below the DMZ; I remember the day. We were surrounded on all sides. It was just a stupid waste. I was thinking from there, you know, "you could build a whole world with what we did here, instead of destroy a country." Build a world. What a waste. Not only was it a waste, but a moral wrong. Those people [the Viet Cong] were right.

His unit was nicknamed "the walking dead" because they had been in the thick of battle so often. The devastation got to Kurt: "You had to be some kind of zombie not to be affected." He and his fellow enlistees "hated the officers" who pushed them onward in missions of now dubious morality. Some officers had "bounties on their heads," financed by soldiers who would chip in money for the enlisted man who killed the officer. Stateside rumors of such fragging were understated, according to Kurt.

Coming home with changed beliefs was a "weird" experience. He resisted joining the antiwar movement for six months, unwilling to reject completely all he had believed and done. He enrolled at a Los Angeles community college to study psychology and history and earned grades good enough to transfer to the university near Santa Teresa at the peak of protests. Kurt gradually became more and more active against the war. After a year in graduate school in northern California, he returned to Santa Teresa and became a union organizer. He went to work at a "sweatshop" microchip electronics firm that employed illegal aliens at minimum wages. This work, he said, was satisfying compared to the "humanist" ethos of a rural graduate school where "money was an abstraction" because people there "already had it."

The day after the company fired him for trying to organize a union he got a low-level job at CSS. Kurt had remained there since, moving up the ranks of eligibility workers and being elected local union president four times. His coworkers knew he was a socialist, but they kept electing him because, as Karen Mullavey put it, "He works hard and does a good job for us." Kurt enjoyed his job very much. He liked "working with winos, junkies, prostitutes, crazies, and people who are just like you and me [but] who maybe had an accident and ran out of money." Despite offers of promotions from both CSS and the union, and despite his frustration with county management and the welfare bureaucracy, he had no intention of leaving.

Kurt's worldview was now decidedly socialistic, although he opposed "very adamantly" forms of socialism (like the "bureaucratic dictatorship" of the USSR) that he did not consider true socialism. His perception of the market went beyond the intuitive assumption of corporate plutocracy held by most of the others to an erudite and internally consistent critique of capitalist systems. By Converse's (1964) definition, Kurt was an ideologue—the only one in either group aside from Buford Schmitt. According to Kurt, corporate political action committees largely determine U.S. policies; politicians are cutting back democratic rights because, despite elections, officials "are gonna obey who put them there, the class they represent." Although careful to say that the United States is "better than most" where rights are concerned, Kurt argued that true democracy entails basic economic rights, not just political rights, which for him are "the form without the substance."

The cause of poverty, according to Kurt, is the "class system" which maintains a maldistribution of wealth. Isn't talent rewarded? In some ways, yes, but so are what he called the "Harvard-Yale contacts" of elites. Don't some dropouts become millionaires? "Sure, 1 percent, but 90 percent don't." Unemployment is caused specifically by labor-saving machines and generally by capitalism's need for a certain level of unemployment to depress wages and "keep unions in line." "Everybody can't be employed since they couldn't discipline workers." Inflation is caused in part by the "militarization" of the economy ("By spending all this money on goods that can't be used—hopefully they'll never be used—there's a lot of money circulating but no products to absorb it"), and in part by "monopolization" ("big corporations" need not lower prices "when demand drops"). Kurt believed that the market simply no longer responds to supply and demand in any real sense and that it has in fact ceased to meet adequately a host of human needs. "To me, the great engine of capitalism died out in the 1930s; what's held [living standards] together since then is the welfare state."

In keeping with these views, Kurt advocated the broadest social charter of all twelve subjects. He would increase public spending in most areas, maintain current levels in some, and decrease only military and local administrative spending. Rather than continue to "subsidize poverty," he would broaden welfare programs to "teach people how to work and have the skills to get off welfare." Where would the money come from? Kurt would sharply cut military spending, for him the most "wasteful" category of all public expenditures, and use profits from businesses run by government after they were abandoned by corporations. (Wouldn't these be less efficient and profitable owing to the lack of incentives for cost reduction in the government sphere? Kurt argued that the Tennessee Valley Authority, for example, makes a profit *and* provides cheaper power than its corporate counterparts and that publicly owned enterprises can function competitively. The post office, like a highway repair department, he said, is a service with goals other than profit and so cannot fairly be compared to a business.)

Kurt was well aware of the opposition to more state spending and taxes but felt sure that popular resistance is selective:

> Prop 13 passed because inflation, speculation, and rising [property] taxes were taking home ownership out of working-class hands and it scared [people]. Prop 9 is a good example. People aren't opposed to taxes. People felt their state [income] taxes were fair for what they got in return, and that is why it lost overwhelmingly. . . . I think it was a very intelligent choice to make. . . . I don't mind my taxes going to services; I don't think most people do. They don't mind building roads and schools. There's a backlash because [welfare] is readily accessible for a backlash. But to build a B-1 bomber or something to destroy the world, I think ultimately people will object to that.

Kurt opposed each of the Reagan cuts I asked about. He called the administration's attempt to cut miners' black-lung benefits "a crime" and vehemently protested Reagan's cuts in school-lunch programs: "I don't know what he's talking about. I mean, what the hell's the 'truly needy' as opposed to the needy? He throws out camouflage slogans that don't [refer to] a goddamn thing." Kurt was also against all of Reagan's deregulation plans because most regulations have "clearly improved the quality of life" and because the only reason to worsen it with deregulation is to "fatten corporate coffers." Corporations that get the profits, he argued, should have to pay the "full social costs" of their production—including cleaning up water, air, and land pollution. Having spent years filling out forms, he was sensitive to paperwork burdens, but insisted that we must "look at what regulations are *trying* to do. I understand the frustrations [business people] feel and I think it could be streamlined, but the world *is* really complicated [and] democracies are very inefficient."

In Kurt's eyes, Reagan's deregulation efforts amount to additional corporate subsidies. He thought the billions of tax dollars that now support the tobacco, cotton, oil, and nuclear industries (many of which might not be profitable without such "corporate welfare") should be used to finance public services that directly meet human needs. Kurt believed that the impetus behind deregulation was not so much the costs of regulatory paperwork as "the oil companies holding a gun to the head of the national economy." But wouldn't spending cuts and deregulation improve the economy and thus provide jobs? Kurt said that this is a "bullshit theory" designed to conceal a policy that redistributes national wealth both upward to big business and into "war industries," which exist to protect the "interests of the corporate capitalist class" abroad.

Kurt's political behavior was consistent with his political beliefs. He voted for a state tax on oil company profits, worked actively against the two tax-cutting propositions and for the local rent control initiative, and supported leftist Citizens' party candidate Barry Commoner for president in 1980. By voting for Commoner Kurt hoped to "open up an alternative" to Carter, for whom he found it morally difficult to vote. This may have been a "mistake," he said, since Reagan is so "dangerous." I asked him what good it did to vote for candidates who may have great ideas but are not electable. He agreed it was a good question but maintained that when "the system is hellbent for disaster . . . the few voices in the wilderness are important. . . . If you're not going to try to avoid disaster, why win?"

By "disaster" Kurt meant the combination of the Right's "reckless warmongering," which in his view is edging us toward a nuclear showdown, and its economic policies of "upward redistribution" of wealth and power in which the symbol of free enterprise remains real for conglomerates and multinationals but less and less so for a local grocer or neighborhood carpenter. The problems he saw on the front page and in his office stem largely from the growing power of big business to exploit workers and communities and to dump both whenever the profit picture looks brighter in developing countries. Whether there or here, those affected have no democratic say over the processes that structure their lives.

For Kurt, the state surely has its problems, but what others reverently refer to as the free market has lost its claims to legitimacy in the measure that it actually occludes the opportunities it claims to create. Interestingly, his criteria for accepting the equation of capitalism and democracy was similar to that of the more conservative NDC workers. It is on the evidence that they would differ: for most of the NDC subjects the market creates enough opportunity for ordinary folks; for Kurt it does not. And this is why he believed strong state support and a radical restructuring of power are essential.

Long into my second interview, I began to wonder about two things. What was it about Kurt that made him so fervent in his political beliefs, first on the Right and now on the Left? I could not know for sure, but I came to suspect that his ostensible need for strong ideological commitment began with his parents— their blend of passionate humanitarianism and equally passionate anticommunism. Also, there was his conservative Orange County environs. Then, having undergone a profound transformation in Vietnam, perhaps he felt some need, on top of that for duty to others his folks had taught him, to be as committed a socialist after seeing the error of his ways as he had been a conservative before. Whatever had driven him to ideological commitment in his teen years, he may have felt some need for consistency or continuity of commitment after his conversion—that is, the need, if he was going to feel good about himself, to make up for the political past he had rejected. I could not help but wonder, too, how Kurt could reconcile his desire for fundamental social change with the incremental and individualistic nature of his chosen work:

> I know the Social Services Department, without mass political and economic change, is not gonna deal with poverty. I don't kid myself about that. [But] I have individual cases where I can work with people, get them on SSI, stabilize them, give them the right doctors where they can work again, and that's very satisfying. But I don't kid myself. I don't do that for the majority of my cases.
>
> The worst thing America does is give people nothing to believe in. If you don't believe in something, you can't deal with anything. If you have a system to absorb your experiences and change the world a little, you can accept a lot of things.

His union work, his efforts in local grass-roots politics, and the broader democratic socialist movement with which he identified all seemed to sustain Kurt in what must be called his uphill battle to make a difference for people through (and despite) the welfare bureaucracy. The converse also seemed true: that to be able, even occasionally, to provide concrete help to one of capitalism's casualties, to meet a living breathing human's needs, helped sustain his hope when in the big picture progress seemed far off indeed. Thus, it was not that he felt some need to reconcile one with the other but rather that the *interaction* of the two was self-reconciling. However precarious it seemed, this sort of balance may account for how Kurt sustained a wearying array of political work across both professional and private spheres and for why he could disdain an electoral system that preserves what he thought of as an unjust status quo and yet still vote in every election. As he put it,

> I guess it would come down to a statement Gramsci once made: "Pessimism of the mind, optimism of the will." To me, that always meant that you look at things and you go, "Everything's really fucked up, nothin's gonna work," but you don't change something by not believing somewhere in yourself that it can be changed. And I guess it's a moral thing, an obligation to vote, to exercise a right ordinary working people struggled for centuries to establish.

RON JAMISON grew up during the Great Depression on the outskirts of St. Louis. While his mother raised the children, his father traveled, selling farm products and "during tough times" straw hats or "anything to make a buck—we never went hungry." His Scotch-Irish and Polish family was heavily Catholic. At the age of fourteen Ron left home to study for the priesthood at a nearby Maryknoll seminary, a decision he attributed to both his mother's urging and his years as an altar boy when the parish priest provided as much of a role model as his traveling father. After ten years but before being ordained, Ron left the seminary—"didn't like the life," he told me.

He then enlisted in the army and, in a jarring change of pace, was sent to Korea as a machine gunner. Although he came to "question" his faith there, he soon arranged a new job as a chaplain's assistant, work more in line with his Maryknoll past and his desire to "do good for people." (I asked Ron what he thought of the role of Maryknoll missionaries in the current civil strife in Latin America: "I always thought we should be with the poor; never was a monsignor type.") After the war he finished college and earned a master's degree in social work. He began his career in the settlement houses of New York's Lower East Side, working with young people and doing community organizing. He had continued such work in several capacities on both coasts ever since.

His folks were Democrats and his father often talked positively about unions, "even though he never benefited from them himself." Ron's years in the seminary helped develop his "concern for people," but they also sheltered him from politics. He remembered coming home and hearing rumors that Willkie had won, only to wonder who Willkie was. Later in New York he discovered the populist progressivism of Henry Wallace. He grew to prefer Wallace over Truman but remained a lifelong Democrat.

Ron became a member of the Sierra Club in the early 1950s and met his wife on one of their outings. They had been married twenty-seven years in 1981 and had two grown children. His wife was a nurse, and they shared a comfortable three-bedroom home in a quiet suburb. After moving to California in the 1960s to be near his wife's family, Ron worked in a succession of social work and community service agency positions. In the early 1970s he took a job at CSS working with disturbed children who received welfare and their foster parents. At the time of my interviews Ron was in the middle stage of Parkinson's disease, thankful to have a secure job in his calling that he could still do.

Ron's beliefs about the world's problems were centrist compared to Kurt Wilson's. Like Karen Mullavey, Ron noted in several contexts that free-market capitalism did not work as it was supposed to. He was puzzled by "inflation" that disproportionately afflicts "the essentials of life" like housing, energy, and food. It is strange, he thought, that this inflation seems immune to the laws of supply and demand: "For the first time you've got manufacturers who can't sell their products and still keep raising prices. . . . That's different than the 1930s." He singled out unemployment as the other major problem facing the United States. He touched upon both the psychology of joblessness, noting that some groups like blacks "have been unemployed so long they've given up trying" to find work, and its structural sources, saying he had just read of a major plant closing nearby.

Ron was no socialist, but neither did he believe, as capitalists since Adam Smith have claimed, that the unencumbered pursuit of private gain will some-how yield public good. He attributed America's economic woes to "a number of people wanting to get rich." He named "stockholders" as the current culprits but also noted that in the past some unions had pushed a bit too hard for a larger share of the pie. He saw the stockholder class as "controlling government policies" now (for example, the "big break" Reagan "has given the oil industry") and implied without ever quite saying so that this was behind the persistence of poverty and the failure of the state to eliminate it. As with his view of unemployment, poverty had two aspects for Ron. At the individual level, poverty, he said, is caused by "an inability to do your share of work that pays off," an inability rooted in "lack of education." At the systemic level, modern poverty began "when they started charging interest around 1400 A.D.; then man started benefiting from the work of others without doing work themselves, through ownership."

Like his younger coworkers Karen and Kurt, Ron maintained that "big business has too much power" and that "monopolies" are an obstacle to democracy. Unlike them, however, he did not think the country as a whole is run for their benefit alone. In his view, "more Democrats" would change the power imbalance by "working" in the interests "of all classes." Democrats also "have to have fiscal responsibility, [but] would invest in people programs, not war industries." Reagan's cuts in social programs will do nothing, Ron said, to solve economic problems, because they will result only in "less money to spend by people who have no money. . . . There won't be as many contributing members of the economy. . . . [and] the rich will just get richer."

In keeping with his views, Ron advocated a broad social charter; his spending preferences were those of a classic liberal Democrat. His life experience as a social service professional had convinced him that state programs have done for the masses of low-income people what the market had manifestly failed to do. Thus he supported increasing or maintaining current public spending in nearly all areas. Like most liberals, he would cut funding for the military. He remembered from his army days that officers were:

> just waiting for World War III . . . trying to keep the spirit up in us. Just like a car salesman will promote his product all out of reason, I'm thinking that the military industries are promoting Red scares. And if you spend all your energy and money on something like that, there's not enough left to live a good life. Silly stuff like taking battleships out of mothballs—that's enough money to support a medium-sized city!

Aren't the Soviets getting ahead of us? "I don't think we can afford it and I don't buy it either."

So far, the consummate and consistent liberal, I thought. But then, unlike most liberals and unlike even most of the NDC subjects, Ron said he would also cut spending for higher education and job training. Although he had two sons in college, he believed higher education is "overspent" because "so many professors get research grants like you instead of teaching."[1] Although such a policy preference might put him in the conservative column in a survey or poll, in Ron's mind it was clearly grounded in antielitist, populist sentiments very much in line with his liberal principles. As to his choice of cutting funds for job training, I wondered how a person who had spent his life attempting to arrange gainful employment for the poor could have arrived at such a policy preference. Simple: he thought job training programs are "a waste of our money 'cause the tendency is to get people *prepared* for employment, and that's as far as it goes." He explained:

> There's been no real breakthrough in jobs programs like the CCC. Those were jobs. They didn't tell young men and women they'd have to rise and shine at 8 A.M. and have their shoes polished and so on. They just offered

---

1. I offered Jamison neither a defense of my research and career nor any ideological work to justify "professors who get research grants." As a young, untenured sociologist, I sometimes harbored similar feelings about some of my senior colleagues. Besides, I was not personally offended by his comment since my research was largely unsupported by grants.

jobs that people went out and did. . . . Employment counseling and training is good in itself, but it's something private industry used to handle for themselves. And the unions used to have their own schools, for example, on ships. I worked with the maritime union and they'd train their own apprentices. . . . I'd like to see private industry take care of it.

Thus it was not that he opposed public job training on principle as many conservatives do, but that like the more conservative Greg Larson and even Buford Schmitt at NDC, he would rather see a *better* program like the CCC of the 1930s and more training responsibility assumed by the private sector. When Ron's reasoning is examined, such anomalous ideas about spending cuts appear consistent with the broader body of his liberal beliefs.

He had grown up believing in something like economic democracy, although "without ever using the term." As a young man in the 1940s Ron had entered an essay contest on "How to Improve Your State" and won a trip to Hawaii with his article on industrial coops and worker democracy. He had carried such ideas with him since. So, for example, the use of public funds for loans to reopen the abandoned Youngstown steel plant as a worker-community enterprise sounded "logical" to him. The Chrysler bailout, on the other hand, he opposed as simply a public subsidy of private profits.

These are the traditional beliefs and policy preferences of a New Deal–Great Society liberal Democrat. Ron offered many others. He supported raising welfare benefits from current "miserably low standards" and favored universal public health care—not only because it would fulfill a human need but because it would be cheaper overall and "I just never have been sold on doctors being our wealthiest class." Ron felt the tax system is unfairly skewed to favor the rich. He told of elderly couples who "had to live without benefit of marriage" in order to make their taxes affordable, while President Reagan's ranch, called a business "for tax purposes," gets an IRS refund. His list of benefits all citizens receive from public spending was a long one.

The social charter Ron envisioned, however, was not at all unlimited. Although he considered himself a man of the Left, he thought socialism amounts to "government control of all aspects of life" and is therefore undesirable. Ron said, for example, that he had "always stood for being overcautious on [job] safety" and he would maintain public spending on it. Yet he later mentioned that Reagan's moves toward deregulation in that area did have some appeal for him: "Sometimes you see on the highways there's two flagmen for every two or three construction workers. Sometimes I wonder if that's necessary." He went on to contrast black-lung disease ("it's been proven that [in] mining companies that don't keep to safety standards, the miner is the victim") with excessive concern over baseball ("I remember a story about the boy who was hit by a baseball and killed. . . . Others said baseball is a dangerous game and that kids should never be playing baseball, [but] that was one boy in a million"). For him, safety regulations in mines "need to be enforced as much as possible," but in other areas "cost effectiveness would be a factor." The line Ron drew was selective. He approved of Reagan's general idea of deregulation because "there seems to be more regulations on transportation than are necessary. How safe do you want to be?" But he was quick to add that if corporations took the opportunity to "go for making extra profits out of the lack of government control," they should "stay regulated."

Ron's liberal social charter was delimited in other ways as well. As an environmentalist and outdoorsman of long standing, he strongly favored environmental protection regulations. "My sons and their children, they have full lifetimes, and if we don't start preparing things for them they won't enjoy this mother earth." Yet, *on the same grounds,* he had "mixed feelings" about the land-use and growth-control laws that preserved the beauty of Santa Teresa. He believed such regulations tend to make housing prohibitively expensive for young families like his sons'. Similarly, I did not expect that a thirty-year member of the Sierra Club would want to hold the line on spending for public parks, but in a context of economic recession and compared to basics like food and medical care, Ron considered them "a luxury." School-lunch programs were "sacred," but food stamps were another matter because "undeserving poor" like college students could get them, and besides, he told me, "Food stamps is an Agriculture Department program to promote the sale of American agricultural products." Cuts in funding for public television were also acceptable to Ron, even though he enjoyed its programming regularly, because its shows are often "highbrow" like "opera" and thus "can attract private donations."

Ron had seen too many "pork-barrel dams," too many "cost overruns" in military contracts, and, after a lifetime in public-service work, too much waste and red tape in his own end of government to give the state carte blanche. Like his coworkers, however, his analysis of the source of waste centered on the paradox of accountability:

> You see waste in the welfare departments where people want only the "deserving poor" to benefit, and then you set up all kinds of rules to make sure it's the "deserving poor" that get it. But you have federal inspectors watching state-level people. . . . It's costing us taxpayers so much extra, and inspectors are not the ones who are producing services. That's part of the waste of our system.

Ron's liberalism, his vision of a broad social charter, remained strong, albeit tempered by experience ("within reason" was a phrase he used often). He never advocated more government for its own sake but always held that human needs left unmet by the market must be met nonetheless. His preference for more spending on public housing, for example, was rooted in his knowledge that homes are no longer affordable for most families. He never said that housing, as a basic necessity, should no longer be a market commodity; he presupposed only that *because* the housing market now fails to meet the needs of the most vulnerable people, other modes of shelter must be available. In short, Ron assumed neither that the free market is sacrosanct nor that state programs are the only solution for America's problems.

Such beliefs translated into votes that fell consistently along traditional liberal Democratic lines. When I asked why he voted against Proposition 13, Ron noted first his "job interest" and then the fact that the measure would "cut out money for [welfare] program support." "Sure," he said, he liked the property tax cut he got when it passed, but he would vote no again because the distribution of those cuts created "injustices."[2] He lived outside the city and so could not vote on the rent control measure, although he said he favored it because it "benefited the elderly and the poor." He also voted for the tax on oil companies, "naturally," because, he said with characteristic understatement, they had "managed to absorb quite ample profits." With Ted Kennedy, his first choice for president in 1980, out of the running, he had simply "voted Democratic," with neither enthusiasm nor hesitation. He seemed to me to be saying that candidates good and bad come and go, but the ideals and values most important to him always stand a better chance with Democrats.

I asked Ron a general closing question about whether he did anything aside from voting to, say, live out his political beliefs. He smiled just slightly through lips that had begun to twitch as the long interview taxed him and said, "Not really. I have Parkinson's disease, so I have a built-in excuse for not being active, [but] fifteen years ago I was on projects connected to city government, and before that I was in a settlement house, so community action was part of my life." When I last saw him in 1981, Ron was sixty-two years old and slowly dying. He had little hope of seeing his vision of the social charter realized in public policy because, as

2. Upon transcribing this response, I wondered whether, by citing his personal "job interests" right away and only then mentioning cuts in public aid, Ron had been trying to avoid any pretense of having voted against the Proposition 13 tax cut for purely altruistic reasons. He knew, after all, that I knew that he also had more self-interested grounds for doing so. When the measure passed, he received a substantial reduction in his property tax assessment; yet its passage also threatened funding for public aid programs. While his "interests" were mixed, his choice of response implied a concern with a particular presentation of self: modest, not excessively idealistic, reflexive about having made a good living helping others. While there is no way of knowing, I suspect this choice of response, as well as his vote against a bill that would net him hundreds of dollars per year, served his *identity interests* well.

he put it, there were now "more business-oriented Republicans than Democrats like me, so it won't happen." Ron gave no indication, however, that he was a disappointed or frustrated person. American democracy had worked "pretty much as designed," and he had played his part over the years to make it work a bit better for the underdogs. He seemed to me content: his job at CSS offered security and, at least as important, the satisfaction of continuing his work.

MARC DRISCOLL was a handsome man of medium build with dark curly hair and brown eyes who came from what he called a conservative background. His father was a career military man, a noncommissioned officer in both the army and the air force. Marc felt his childhood experiences tended to be "military and patriotic" as a result. The family had moved a lot when he was growing up, but most of his school years were spent in Massachusetts and Hawaii. Marc and his seven younger siblings were "encouraged to think for themselves" in part because of the background differences between his folks. His mother was a Boston-Irish Democrat, his father a southern Republican. This may help explain Marc's self-description as a "pragmatist" who prided himself on his "objectivity."

He attended the state university in the mid-1960s, earning a B.A. and an M.A. in political science before going to work at CSS. He later took a leave so he could get a master's degree in social work. He married a professional speech therapist, and after launching their careers, they invested in a duplex as a tax shelter just before housing prices soared. With the appreciation in value they were able to finance a beautifully appointed four-bedroom house with a solar-heated pool in a well-to-do neighborhood a mile from CSS.

Unlike most of the others in both groups, corporate power was not central to Marc's worldview. America's biggest problem by his account is "bad leaders," politicians who have eroded our "national trust and spirit." When I asked what caused this, Marc then mentioned the role of big campaign contributions. He wanted to see the United States move toward a parliamentary system and away from a two-party system, but he believed given the poor showing of third-party candidates, that we are "stuck" with the present setup. Our next most important problem is economic: capital does not get invested, he argued, because "people just don't save"; then he added that because people expect inflation to continue, saving makes little sense.

Marc's logic struck me as noteworthy. He started with "bad leaders," but then he worked toward the problem of big campaign contributions. Economic problems are rooted in *individuals'* failure to save and are caused only secondarily by the economic circumstances under which saving is perceived as irrational. Similarly, Marc claimed the cause of poverty is a parental "failure to instill the right values" in their children ("the value of work" and "getting an education"). But when pressed, he explained why parents might rationally neglect to instill such values—that they "see no light at the end of the tunnel" and therefore conclude "what's the use?" His initial reasoning, however, seemed to give primacy to individual choice as the principal cause of social problems.

More than any of his five coworkers, Marc held a meritocratic philosophy. He volunteered his support for free enterprise, whereas the others saw it as more or less an ideological myth. Although he was a "good union man," he supported free trade and argued that "unions are just going to have to make a choice between high wages for a few or jobs for many." High wages of American workers, he noted, contribute to inflation, unemployment, and rising imports. Marc supported "free-market policies" that would reduce workers' living standards in the interests of "lower prices" and "efficiency." In his own work sphere he detested "civil service rules which protect incompetence." Incompetence offended his sense of professional pride, although the incompetence he complained about was that of administrators. He would like it if the nation's wealth were somewhat more evenly distributed so as to better meet basic human needs, but he was as opposed to limits on how much wealth a person can accumulate as he was to the inheritance of great fortunes. For Marc, these last two beliefs were ideologically consistent in that both followed from the same meritocratic principle: an *individual* should be able to "go as far as his abilities can take him":

> I hate to place limitations on anyone at the upper end. [That is] what keeps the Soviet Union from achieving much more than they have. . . . What good does it do you to be ambitious? . . . On the other hand . . . I don't believe in great wealth being passed on from generation to generation. That's what I'd tax against. I think that, individually, anyone should be able to achieve whatever they can for themselves and . . . to leave a legacy (for their familes) which is significant. But the Rockefellers—Nelson, governor of New York and vice president, Winthrop was governor of Arkansas—I mean, on whose money? Old John D.'s! And if they didn't have old John D.'s money, would they be in the positions they're in? I don't think so.

Such ideas seemed to mesh well with Marc's life experience and training. He rose from a large working-class family to earn two master's degrees, achieve professional status, and sustain an upper-middle-class life-style. His graduate education in political science stressed pluralistic voting patterns at the expense of structural economic influences. And his more clinical training in social work was designed around the individual case as the unit of understanding.

His meritocratic beliefs took on a different and intriguing hue, however, in Marc's view of the social charter. Like most of the NDC workers, but unlike the other five CSS workers, he thought there are jobs available for those who really seek them. Yet he would drastically *increase* the welfare, unemployment, and job training benefits available to the poor *in order to* be able to require that they work. "The trouble with conservatives," according to Marc, is that in their attempts to make welfare unattractive they hamstring state supports so much that they cannot then rightly "get tough" with recipients. Instead, he thought,

> we ought to say, "Here's $500 a month to support your family, instead of $322 a month. Here's sufficient money to live, to get a decent place to live, to put food on the table; here's a training program that's meaningful; we'll pay your way through that, but this is it. . . . Here's your skill, we'll support you for X number of months till you get a job. If you can't get a job here we'll send you to where we'll get you one for sure and pay your way there. And now you're on your own."

Marc advocated this approach because in his experience "a significant number" of those receiving welfare benefits "are very capable people who, given half a break, could really make something of themselves." Current policies, he argued, provide only "disincentives" for those who "want to get back on their own." Such people "need a little extra help, but the message we're giving them is 'OK, well, if you want to become a schlepp, we'll give you just enough money to schlepp by.' That's not a truly helpful message." Marc's central frustration with the welfare state, then, was that it "never gets people over the hump" to where they are "situated, motivated, and *enabled*" to work toward what Marc saw as the basic goal, "middle-classdom."

There is an irony here that has to do with the malleability of ideals. Marc repeatedly professed his belief in individual achievement and self-sufficiency. Conservatives invoke this belief in their attacks on excessive public assistance, arguing that welfare erodes the great American work ethic and creates dependency. Marc, on the other hand, invoked it to condemn "half-assed" social programs that provide *so little* assistance that progress toward self-sufficiency is thwarted and greater dependency results. Was Marc doing ideological work here by, for example, justifying his preference for expanded public assistance (more resources for his work?) in terms of traditional values that carry greater moral legitimacy than simply saying basic human needs should be met? If he was, he was doing no more than conservatives who justify cuts in public assistance on the ground of fostering self-sufficiency rather than argue against aid on the ground that it redistributes income or gives the poor some minimal alternative to low wages. Whether one chooses with Berger (1981) to see such forms of reasoning as ideological work or to conceive of them in other terms, it is clear that the same value premise or moral principle can be put to strikingly different ideological and policy ends.

For Marc, the notion that good-quality universal entitlement programs like national health insurance would make for unhealthy reliance on government was "silly." He had worked with poor people everyday for a decade and knew, he said, that most welfare recipients "want to get off." A confirmed Reaganite like Buford Schmitt dismisses Marc's case for a more generous (albeit more strict) welfare state as liberal nonsense. Although they might well agree that excessive and wasteful dependency indeed exists, they would disagree as to its source. Marc would probably cite conservatives' historical stinginess as the cause, whereas Buford would cite liberals' long-standing largesse. It is hard to imagine how a survey analyst looking at answers to a question on welfare dependency would distinguish between identical "yes, too much of that exists" responses, but to the extent that political implications are inferred from polls it seems critically important to try.

Marc was no leftist. The social charter he envisioned gives the free market a central place. Yet here again a capitalist principle was put to paradoxical purposes when, on free-enterprise grounds, he adamantly opposed federal loans to Chrysler:

> I hate it. It's a terrible precedent, terrible, terrible. I have a belief in free enterprise. I have a belief in the free market, and I do believe, with certain limitations with regard to monopolistic stuff, that it operates pretty well. People didn't want to buy Chrysler products; they were dinosaurs. Why should we as a whole have to pay? . . . Heck, they don't do that for the small businesses that close in this country year after year.

In most of his other opinions Marc approved of job-creating policies, but he clearly disapproved of loaning tax revenues to auto companies who have "had their heads in the sand for a decade" in order to "bail them out for such obvious gross blunders." Contrast this with his stance on the worker-community proposal to buy Youngstown Sheet and Tube from a parent conglomerate intent on closing it:

> That's entirely different. I don't like the corporate practice of take over and bilk. It's real nasty to let [that plant] fall into disrepair. They don't invest any money in it, and eventually it folds up. That's ethically terrible. But for [the workers] to try and internally maintain an organization that is significant to the town—and to do it themselves—I think that's a constructive thing for the government to do.

Although Marc's vision of the social charter was based on free enterprise, he believed not only that the state has some mandate to make up for the market's shortcomings but also that there are moral limits on the market. He made it clear that the license he gave to capitalism was not without its leash when I offered the argument that economic decisions are best left to the market: "Oh, that's crazy. That's stupid. I'm idealistic, but I'm not an ostrich. There are people out there that aren't that nice! I think we need some basic protections; that's what government is for. Otherwise we'd have a Hobbesian society. That's not civilization."

Marc's support for government, like his belief in free enterprise, was not uncritical. The incompetence he saw above him at css offended his sense of professionalism. The "insane" eligibility rules, programs that fail to live up to their intent (AFDC, job training) or move beyond their intent (food stamps and Social Security), and the failure of policymakers and administrators to get advice from those who "actually operate the programs"—all tempered Marc's support for a broad social charter. Indeed, among the six css subjects, he was the lowest spender and had the fewest objections to the Reagan cuts. However, just as he desired a welfare state that takes seriously the goal of self-sufficiency and avoids the punitive red tape that creates dependency, so too he desired more "real" free enterprise, less corporate "irresponsibility," and democratic participation in workplaces. And although he remarked that "50 percent of our tax dollars are wasted," he hastened to add that "private industry probably wastes 47 percent."

Thus Marc's political beliefs did not fit neatly in any one niche along the liberal-conservative continuum, and they were not clearly related to his material interests either. He voted against both Proposition 13, which would have (and did) saved him about one thousand dollars in property taxes annually, and Proposition 9, which would have saved him at least three hundred dollars a year in state income taxes. True, symbolically, such measures were explicitly antigovernment and posed concrete threats to social services. But Marc's job would not have been affected directly. He and his wife had no children and they did have significant property and income, so they paid relatively high taxes. Yet, Marc had no complaints about his taxes and criticized the tax structure as "very regressive." Thus, on issues where there appeared to be conflicts between pocketbook and principle, his voting behavior and policy preferences clearly leaned toward the latter.

As a landlord, Marc had a more difficult choice on the rent control initiative. He thought "long and hard" before concluding that landlords as a group had "abused their power" and worsened the housing crisis for thousands of families in Santa Teresa. He was unmoved by dozens of campaign fliers from the landlord association ("Just 'free enterprise' scare tactics—'they're gonna tell you what you can do with your home' stuff"). The proposed ordinance was "a moderate measure with a moderate amount of flexibility to adjust things." Perhaps, too, because the rents he charged were already below market, and perhaps because of the psychic rewards of a clear conscience, he voted for it. But the clarity and moderation that appealed to him in the rent control law was not apparent to him in Proposition 11, the "tax big oil" initiative. He voted against it, not because he objected to state intervention in the market per se but because he objected to "poorly designed" intervention.

Marc hinted at no class or group ties except "professional" and resisted any political identification save that of "pragmatist." He wished to preserve his sense of integrity through independence. Indeed, a theme running through Marc's ostensibly contradictory comments (disliking "incompetence" in civil service and public programs yet backing both, supporting well-crafted policies regardless of political valence) was that integrity, consistency, and intelligence, qualities that would place his beliefs above the partisan fray, were the most important. It struck me that his affinity for such ideals as professionalism and quality gave him the ideological elbow room he needed to feel independent, to feel that he had personal integrity. Such largely unexamined strategies thoroughly complicate the analysis of ideologies, but if Marc is any example we would do well to look at how they affect political belief systems.

His voting history placed him in the Democratic camp, but the fit was not perfect. In 1964 he worked for the Goldwater campaign ("he was honest and principled, . . . someone you could disagree with, but walk away respecting"), and he still admired the man. In contrast to Goldwater, Marc dismissed Reagan as simply "a hypocrite." After flirting with the idea of voting for Libertarian candidate Clark, Marc "reluctantly" voted for Carter in 1980:

> I don't like the two-party system, but, boy, we're sure stuck with it. I thought a vote for anyone but Carter would enhance the chances of Reagan winning. My strongest feeling about the last election was that I didn't want Reagan winning. If I'd thought that voting for Barry Commoner [known to Marc as a democratic socialist] would have worked against Reagan being elected, I would have.

Despite his "disillusionment" with the political system, Marc reasoned that the probusiness, antigovernment philosophy Reagan had shown in eight years as governor represented more of a threat to his basic values than the "incompetence" he saw in Carter. To judge from his voting behavior, Marc's notions of meritocracy and free markets were more in accord with those of his left-liberal welfare state colleagues than with those of the business-Republican right. It would be inaccurate, however, to categorize someone so supportive of free enterprise and critical of unions and Social Security as a welfare state liberal. He was both less and more than that. If forced to hazard a one-line summation, I'd say Marc wanted everyone to be able to enjoy the *opportunity* to achieve as he had. Even though he seemed sure that neither state nor market institutions work very well toward this end, that is what he, both personally and professionally, was about.

CHENTE PALACIOS described the small agricultural southern California town where he was born as "a real nice place to grow up." He was a soft-spoken, thirty-two-year-old single Chicano with an athletic build and rich brown eyes. His parents worked in a local explosives and plastics plant, while the three children were watched over by his grandmother who taught them the Spanish language and the Catholic catechism. Chente would later reject organized religions— "Adam and Eve stories," he said, never "answered" his questions about "cave men" and seemed to him to have played too large a role in war throughout history. He grew up on Superman comic books (still holding a now-valuable collection of five hundred) and science fiction and preferred to read in his room rather than go out and play. His earliest political memory was of a scolding from his parents, lifelong Democrats, for wearing an IKE button he'd found on the playground. He had no idea who Eisenhower was and so shrugged it off.

Chente was the only Chicano in the above-average track in junior high school. Since all his friends were below him, he was not very happy and never studied. The B and C grades he received pushed him out of the college prep track in high school, but this did not bother him, he said, because he was a first-string varsity football and baseball player and had his science fiction. Teachers often told him he "belonged in college prep" because math and science came easily to him, but he had little desire for higher education. He did enter a local community college in 1967, however, where "you could count the number of Chicanos on your hand." There he was struck by a "radical" Chicano whose comments in a political science class were highly critical of racial stratification in the United States:

> I used to sit in the corner and I was tripping out on him. At first I didn't know what to make of it because where I grew up these problems didn't even flash on me. . . . Chicanos would date white girls. I never saw any discrimination. The Okies used to give us a bad time, but we gave them a bad time, too, you know? There wasn't anything blatant. . . . Even to this day all the stores [there] are owned by whites, but I just never used to notice that stuff. And I used to hear this guy [in class] talking, and at first I didn't agree with him . . . but at that time it just kind of planted a seed in me. . . . I think I liked the fact that he was speaking out. Here it was, just me and him in a class of forty people, and here he was speaking out. Myself, even through high school, even now, I just keep my mouth shut.

Chente "smoked lots of weed," let his "3.0 average" slip, and spent much of his time "hanging with, I guess you would maybe say, not a very good crowd." He never applied for a student deferment, figuring the army was "unavoidable," and was drafted in 1969. Like Kurt Wilson, this was to be a critical educational turning point in his life. He scored well on army aptitude tests and was put in the radio corps instead of the infantry; "lucked out" was his phrase for the fact that this may have saved his life. In Vietnam Chente developed a radical resentment:

> I really resented being in the army. For one thing, I was drafted. . . . I did what I was trained to do. I lucked out [because] in the army they train you for something and they put you in something entirely different. The army is famous for that. I lucked out the whole time 'cause I don't know what I would've done if I'd had to shoot somebody, if I'd have shot back. I probably would have. . . .
>
> I really sympathized with the [antiwar] protesters 'cause I was thinking, 'Hey, maybe they'll help the war end and I won't have to go.'. . . You gotta understand, a lot of us vets felt that way. The majority of us got drafted; we didn't want to be over there. Maybe some felt [angry at protesters], but I didn't. I thought it was great. In fact, when I got back I got into the antiwar movement. I used to go to demonstrations wearing my jungle fatigues to show 'em that, here I was, a vet, opposed to the war. A lot of us vets used to do that. In fact, when I was in Nam that was when the students got killed at Kent State. A lot of us over there were really pissed off at the National Guard, that they'd go do something like that.

Until his stint in the service Chente never thought much about social class issues. He had assumed that, like his family and friends, most people were workers. His identity became clearer in Vietnam:

> I still consider myself part of the working class. So what if I went to college? Probably about the time I was in the army I started that stuff, started forming radical opinions. [Q: Why then?] Because there were a lot of Chicanos, blacks, Puerto Ricans, and poor whites in the enlisted ranks, and a lot of the officers, man, they all had southern accents, like they were all southern aristocrats or something.

Reflecting on how their lives had led them to this strange land, Chente and his soldier buddies often "rapped" about the war and the United States. Most were critical. "You'd have to look hard to find somebody that was really gung ho about the war." His unit leader was fragged for repeatedly ordering them out on "insane" missions. "We had a sergeant, a complete jerk, thought we were still in basic training. They threw a grenade in his hooch [tent], tried to blow his shit away. They got rid of him; otherwise [somebody] would've killed him."

Upon his return to college, he had a "bad experience" with a radical Chicano group on campus:

At the time I was there, they were really nationalistic. If you didn't speak Spanish perfectly, they didn't consider you a "real" Chicano, and that kind of bullshit. Well hell man, here are these guys, Chicanos coming from like almost middle-class families, tellin' *me* that I wasn't a real Chicano! Here I grew up with V*atos*, you know, V*ato locos* [Chicano street slang for "crazily daring dude"]. They were gonna do everything themselves with no help from whites, blacks . . . and I didn't agree with that, especially just having gotten out of the army where I worked with whites, blacks, Puerto Ricans, you know, it wasn't just Chicanos. I just split—quit school and said "fuck you guys."

Chente had good experiences, too, in college. He helped start a community college branch for migrant workers where he taught English, did peer counseling, and painted murals symbolizing local culture. These did not, however, outweigh his negative experiences. He dropped out of school and worked for two years in a defense plant, "polishing nose cones" for four dollars an hour and in the process getting "heavily into reds" (barbiturates) and other drugs. After two car wrecks he began thinking hard about his life and about regaining his athletic prowess. He started to run every day and continued to at the rate of fifty miles a week. When he entered the university, Chente switched his major from business to sociology and Chicano studies and got a job as a clerk in the Veterans' Assistance Office. So few veterans came in that "I felt like I wasn't really earning my money." He was eventually laid off. Chente graduated in a special Chicano studies ceremony, which his mother and sister proudly attended, meeting his professors and generally relishing the family's first college graduation. After collecting unemployment for two months, he landed a job at CSS as an eligibility worker. Although he felt tired and frustrated, he enjoyed the work and hoped to get graduate training in counseling and make a career in social service.

Despite his personal achievements, Chente's view of the U.S. system cannot be described as hopeful. Beyond the corporate plutocracy noted by most of the others, he saw an elite few "pulling the strings" from which politicians of all stripes dance. He was not what Lane (1962) calls a cabalist, one who sees the world controlled conspiratorially by powerful forces that are difficult for ordinary people to see, but he did subscribe to a ruling-class conspiracy theory. Unemployment, in Chente's view, may be created "on purpose" to ensure a supply of "cheap labor." He had sometimes suspected landlords of conspiring to "drive out undesirables" like "poor people" and "people of color." Government is most unlikely to do anything about these problems because politicians "were voted in by people who want the same thing, same as the people with money." Poverty is caused by "too few people having control . . . and the rest having none, too few people hoarding the wealth." People should, he said, "be able to control their own lives," but that is not possible for too many in the United States today and won't be without "massive protests" like those of the 1930s and 1960s. The Chrysler loan guarantees were, for Chente,

> just another example of Reagan being more concerned with big business than he is about the people, the poor.
>
> Q: But Carter was the one who first . . .
>
> He's no different. Republicans and Democrats, when they get to be president, they're just the same. I didn't even vote last time; and the time before that, I knew I was wasting my vote but I voted for what's his face, the Socialist Workers' party candidate. . . .
>
> Q: But, on the Chrysler thing, I think Carter's argument was that the loans were needed because so many auto workers were already unemployed.
>
> Carter said that? Well, if it's gonna create jobs, then maybe it's good. If 300,000 workers work there, I would be for it, but I don't know, I just don't believe [saving jobs] is gonna happen.
>
> Q: So you don't think it was a decision made for the workers?
>
> No. It never is, man. . . . If it was just some other business they wouldn't get it. They're gonna want to save these big corporations.
>
> Q: What about the Youngstown case I mentioned?
>
> That sounds like a good idea. That'd be a great idea, but it sounds like they wouldn't get the loan. They'll give it to a Ford or a Chrysler, but not to the workers and the town.

Chente's class-conflict logic was evident in his beliefs on a host of other issues. Low- and moderate-income groups pay too many taxes while "people with money have a lot of loopholes." He would tax "the poor less" and tax "the hell out of the corporations." Wouldn't this just be passed along to consumers? "There's nothing you can do, man." For Chente, the system is simply rigged for the rich at best, a class conspiracy at worst. Such suspicions surfaced again when I asked about Reagan's proposal to cut the number of weeks of unemployment benefits:

> It just throws more people out in the streets. Is that what this guy *wants* or what? I don't know, I was in my room the other day just thinking about it

and thinking about it. "What does this dude want?" Maybe he wants to create, what do you call it, so much unrest, where all the minorities, blacks, Chicanos in the barrios, ghettos, maybe they're gonna start rioting again. Then he'd have an excuse to send in troops and start killing people. Not just them—poor whites, too. All the "undesirables" in this country. I don't know, it was just an off-the-wall thought. He may not be planning, but it may come down to that—maybe not this summer, but soon.

The future, then, did not look especially bright to Chente. He expected that five years into the future his life would be OK, but he was not sure about the larger society. "Hopefully there'll still be a world left; I don't know, we might have a nuclear war." He thought that "the cold war mentality" was making a comeback under Reagan ("more nations with nuclear bombs," "arming ourselves to the teeth," "every time [Reagan] opens his mouth he makes the Russians nervous"). Without "a complete restructuring" of government, he saw little hope for U.S. democracy:

> The future of democracy? Bleak. It's just gonna get worse, unless things get really bad and people wake up and start protesting again. Back when I was in college I used to see the 1980s as another 1930s, only this time the people would win out. But unless people start waking up, bleak. Otherwise, before we know it, we're not gonna have *any* say, we'll be so controlled. Hopefully I'm not just being paranoid.

Chente saw the market as dominated by big corporations who typically act against the public interest, so in his eyes whatever good gets done is done through the state (including regulation of industry). Yet his support for it was hesitant because he saw the state as controlled ultimately by officials beholden to corporate interests. He was in a bind: he favored more spending on most public services, but he also agreed with many of the criticisms of the public sector advanced by the NDC workers. Still, he opposed cuts in social spending because he believed cuts cannot discriminate; a 25 percent cut will cut 25 percent of the "truly needy." Were not cuts designed to affect only welfare chiselers?

> There are people I see that fit that description, but I think a lot of them just can't find the work. . . . One of my coworkers has a client who's very selective as to what kind of job he wants. She thinks he might be just saying it so he doesn't have to work, but I don't know because when I got laid off at the university . . . I got unemployment, and I know *I* was being very selective about what kind of job *I* was gonna take, you know? Having been in that kind of position, I think these people too are not gonna want to take just any job. . . . If it was me, and I was on unemployment, why should I take some shit job someplace when I could get this money and be selective? So I

can relate. . . . That's cool because I did the same thing. But there are a few who just aren't gonna work . . . probably gonna be on welfare the rest of their lives, and their kids will probably be too. But they are *very* few.

On one hand, this quote, from the horse's mouth, confirms the worst suspicions of conservatives: a welfare worker's condoning what they condemn as the trouble with the welfare state—selective search for work financed by public aid. On the other hand, Chente, like many CSS workers, spent much of his time preventing or detecting fraud, abuse, or any *extended* selectivity or reliance on the state. He was critical of "irresponsible" clients, actively concerned about the few collecting disability who may not have been truly incapacitated and frank about the "10 percent" on his caseload who may in one way or another have been "bad apples." Surely Chente was drawing the line between legitimate and illegitimate use of public aid more generously than, say Greg Larson or Rudi Ventura. They espoused a standard of self-reliance according to which they had lived. In similar fashion, Chente's position seemed to be drawn from his experience of trying to build a "decent future" while jobless. He had "been in that kind of position," had done "the same thing," and so he could "relate" to people who stayed on welfare long enough to find something better than a "shit job someplace." He had been on unemployment a grand total of ninety days (two months more than Rudi) in fourteen working years; his intentions, he seemed to believe, were honorable enough. He had not "ripped off" other taxpayers by being a permanent ward of the state, so why should he presume that of others? His benefits had paid the rent for a couple of months so he might find a job he could "feel good about," one that would give him "a start." Even if he had not had an ideology that permitted this, I suspect that Chente—to appear consistent to himself—would have shied away from dissuading others worse off than he had been from using public aid to get on *their* feet.

Thus, while Chente followed all the CSS procedures for detecting even minor welfare cheats, he continued to live out his beliefs through his commitment to helping those in need. This commitment struck me as important because he was no longer politically active as he had been after his radicalization during the Vietnam War. He said nothing to suggest that his beliefs had changed but much to imply that, in his view, the times had. His hope waned in the 1970s. He had become quite cynical about electoral politics ("Mickey Mouse" was his write-in candidate for president in 1972). And things had only worsened in the age of Reagan. Like Sally Jones, there seemed to be a certain symmetry between Chente's growing sense of powerlessness and his waning activism, each accommodating the other.

How do people with a "radical" identity live with themselves without being politically active? Like Joe Demski, who shared his cynicism about politics and looked for a way out of NDC and into nursing, Chente looked to his job for a way to make both a living *and* a contribution to a society he thought was badly in need of it. After his active days in the antiwar movement, he had picketed in support of farm-worker strikes and leafleted for rent control, but he was not active even in his union at the time of my interviews. "After a while, I just didn't want to do anything." He didn't seem to know exactly why; he guessed he "just got lazy" and too often felt "pooped." He seemed to manage the apparent contradiction between his leftist beliefs and his political inactivity by adjusting his public identity downward to "just a liberal."

His words *lazy* and *pooped* were used in an unusual and particular way: "A lot of times when the tenants' union or somebody was hittin' me up to [do political work], I'd rather be out running. . . . After coming off work, I have to run to keep from goin' nuts . . . eight, nine, ten miles." This suggests that, as in the case of his coworker Karen Mullavey, work was sufficiently taxing that political activity became too much to bear. Also, perhaps, like many of us, as he grew older, personal concerns and private life loomed larger. A cynic might say that he had sold out, but I think that the growing gap between the social change he believed was necessary and that which he believed was historically possible might have been incapacitating in a way that personal pursuits like long-distance running were not.

Until Chente sees some progress toward social justice, he will probably just keep trying to empower a few of the individual victims of injustice who trudge through CSS, and then go home to read science fiction, party with his roommate, watch the new color television in their funky bachelor bungalow, and run and run.

MIGUEL WHITE was born to Native American and Mexican parents whose ancestors had lived in Santa Teresa since the nineteenth century. His mother had been blind since her teens and his father, who worked at a tire store until his hernia operation and then in the City Parks Department, was also disabled after a stroke. Miguel lived with them in half of the duplex he bought for them in a pleasant downtown neighborhood. He was the middle child between two sisters, one of whom lived in the other half of the duplex with her children. He was a shy, kindly, soft-spoken man of thirty-seven, slightly chubby, gracious and self-effacing in demeanor, with dark brown hair and eyes.

He spent twelve years in Catholic schools but was no longer formally religious. A good student, he enjoyed school—especially sports, although he claimed to have been unathletic. Miguel's earliest political memories were hearing his folks speak against Eisenhower ("always on the golf course") and wondering why Vice President Nixon was pelted with stones in South America. His folks always voted Democratic, but they never tried to inculcate any particular political values in their children. They now agreed "100 percent" with his opposition to Reagan.

Miguel developed a bond with Chicanos as a teenager. His family was part Mexican on both sides, but they were taken to be white because of their light skin. This afforded Miguel a unique view of race relations:

> You always wondered why [Chicanos] always did the janitorial jobs. My relatives have really dark skin, but we'd hear a lot of stuff because people don't realize we have Mexican blood . . . thought [Mom] was Irish or something. I remember [she'd] get really angry [when] she heard like "lazy Mexican" or how they wouldn't "go live next door" to a Mexican. Then they'd find out she was Mexican, they'd get kinda sheepish.

Miguel entered the Los Angeles branch of the state college in 1964, majoring in social studies in preparation for a career in social service. He joined the Young Democrats' Club, and worked part-time at Sears and picked lemons in the summer to finanace his education. When student deferments were dropped he was drafted. He enlisted before his induction in order to have some choice of duty and was sent to Germany as a clerk where he typed reports on troop levels and on "the one or two a month" who went AWOL. When his hitch was up, he returned to California to finish college, but his education was cut short again when his father suffered a stroke. He then took the first job that opened up at CSS, supply clerk. "I knew, since I didn't graduate, I'd have to work two years at something else before I could take the test [for eligibility worker-I]."

In the dozen years between then and my 1981 interviews, Miguel had worked his way up to eligibility supervisor. He enjoyed his coworkers' camaraderie and his "responsibility"—the two things that got him through the frustrations of "being caught in the middle" between conservative critics who were concerned he might be too generous and complaining clients who often saw him as stingy when he gave them "bad news." This bind, he said, had led him to develop "a little callousness" as armor. Occasionally such frustrations had led him to think of other work, but only if "I could find a job that was secure . . . or one that wouldn't end. I'd hate to be . . . out of work; I don't like that feeling." He said he would be "leery" of starting anew given the vicissitudes of the job market and his folks' dependence on him. He was satisfied enough, however, to stick it out at CSS for the foreseeable future, although, unlike most of the others in both groups, he "probably" would accept a promotion to management if offered.

Miguel's personal world was reasonably secure, but he found the world at large less so. The "arms race" seemed "frightening" to him, "not necessary for our defense." He saw the United States as headed back toward a "war economy," a strategy for economic recovery he believed history had shown was "not the right way." He thought it would lead to more unemployment and thus more crime. Moreover, increased unemployment did not seem to him merely accidental:

> It's kinda silly, but I believe [poverty is] created by the upper class. What's coming out of the administration now is eliminating the middle and creating a larger lower class. Poverty is from lack of opportunity, lack of jobs, lack of a way to get out of their situation. If we really cared, there shouldn't be any poverty in this country. Supposedly we're the richest country in the world, yet we have ghettos like Watts and Harlem. And the first thing they cut to save money are economic recovery programs, all the job training programs. . . . To get out of the ghetto you need some help. There are always going to be a few who'll make it with no help, [but] I guess I just don't think the human species is that strong.

Miguel believed the United States is run by "big money" interests, "big oil and steel companies" who "put Reagan in power [by] spending money on his campaign." He wanted to see a more even distribution of wealth, but he was sure this would not happen: "A few people just control too much of the economy or have too much of the money." What he called "the energy monopolies," for example, had succeeded in limiting public investment in alternative energy sources because "they wouldn't make as much money in a solar world." To him, Reagan's free-market policies meant that government helps a few make profits, but these will not trickle down to benefit the majority. What about Reagan's idea about the private sector filling in the gap in funding services for the poor?

> I just can't see these people who are out to make money turning some of it back. Like Prop 13, the landlords were gonna give the savings back to tenants. Well, in [css, clients] have to report their increases in rents, and a *bigger* percentage of rents increased after Prop 13 passed. I don't know anybody who got reduced rents because property taxes were cut in half. I just can't see people who are in the job of making money giving some of it back to the community. A lot of people have to be forced. It's probably a bad thing to say about human nature, but I just can't see people doing it on their own.

Miguel applied such reasoning to most other issues. He did not assume that the market, left to itself, would always hurt people or that the state always had to help them. But he was clearly inclined to believe that without the state watching, the market's natural drive toward private profit tends to harm public interests. It was as if he thought the state's responsibilities should be directly proportional to the market's irresponsibilities. For example, he opposed Reagan's cuts in black-lung benefits to miners because companies never maintain "conditions in the mines"; government had to "force the companies" to meet safety standards. The state had to care for miners because mining companies only discarded them. Miguel was not an uncritical advocate of government control. He had many misgivings about his own agency and about the red tape involved in state regulation. But he adamantly opposed deregulating industries (he cited autos and nuclear power) which, "without somebody watching 'em," had disregarded what is "best for their customers." Hadn't Reagan received a mandate for things like deregulation?

> Yeah, but if you look at it, how many people voted? What is it, less than 60 percent of the eligible even voted. And of that he got 60 percent. If everybody voted, then I'd say a true democracy was happening. Unfortunately, people don't want to vote—they're so fed up with the system. I hate it when Reagan says "mandate" when he actually got maybe 35 percent of eligible voters.

For Miguel, the litmus test of a democracy was whether or not human needs were met, and the United States did not score well: "We just have too much poverty in this country for it to be working the way it should." Ideally, everyone should have a "say" so that "it would be *us* running the country like we want." He saw popular participation as the only antidote to corporate power, but corporate power, he implied, made people feel they could not affect the system. Yet, although the social charter he envisioned was clearly a broad one, he said nothing to imply a desire for state control of the market. Like most of the others, he was no social theorist or political economist who moved easily in the realm of such debates. He did, however, express concrete, reasoned policy preferences in keeping with his definition of ideal democracy. For example, he favored national health insurance because "now you can't afford to get sick unless you're working where you're covered."

He thought the best things government had spent money on were those that made people "better able to work"—higher education, employment training, and job creation. From the first interview, Miguel consistently invoked the enabling qualities of public assistance programs in support of continued spending and in opposition to cuts. In regard to welfare, for example, he said:

> What Reagan's done is to eliminate [aid for] all those that've tried to work to reduce their grants or get off; those are the first people he's eliminated completely. What we [had was] an incentive for recipients to work, where some of their income wasn't counted. Like, say they make $300. We count $150 of it off their grant. What the new regs do is eliminate anybody who's working. . . . The ones who aren't touched at all are the ones who're *not*

working. We have maybe twenty graduate students on the U-Parent [Unemployed Parent] Program who haven't worked in twenty years and haven't even tried, and they're not affected. . . . He's taken any incentive [to work] out of the program. . . . I know the public just sees he's getting people off welfare and that's probably what they want to see. But he's taking [off] the ones who *tried* to get off. . . . A mother and child is eligible for $408 a month. What he's done, if they *gross* $612 a month, they're off. . . . After you take payroll deductions, child care, and all that, they're taking home less than their grant. And I just can't see somebody working for less than their grant, besides [losing] MediCal; it just doesn't make sense.

I have to admit there are people who shouldn't be on welfare, but they weren't even touched by the new rules. He's just basically taking the working mother off. Now, I don't think anything against graduate students per se, but I think that's a choice that, if they can either go off welfare or stay on and go to graduate school, they should not go. It just irks me that the ones he took off are the ones trying to work, who're trying to get off eventually.

Contrary to stereotypes of free-spending, dependency-creating bureaucrats, Miguel advocated generous public services only within clear limits. Although he was a liberal Democrat who favored a broad social charter, he grounded this charter in traditional values like work and self-sufficiency. Social programs should exist to make work possible or to make life possible until one is able to work. It occurred to me that by giving an account of his predictably liberal spending preferences that drew upon values of work and self-sufficiency, Miguel may have been making a strategic ideological concession, giving a nod to conservative criticisms of the welfare state or making an accommodation in his now-beleaguered beliefs.

He did not, for example, oppose Reagan's cuts in school-lunch programs because, like the more conservative Greg Larson, he thought "it's available to a lot of people who don't really need it." He strongly favored education spending, not for its intrinsic value like the less-educated NDC workers, but because "that's going to help us all in the long run." Yet, like the archconservative Buford Schmitt, who complained of "too many dessert subjects" and too few "meat-and-potatoes" subjects, Miguel was hesitant about increasing funding for public schools because "they have so many electives" that seemed to him "a waste of time." "Maybe I'm conservative in that way, that they should go back to more of the basics first."

If he was making such an accommodation, then I suspect there were other ingredients in it aside from the more conservative political culture with which he presently had to contend. The majority of the clients he experienced everyday very much wanted to work and be self-sufficient, but the cutbacks made that even more difficult. Public assistance spending that was wasteful or that went to clients who didn't really need it only made things harder for those who did. He had felt chronically short of resources ever since he came to social service work, so perhaps he felt he had to set priorities. What he did not say (for it would have seemed selfish when he clearly was not) was that his own long-planned *undergraduate* education had been interrupted by the army and by his father's stroke, that this had meant he had had to start at a lower level and work longer to get where he was, and that, therefore, the use of public assistance for *graduate* students, even if they were a fraction of 1 percent welfare clients, was where he would make the necessary cuts. Just as Chente, because of his own stint of joblessness, did not go out of his way to get tough with clients who wanted a decent as opposed to just any job, so Miguel, forced to make choices, seemed to refer to his own experience in deciding where to draw the line.

Although Miguel endorsed a broad social charter, his endorsement had clear limits. He would not, for example, spend more on welfare, just spend more wisely. He opposed the Reagan cuts in unemployment benefits, but would take steps to stop the "few" who were "taking something they're not entitled to." Similarly, he would stop business people from cheating on their taxes (he gave the example of President Reagan receiving a tax refund for "losses" at his ranch).

His support for public programs and state regulation seemed limited in a parallel way by his complaints about bureaucracy. He favored strong job safety regulations, but felt that OSHA had gone to "extremes in some areas, like having so many feet between each desk." He would support doing away with such rules, but only if such regulatory reform would not be merely an opportunity for "reverting back to sweatshops." "Too much bureaucracy," he said, "hurts every segment of America. We have to work with bureaucrats in Sacramento who don't know what they're doing. *Excess* bureaucracy will render any program less effective, . . . but I think we need *some*." Did Miguel agree with conservatives who argue that there is too much waste in the public sector? Yes, but unlike them, he believed that such waste stems from the higher echelons:

> Oh yeah, I think our department, and it's probably true in a lot of government, we're top-heavy. Too many administrators who . . . could be combined into one job. And I think every time we have cutbacks, they're never affected. . . . a lot of government's problem is too many chiefs. We have one administrator who could go away for a month and her in box, when she comes back, there'd be nothin' in it; whereas a worker could go away for a day and the in box is overflowing.

Many of Miguel's detailed criticisms of the state sphere echoed those of his conservative counterparts. Yet these did not lead him to champion the market sphere as the logical alternative. His problems with government did not involve principle but practice—the failure of the state to address adequately the problems left in the wake of the market. He had no objection in theory to the Chrysler loans, but their purpose should have been only to save jobs and not to save a corporation whose management caused the problems in the first place. The Youngstown community-worker group would have been a better investment for public funds because "workers sometimes know more [about] how to run a business than upper management." "Besides," he claimed, "it couldn't be worse than Chrysler" where public money simply "subsidized private profits."

Wherever the logic of the market conflicted with a greater social good, it lost its claim to legitimacy. Profit and loss, the bottom line, were not the sole criteria for assessing the rationality of either market outcomes or social policy. Miguel believed that the Reagan administration's cuts in funding for public transportation, for example, were "a big mistake." When I countered that if such systems were not popular or profitable enough to sustain themselves, then perhaps they did not deserve a public subsidy, he invoked a broader set of criteria:

> Public transportation, if it's a good system, will benefit everyone—the environment, even cars on the road. They'd have to charge too much to be self-sufficient. I don't think there's any public transit system that doesn't get government backing. In Europe they're totally run by the government. That argument doesn't stand. . . . I don't think the purpose of [public transit] is to make money. Besides, some of the real benefits don't show up on the balance sheet, just like a lot of the real costs of private cars get paid for by public taxes.

Similarly, after Miguel expressed his support for stronger environmental protection laws, I asked whether we could really afford clean air. Wouldn't it add to business costs and consumer prices? To this he replied, "What about the costs of sickness, lost workdays, and health?" For Miguel, then, there was more to costs and benefits than narrow notions of profitability.

Miguel's experience in the public sector had led him to place limits on the legitimacy he granted to the state. But although many of his criticisms of public bureaucracies mirrored those of the more conservative NDC workers, they had not led him to embrace the market. For Miguel the market did not consist of the competitive and democratizing interplay of small producers as laissez-faire lore had it. It was organized in terms of corporate wealth and power, and as such it had demonstrably inhibited democracy by making self-sufficiency harder and harder to attain for more and more Americans. Although he would probably stop short of saying the market system was illegitimate, he would doubtless insist that its claims to legitimacy should be proven rather than presumed. In the absence of such proof, he was likely to continue to believe, however reluctantly at times, that the welfare state had its own mandate.

Miguel and the other five public-sector workers thickened the plot. Their origins, family backgrounds, educational and career paths varied considerably. Although all six might be labeled liberal in their political beliefs, these, too, displayed rather striking variations. On the left were Kurt Wilson and Chente Palacios. Both were democratic socialists who held some radical views, but whereas Kurt was very active, Chente was not. Moreover, they differed with respect to their positions on issues. Marc Driscoll, on the other hand, espoused a brand of laissez-faire liberalism that was more conservative in principle and more radical with respect to welfare programs than was that of most of the others. And among the six there were marked differences in voting behavior.

Despite their unique biographies, experiences, and patterns of political reasoning and belief, however, the six CSS subjects shared ideological themes and common visions of what the United States is and ought to be about—to which I now turn.

7

Reluctant Radicalism, Residual Liberalism: Visions of the Social Charter among CSS Workers

THE six political biographies just sketched bore little if any resemblance to conservatives' caricature of welfare workers. They worked very hard for very moderate salaries, coddled few if any clients, and seemed to me to be highly skilled. Not even Kurt Wilson, a democratic-socialist union president, could be portrayed accurately as a plodding bureaucrat seeking greater control over private life for the sake of his own interests. Although each of my public-sector subjects defended the welfare state against many of the recent criticisms, each also had an insider's critique that often paralleled the complaints of the ostensibly more conservative NDC workers. None seemed to be burned-out careerists who produced nothing and were just collecting their paychecks.

Nor do left-wing stereotypes aid our understanding of what the CSS workers were up to. Surely none of the six just described could be seen as a complacent crisis manager whose mission was keeping the lid on the status quo for the powers-that-be. Even if their role was in some way functional for the American capitalist system, the tenaciousness of conservative attacks on welfare programs and workers suggests that there is more to it than that. And if none of the six at CSS explicitly held up his work as essential in the struggle to institute a more just social order, all clearly saw themselves as having chosen work that entailed giving at least some aid to the victims of the current order.

Even among such a left-liberal lot there were significant differences of worldview—of who holds power in America, in whose interests it is wielded, and with what consequences. On one hand was the vision of a corporate cabal held by Chente Palacios: the monied moguls who control the nation's industries and banks also control government and much of the media, and they set the levels of inflation and unemployment that citizens must endure. Even the local system seemed rigged to Chente: the landlord association replaced the Business Round-table.

Kurt Wilson held a more complex version of this view. He saw a bit less black-and-white villainy by big business and a good deal more systemic injustice in capitalism. In his view, it was not so much a matter of direct instrumental control of the state as it was of a historical process wherein reforms won with great struggle and sacrifice by the have-nots are turned to the advantage of the corporate class against whom the struggle was waged. For him, the class system not only preserves the power of the rich but fosters beliefs that lead the powerless to accept it as natural. It is a system in which the basic distribution of wealth has remained remarkably unchanged despite real and imagined mobility. Kurt acknowledged that some in the working class have been able to demand a larger share of the pie, but he argued that the response by those controlling capital has been to shift investment to developing nations where labor is repressed, unor-ganized, and cheap. When liberation movements in those nations make profit-able exploitation difficult, Kurt claimed, our economic growth stalls. People like Reagan then get elected and begin to break the unions' power and enact policies that "lower the standard of living of American workers" so as to better compete.

Neither Chente's conspiracy theory nor Kurt's more complicated critique was embraced by the two social workers. For Marc Driscoll, free enterprise "works pretty well." He believed in it and "with certain limitations" (such as "monopolies," environmental protection, worker safety) granted it legitimacy. Like the others, he agreed that big corporations are too powerful, but unlike most of them he thought that more citizen participation could change this. For Ron Jamison the free market is not inherently exploitative but is no longer really free. The laws of supply and demand no longer function; prices do indeed go up, but dropping demand does not bring them down. The market no longer delivers the "greatest good to the greatest number" because of "too many people wanting to get rich." Socialism, which he saw as Soviet-like "state control of all aspects of life," was not an alternative, but "more democrats" and better human services were.

Miguel White and Karen Mullavey did not offer Kurt's depth of historical and political analysis, but they tended to share his values. Like Ron, Karen believed that the United States no longer has a system of free enterprise but rather one of "monopolies," a term she used loosely to connote all big businesses that are relatively immune to consumer or citizen concerns. For Miguel, the United States is "run for the big companies" who basically control government with campaign contributions. Unlike Marc and Ron who held that more democratic participation could make capitalism meet human needs, Miguel and Karen saw more basic structural problems that are not amenable to reform because politicians are beholden to corporate interests.

With the partial exception of Marc Driscoll, then, none of the CSS workers equated capitalism with democracy. Democracy meant more to them than having the chance to vote for one of two elites; it had to do with a system that meets human needs, and this standard the United States does not meet. Most would concur with Kurt: political rights without economic rights is not "real democracy." Karen defined "real democracy" in terms of "shared wealth" and "individual freedom." This seemed to me particularly significant in light of the long-standing axiom in American political culture that shared wealth means socialism, which means the *loss* of individual freedom. It is noteworthy, therefore, that individual freedom stood as the standard of democracy not only for the meritocratic Marc Driscoll, who favored free enterprise, but also for the socialists, who did not.

All save Marc, however, also believed that the market portrayed in American folklore as the bedrock of individual freedom and democracy has become a *fetter* on freedom and democracy for millions of people. And even Marc would agree with Miguel White's assertion that corporations would not "look out for the public interest" unless "forced to by law." In fact, perhaps because Marc granted somewhat more legitimacy to capitalism, he was more adamant about punishing businesses that "take advantage." He had little use for regulatory agencies that "seem to spend the most money procreating themselves," but when corporations violate "reasonable" standards and treat fines as "simply a cost of doing business," then he would "take the president of the company and throw his ass in jail for thirty days." Most of the others tended to assume that regulatory agencies are captives of the industries they supervise. With the partial exception of Ron Jamison, the others believed that the market, left on its own, would run roughshod over citizen and community rights.

Like most of the NDC workers, at least four in the CSS group believed that real power in the United States is held by a corporate plutocracy. Marc employed his knowledge of political science to qualify this notion, and Ron had been part of enough reform movements and public programs to believe that there are worthwhile democratic constraints on corporate power. Karen, Chente, Kurt, and Miguel, on the other hand, were more unequivocal. For them, "the free market" amounted to a code phrase signifying government acquiescence to corporate prerogatives. At a minimum, all six shared the belief that the market simply does not function as it is thought to in capitalist theory and that it fails for many less-than-inevitable reasons to yield the greatest good for the greatest number. Thus, although they would certainly debate the details of the best means and the appropriate extent, all held that intervention in the market was essential.

In this respect their beliefs were distinct from those of the NDC subjects, who tended to take the market and its injustices for granted while holding government at fault for what is wrong in both state and market spheres. The CSS subjects, conversely, tended to take the state and its inefficiencies for granted while holding business (corporate power, for example) responsible for both market injustices and the inability of the state to do much about them.

For me what was most striking about such left-liberal perspectives was how often they were drawn from traditional American values—the same values, in fact, held by most of the NDC workers. Marc Driscoll, whose own movement into a professional career seemed to sustain his meritocratic philosophy, criticized the welfare system precisely because he felt it robbed his clients of "incentives for individual achievement." Kurt Wilson spoke at length about how "plant closures" and "capital flight" rob people of any control over the major economic decisions shaping both their opportunities and their communities. Chente Palacios observed that individual freedom and security are "impossible" when "rent gouging" by "conglomerate landlords" drives "working families out of town." All the others offered their own examples of how a market world, organized for corporate profitability, had sapped the abilities of ordinary people to build their lives by the fruits of their labors. An irony that seemed to anger Kurt, Chente, Karen, and Miguel was that corporate policies that "raped the environment" and "exported American jobs" were justified by "corporate PR men" in terms of "freedom of individual initiative." And all six in one way or another argued that industry political action committees have corrupted the electoral process with millions of dollars in campaign contributions and then have rationalized this by reference to freedom of speech. In short, they rooted their criticisms of the market as it now operates in what they saw as its *perversion* of values that they, like most Americans, claimed to cherish. To the extent that most of the CSS subjects held "radical" political beliefs, it was *not* because they had abandoned traditional values for any foreign or anti-American ideology.

They surely would get an argument from their NDC counterparts on the size of the gap between the ideal and the reality of America. But there would be little disagreement on either its existence or the standard according to which it should be measured. For most in both groups, the system should be judged according to how well it leads to what I have called democratic ends—real opportunities for everyone. This did not, even for the socialists, imply leveling as such, only that there should be a truly level playing field. There would also be debate, of course, on what constitutes "truly level," but there would be little disagreement between the two groups that equality can no longer mean the false or ideological equality that blames individuals for failures that are plainly structural in origin. Free enterprise was acceptable, even among the more left-leaning CSS workers, insofar as it actually broadened the structure of opportunity without exploiting others abroad. But the political-economy of the United States in 1981 could *not*, in their view, make that claim. They had seen it generate enough poverty, unemployment, and personal hardship to look skeptically upon (Ron and Marc) if not reject outright (Chente and Kurt) the market's claim to moral legitimacy.

Public Workers on Public Spending

When my questioning turned to specific spending preferences, it was clear that the CSS group was more likely than their NDC counterparts to support public programs. The differences in worldviews just described tended to disappear behind a basic consensus supporting the legitimacy of the welfare state on the grounds that the market left to itself too often failed to meet basic human needs. Predictably, in all areas of spending, the CSS people were nearly unanimous in their support for public programs. Again, I asked each of the six about ten types of spending: public schools, higher education, welfare benefits, medical care, mental health services, environmental protection, public transportation, public housing, job safety, and employment and training programs. In almost every instance CSS workers not only supported public programs but were nearly twice as likely as the NDC subjects to prefer increased rather than maintained levels of spending. There were only four responses in which lack of support or opposition was expressed, none of which I would not have predicted.

Ron Jamison, with two college degrees and two sons attending public universities, believed strongly that higher education is essential for reducing poverty—yet he favored *decreased* spending on higher education. The less-educated, more conservative NDC workers all favored maintaining or increasing public spending in this realm, as did the other five CSS workers. Ron objected to what he saw as the elitism in a system of higher education where research is given priority over "teaching taxpayers' kids." Similarly, only Ron would lower spending on employment and training programs, not because they were unnecessary—like most in both groups he favored *federal* job training programs and *guaranteed* employment—but because such programs he felt have been reduced to mere "preparation" for the job search. Although such spending preferences may appear anomalous to Ron's otherwise liberal beliefs, the moral-political reasoning he invoked to account for them does not.

All the CSS workers except Driscoll supported spending on job safety programs. Marc thought them "mired in appeals procedures and delays," and he objected not to state regulation of occupational hazards per se but to weak enforcement. He would give OSHA less money but more "IRS powers" to levy "steep fines and jail terms" so as to get "more action." Five of the six in each group supported spending for mental health services, but Marc joined Buford in opposition because, he said,

> professionals there are more concerned with their *own* processes and problems. . . . Direct service is what gets cut. . . . Everyone wants to be a consultant or . . . the kind of therapist that sits in their office and has people come to them. Now give me a break—*public* mental health? That's not where it's at. They're supposed to be out there in the community. . . . The way it's administered, I wouldn't spend a nickel.

Whereas Buford had opposed spending tax dollars on mental health services because, like most things, it "was not the government's business," Marc objected to what he perceived to be the professional elitism of the mental health department's therapists.

Thus in the four responses out of sixty in which public programs were not given clear backing by the CSS workers, we find not anomalous nuggets of conservatism in otherwise solidly liberal veins of belief but rather a leftist critique of the way public programs are currently run. These exceptional responses might appear inconsistent if viewed as isolated answers to survey questions. But seen in the context of the respondents' reasoning they are consistent with their other policy preferences. The desire expressed when explaining these choices was always for more and better public services. It was not that mental health, job safety, and the like, were not the business of the state but that the state was not adequately taking care of its business.

The liberalism of the CSS workers was more difficult to discern in their answers to questions about spending for the military, police, and prisons. Less support for such "public security spending" has been found to predict liberalism, whereas more support correlates with conservatism (see, for example, Smith and Citrin 1978). Indeed, the CSS group voiced less support for spending in these three areas than did the NDC group. Only Marc Driscoll, perhaps the most conservative of the six and the son of a career serviceman, favored more military spending, and he was at pains to point out that his support was for higher wages for enlisted personnel rather than for more nuclear warheads. The others saw the military as "out of control," robbing resources from the private economy and government alike for foreign policy purposes most saw as dubious if not imperialistic. Although none of the six questioned the need for a strong national defense, all were plainly worried, as Karen put it, about "Reagan's warmongering" or, in Kurt's phrase, the Right's "reinvention of the cold war."

In contrast, four of the NDC workers supported military spending. This difference, however, would be easy to exaggerate if one looked only at yes-or-no responses to my initial question. Buford believed that military "protection" from imminent communist invasion is the very best thing government spends money on, yet even he thought "we have enough nuclear warheads." Rudi was generally a foreign policy hawk who was enthralled with the power of America's military technology, and he supported more military spending so as to keep up with the Soviet Union. Greg Larson, the self-professed conservative and former marine, was "frightened" by Reagan's "star wars" program and would spend more only if he could be sure it would go to "GI wages." Although José would not cut military spending, he was sure current levels were more than adequate. Moreover, Greg and José joined Sally and Joe in voicing the same sort of fears of excessive militarism expressed by the CSS group.

The differences between the liberalism of the CSS people and the conservatism of their NDC counterparts become still more complicated when spending for police and prisons are considered. Four of the six in each group supported police spending. Does this mean that the liberals were as law-and-order-minded as the conservatives or that there is truth in the old joke about a conservative being a liberal who has just been mugged? No, the CSS workers who supported the police did so reluctantly and justified their preference for such spending in terms of a leftist analysis: if more progress was made toward social justice, there would be less need for police; since, however, such progress is not likely, the police are necessary. Kurt Wilson supported more police spending because he believed Reagan's economic policies were generating "a rising level of social hardship" that would increase the sorts of crimes of which "working people" are the most likely victims. Others retained left-liberal reservations about "unjustifiable force" (Jamison) and "bad priorities" like "repression of gays" (White). Their complaints against the police, then, persisted alongside a recognition of the need for police. To them this seemed the only rational choice, not an ideological reversal, although it might well be interpreted as an anomalous conservative position if examined apart from their accounts of it.

(One of the properties of accounts, it seems, is the ability they give to their authors to situate an issue position or opinion in a broader body of values—to offer reasoning that makes it make sense vis-à-vis other opinions, to reach an accommodation among and between beliefs. Such properties and what they imply about the study of political ideology are discussed in later chapters. Suffice it to say here that whether a belief can be defined as anomalous or inconsistent, and where it might accurately be placed on any liberal/conservative continuum, depend largely on how much of an opportunity the holder is given to offer an account of what is meant by it.)

I have shown that the public-sector workers fell rather consistently on the left side of the ideological spectrum when asked about spending for most programs of the welfare state, and that this tendency remained strong even when hidden in the reasoning behind what appeared to be exceptions. I think this also holds for their beliefs about the Reagan administration's funding cuts and deregulation proposals, although here, too, there were telling twists and turns. In chapter 4 we saw that four of the NDC workers approved of the general idea of spending cuts. As might be expected from welfare workers, none of the CSS workers liked the idea. Yet when asked about specific proposals for cuts in food stamps, black-lung benefits, public television, and extended unemployment benefits, the two groups differed less drastically. Only two of the public-sector workers would entertain any cuts at all, but most of the NDC workers also opposed most of the cuts.

Among the CSS group, Ron Jamison and Marc Driscoll had no strong objections to cuts in funding for public television as long as its existence was assured. They considered PBS programming sufficiently highbrow to make it a luxury when more basic government services were being cut. Miguel White would support just enough cuts in the food stamp program to eliminate what he saw as abuse by college students, although he noted that the Reagan cuts would "hurt primarily working mothers." These three exceptions, then, were not so much touches of conservatism as they were tough choices made according to what the subjects saw as progressive priorities. I could not find in their accounts of these choices any suggestion of support for a reduced role for government in these four or any other spheres of spending.

The State as Regulator

The final set of data bearing upon the social charter concerns state regulation in the market. Here again each subject was asked about both the Reagan administration's general idea of deregulation and about four specific deregulation proposals—environmental protection, the oil industry, occupational safety, and land use. Again there were surprising similarities with the more conservative NDC workers. Both groups were evenly split on the worth of the general concept of deregulation, but there was very little support in either group for the specific forms of deregulation being proposed in 1981 by the administration. No one in either group, for example, favored loosening of environmental safeguards.

Recall that in the private-sector group Greg Larson and José Bustamante joined Buford Schmitt in supporting the deregulation concept. For Buford, the free market was a sacred totem and any form of state intervention in it a profane taboo. José and Greg liked the idea of deregulation because each had been frustrated by "bureaucratic red tape," as José put it, on those few occasions when regulations had touched their lives. Unlike Buford, however, they expressed no hostility to government regulation as a matter of ideological principle. Neither Greg nor José supported any of the specific proposals for deregulation, nor did either place much faith in Buford's claims for the automatic benevolence of an unregulated market. Sally Jones, Rudi Ventura, and Joe Demski endorsed neither the idea of deregulation nor specific proposals. Despite their skepticism about the costs and efficiency of state regulation of business, they were more skeptical about the public consequences of unsupervised private enterprise.

Among the public-sector group, support for deregulation was also meager. There were four votes of support for specific deregulation proposals among the CSS subjects, to my surprise, one more than in the NDC group. The two social workers appeared to lean slightly further toward the antiregulation side of the spectrum than their colleagues. Driscoll repeated his disdain for "confusing, ineffective" regulations when asked why he supported the concept of deregulation. Jamison noted that "air bags in cars are ridiculous" and that he had sometimes seen "two flagmen for every two or three [highway] workers." Miguel White said the idea had some appeal for him because "too much bureaucracy" can "ruin any program." All three added, however, that their support for the idea did not entail license for "excessive profits" at the expense of "the public interest." None believed that big business could be trusted without, as Miguel put it, "somebody watching 'em." Miguel rejected all four specific deregulation proposals.

Marc alone supported the deregulation of the oil industry (and all other forms of energy) on the grounds that this would spur development and reduce U.S. dependence on foreign oil. He added, however, that "this would also mean getting rid of the oil depletion allowance" and "other hidden subsidies and tax breaks." Both Marc and Ron supported fewer local land-use regulations but not on the basis of the laissez-faire logic they had heard from local developers; if they opposed land-use regulation because it infringed on property rights, they did not say so. Each cited the need for more affordable housing as his justification. Marc voted for growth-control measures, yet he was also aware of the local housing crisis. Ron, the thirty-year member of the Sierra Club, felt obligated to indicate priorities: keep Santa Teresa pristine and free of Los Angeles–style sprawl, but do not make it so "difficult for young families to live here."

Given such reasoning, I found it difficult to construe what little support there was for deregulation among the CSS group as a laissez-faire critique of state regulation or a sign of latent conservatism. Perhaps it reflected their experience in bureaucratic work settings where red tape tends to tie up promising programs or where, as Weber suggested, formal rationality tends to overwhelm substantive rationality. Perhaps, too, as citizens, they had simply sifted the conflicting claims such issues inspire and arrived at what they thought was fair. My point is simply that the accounts they gave of their decisions, preferences, and beliefs drew upon a left-liberal logic—a sense of fairness rooted in what they saw as broad public interests rather than what they saw as narrow private ones.

As we saw in the previous chapter, there were clear differences of belief on these matters among the six public-sector workers. At least one theme, however was clear, regardless of the issue we were discussing: there was consistent (though not uncritical) support for the full panoply of welfare state functions and a shared (though varying) skepticism toward the market. Thus, their visions of the social charter were more sweeping than those held by the NDC workers, although the differences would be easy to overstate. The NDC group expressed surprising support for the state and often criticized radically the market world in which they lived and worked, but their multifaceted ambivalence, toward government in particular, tended to inhibit both their state support and their market criticism. The public workers of CSS often criticized the government, too, but they consistently granted the state greater legitimacy.

The Experience of the New Moral Economy: Affinities and Estrangements

What I have been calling the social charter is not a clearly definable or understood concept. It is not a bounded body of beliefs that is easy to identify, nor even a part of the currency in social science such as party identification. To the extent that my subjects could be said to perceive a social charter, then, it was generally tacit in nature, a construct whose features must be culled inferentially from the moving targets of values, beliefs, and behaviors. Indeed, the purpose of the social charter construct is precisely to give some order to this culling and inferring process. Clearly, even if asked, most people would not say, "My sense of the social charter is . . ." My hope, then, has been that by asking specific questions about issues and policies that bear upon the state-market relation, and by giving my respondents room for discursive detailed answers, I could elicit from them a more explicit sense of how they see that relation.

I leave the evaluation of this effort to my readers, but it is certain that beneath traditional categories used to make sense of political beliefs lies something more "gaseous" than such categories imply. I mean "gaseous" in the sense that a gas changes its size, shape, and volatility according to its location but does so without loss of identity. Elements of a vision of the social charter will vary historically and situationally, although neither freely nor randomly. With the exception of the ideologues—Kurt Wilson on the Left and Buford Schmitt on the Right—most of my subjects' conceptions of the social charter consisted of subtle *leanings*, the personal and political meanings of which can be grasped only in a contextual or relational sense. What follows here is an attempt to identify some additional dimensions of such leanings and to trace the web of affinities and estrangements that entangles them.

By any standard in American political culture, the social charter envisioned by the CSS workers was a broad one. A few exceptional opinions or beliefs appeared to suggest otherwise, but when values and reasoning were examined it was clear that the group as whole sat squarely on a left-liberal terrain. Kurt Wilson, for example, was no less a socialist for favoring more spending on police and prisons, just as Buford Schmitt was no less a hard-line conservative for wanting to spend less on them. Although the NDC workers by and large accepted the premises of the welfare state and did not assume the market was sacrosanct, the CSS subjects clearly favored more spending on more public programs and supported fewer budget cuts and deregulation proposals than did their private-sector counterparts.

Part of this greater affinity for the state sphere stemmed from their everyday experience of a ceaseless stream of human evidence, their clients, that the market was failing to meet the minimal needs of a sizable and growing segment of the citizenry. From Marc Driscoll, the laissez-faire liberal, to Chente Palacios, a radical if resigned leftist, all the CSS people offered anecdotes about the abdication by business of what they saw as its social responsibilities. Karen's phrase "inordinate profits" was standard linguistic currency for these public-sector workers, a unit of their discourse requiring no explication. In Buford's home, as in any meeting of any chamber of commerce, this phrase would be seen as the definition of a contradiction in terms. In the same vein, Driscoll said it was "ethically terrible" for a parent conglomerate to "bilk" and then "abandon" a subsidiary just for profits or tax advantages. For him as for the others at CSS, the notion that investment decisions are the exclusive prerogative of corporate executives was not written in stone; it did not encompass the right to damage the lives of workers and communities who had helped generate the very capital executives could suddenly move elsewhere. Although there were six distinct visions of the social charter in the views of my six subjects, they all shared a theme: *there are moral limits on market forces*. This was so even if (and perhaps because) such limits seemed to them to have little political or legal force at the moment.

Various theorists have argued, however, that political beliefs cannot be understood at face value. Marx, for example, argued that ideology was a function of social class, and Weber held that political beliefs result from the interplay of economic position and status group membership. Lane, among others, has made a persuasive case for the notion that basic psychological needs (to be liked, to have self-esteem, to appear moral, and to sustain an identity that is both continuous with and autonomous from one's family) exercise a strong influence over one's choice of political ideas. "Political thought," he wrote, "like other 'acts,' is a self-serving activity . . . functional for [one's] life purposes as [one] experiences them" (1969, 18). Though Lane was focusing upon the social-psychological factors that influence the choice of political beliefs, his point is also relevant to the objective material interests and subjective bonds to status groups that Marx and Weber, respectively, saw beneath ideology.

Such theories suggest an important question about the character of the css critique of the market. Some believed that the market system was bankrupt, whereas others held that it was only seriously flawed. All six, however, shared basic elements of the leftist critique of capitalism. Were such beliefs rooted in their work experience, where, as they saw it, the market's victims were every-where in evidence? Or were such ideas self-serving conveniences that justified their existence as social service workers?

There is little doubt that their solid support for the state was bound up with their occupational relation to it, although their biographies show that their liberalism informed their initial choice of occupations. Their need to feel that their work was necessary and valued must have made their awareness of capital-ism's faults more acute, but by the same token their experience of the need for and value of their work must say something about the reality of capitalism. They were candid about their desires for greater public resources, but these were always rendered in terms of human need and pride in craft rather than the pursuit of power or pay. Indeed, only Miguel and Karen had considered promotions; the others had refused such offers of greater power on the grounds that it would take them away from what they were "about" (helping their clients) or put them in league with what they saw as a wasteful, corrupt, and excessively bureaucratic management. Moreover, the variations in ideology among them and their support for small business and spending for police and prisons indicated that they were not at all "knee-jerk" leftists.

Although the preponderance of their experience had been with the casu-alties of capitalism and they would place moral limits on the market, they had had many dispiriting experiences in the state sphere, too, and wished to place limits on it as well. They were too familiar with the public sector's warts to advocate state expansion uncritically, even when they saw the need for it as overwhelming. They restrained themselves from such advocacy in deference less to the legitimacy or even the momentum of the market than to their own insiders' critique of the state. They had seen too many unproductive administrators, too many irrational rules and regulations that created waste in the name of efficiency, and too many potentially useful programs "set up to fail" by virtue of means tests that enhanced their punitiveness but not their accountability. Although their detailed insiders' knowledge of the origins and implications of the state's faults had led them to different political beliefs and behavior, their critique shared many essential features with that of the NDC workers.

Thus, if their leftist beliefs and support for the state were in some ways self-serving, they clearly were not reducible or attributable to that alone. Perhaps more important, even if I could sort out those elements of their beliefs that rationalized their interests from those firmly rooted in their lived experience of social reality, I am not certain I would be accomplishing anything analytically useful. As Berger (1981, 183–88) has argued, it is in the nature of belief to serve holders' purposes; thus, beliefs cannot be impugned by showing somehow that they do so. It is not the self-serving character of ideas that casts doubt on them, but rather, Berger says, the extent of consensus regarding the legitimacy of the interests they represent and the degree of "reflexive candor" with which these are expressed.

By these standards, I submit, the CSS workers look no worse than the NDC workers who elevated the individualist code of the market world to a height at which they derived some dignity for having lived up to it. The private-sector group tended to see through laissez-faire lenses, but they were far from blind to the market's flaws and the need for a full welfare state. Similarly, the public-sector group was more apt to support the state, but they did so neither uncritically nor ideologically. Kurt Wilson would have local governments run businesses abandoned by capital flight, but he would have the workers run them as small businesses; he held that government as currently constituted could not be trusted to meet human needs democratically.

Marx, Durkheim, and Weber each suggested that the great transformation from feudalism to capitalism revolutionized not only the mode of production but modes of language, thought, and culture as well. Weber, for example, noted how the spread of "economic rationalism" led profit-and-loss calculation to permeate the culture of market societies (1958, 26). Surely one current illustration of this is an expression widely used in the United States—"the bottom line." This small piece of linguistic currency has a large number of significations: what a controversy "boils down to" or hinges upon; the fundamental criterion, "when all is said and done," for decision and action; or, simply, "the point." "The bottom line" derives its connotative meaning from business accounting wherein the ultimate measure of value and achievement is found on the bottom line of the ledger—net profit or loss. Despite the many specific uses to which the expression is put, its conceptual meaning seems taken for granted. That television news reporters, political leaders, and citizens all routinely say "The bottom line is . . ." suggests that the term requires no explanation.

The point of this excursion is to suggest what I see as an inchoate principle running through the beliefs of the CSS workers: the bottom line is *not* "the bottom line." Faced with a choice between meeting human needs or allowing the market to work its will, all would opt for the former. The outcomes of market processes simply had no status as sacred standards of social rationality. The service careers to which they had committed themselves revolved around the production of *use value*, not exchange value. That is, they were in the "business" of directly satisfying human needs rather than producing commodities that would indirectly satisfy such needs via market exchange.

This principle was intrinsic to their estrangement from the laissez-faire moral economy. That estrangement had several sources, only some of which bear reiteration here. First, the concrete practices of their work involved attempts to meet needs either created or left unmet by the market. Apart from whatever drew them to their careers, such a stream of experience tended to highlight the ways in which the business system violated their visions of the social charter. Second, work experience aside, there was for them ample evidence in our political culture that the market is indeed flawed. Jamison was neither a critic of capitalism nor a fan of socialism, yet he was certain that the classical laws of supply and demand explained less and less about our economy. As he watched a severe recession build and consumer demand plummet, he saw prices continue to rise. Each of the others gave their own examples: tax breaks, oil depletion allowances, tobacco subsidies, export loans, chemical spills left to the state, and so on. At the level of common sense, then, laissez-faire laws were being broken routinely. Finally, it seemed likely that the current attacks on public services by free-market conservatives—attacks that impugned the economic value and moral merit of their labors and, thus, their self-worth—would further alienate them from the market and spur them to collect evidence of its sins.

Their estrangement from the market was demonstrable and understandable. What was more difficult to grasp was their affinity for social *ends* drawn from laissez-faire traditions. Even a socialist like Kurt Wilson espoused ends identical to those of Adam Smith, John Stuart Mill, and Milton Friedman: economic self-sufficiency and individual freedom. The political-economic *means* to such ends were another matter. When they were asked questions about the best methods for maximizing self-sufficiency and individual freedom, their affinity for a democratic moral economy rooted in the state came into bold relief.

There were several reasons the CSS workers retained laissez-faire goals. They were, after all, organically grown Americans, immersed in its culture and reared on the rhetoric of individualism. They also had good reason to temper the radicalism that sometimes beat in their hearts. None had anything good to say about Soviet-style socialist states; neither the ends nor the means by which the ends were pursued led to outcomes that looked to them any more just than what the market-state blend in the United States had achieved. Indeed, even the CSS socialists held that existing socialism was, all in all, worse than the constricted democracy possible under capitalism. As a matter of lived experience, moreover, the CSS workers knew well the gap between what the state might do, given enough support, and what it is now capable of given the support it gets. They had not abandoned the often radical goals they brought to, and/or developed during, their social service careers. But they were acutely aware of the ambivalence toward the state expressed by the NDC workers and so many other citizens. They lived the limits of the state everyday. They shared with the NDC workers a worldview that took for granted the power of a corporate plutocracy, and they believed, much more so than did their private-sector counterparts, that this constituted a constraint on the state's ability to provide for social justice. The results, it seemed to me, were a radicalism that was as reluctant as it was pragmatic and a liberalism that was residual rather than ideological in nature.

The NDC group witnessed little need for public services in their daily rounds. After ten-hour days of short stops at local businesses, they returned to their private worlds in the suburbs. But they did hear welfare horror stories often enough to suspect that what the CSS workers claimed is a tiny fraction of cheaters signified an entire class of "people on welfare." On those rare occasions when they did experience state agencies firsthand, they encountered enough red tape to confirm their suspicions that "waste" is, as Reagan and the Right claim, rampant. Thus, there was greater ambivalence about the state among them and more hesitation about the breadth of the social charter.

The CSS workers, in contrast, saw a constant need for the whole gamut of public services not only in their work lives but in their community generally. All but one lived in the downtown area, and most were involved to some degree in local politics or community groups. Yes, they knew all too well that a few of their clients in one way or another got a little more from the welfare state than they had coming; they spent much of their energies trying to stop this. Their knowledge, however, of "welfare cheats" was fused with their knowledge of limited market opportunities and "insane" rules that "manufactured" cheaters and dependency out of their restrictiveness.

Thus, the CSS subjects drew inferences about abuse and waste that were, like their views of the social charter, measurably different from those drawn by most in the NDC group. "I don't blame clients," said Miguel, echoing Chente and most of the others, "for trying to improve their situation." That a welfare mother failed to report an extra $50 of income in order to save her welfare grant seemed to him "just human nature" when such grants totaled $380 per month. In his view, the social charter was strong enough, or should be, to stand this. Improving one's situation, after all, is precisely what all workers and business people know to be the American way, although many would argue against such use of "my tax dollars." Miguel and his coworkers resented the few who cheat, but this resentment paled beside their knowledge of unmet legitimate need.

Despite their myriad criticisms of the state, then, the CSS group more actively and consistently embraced a new moral economy. They advocated a work ethic, but they would not leave subsistence to the labor market alone. They had seen too many market failures, too many capitalist "cheats," and too many radical deviations from the democratic ends that were supposed to flow from free enterprise to bestow upon it any presumption of legitimacy. Even for the meritocratic Marc Driscoll, market outcomes had little air of inevitable justice about them.

Like the NDC group, these six workers seemed to me to be suspended in a dialectic of ambivalence of their own. However, theirs had to do with a tension between more or less radical ideals and the limits of liberalism—between what they believed the state in a capitalist society should be, needs to be, and what they believed it is and is capable of being under current circumstances. They were estranged from a state they knew was flawed, yet their affinity for the idea that this state should attempt to meet the basic needs of its least fortunate citizens was stronger. Their work lives constituted an implicit assertion of the moral supremacy of a social charter based on a standard of human needs or use values rather than a strict market standard based on exchange values. Although the CSS subjects retained clear affinities for the ends of the laissez-faire moral economy, their experience of it provided so little support for its means that estrangement was the net result. To the extent that such runs of experience continue and that these public workers continue to have even minimal success in making the state incrementally more responsive, their affinity for the new moral economy will be sustained.

8

Interests, Identity, and Ideology:
The Work-Life Relation and
Political Consciousness

I have thus far tried to make sense of how a dozen unique men and women made sense of U.S. politics in the early 1980s. Their folk epistemology has been rendered; my understanding of the origins and workings of their various understandings of how state and market function has been described. Now the question is at hand: what can even a detailed rendition of the lives and beliefs of a mere twelve people tell us about, say, any larger theoretical issue? If my goal had been "generalizable findings," then the answer would be "not much." But that has not been the objective.

The analytic descriptions presented in previous chapters treated the two groups separately, as if their very different types of work were central to the formation of political consciousness, as if, in keeping with the dominant traditions of political sociology, ideologies were explicable in terms of class interests that were a function of one's place in the division of labor. In this chapter I look *across* groups to show why I believe work does, if viewed in relation to private life, shape political consciousness and why interests, if they are understood in relation to identity, do inform ideology. My comparative case study approach, of course, cannot claim adequately to test much less prove any of the hypotheses explored. But it can generate new hypotheses or new outlooks on old ones and thereby contribute something of value to theoretical debates that have raged at least since Marx raised the question of false consciousness.

Up to now I have stuck as closely as possible to the accounts my subjects offered of their lives and beliefs. But the journey from the biographical details of individual cases to group themes entails a methodological shift that must be made explicit here. So far I have tried to provide enough "thick description"

168

(Geertz 1973) to show empirically how beliefs that often appear incongruous can and do cohere within the lives of concrete individuals. But in moving toward a thematic analysis capable of uncovering the *social* sources of ideological variation, I ran into a methodological wall. Close scrutiny of the particularity of my subjects' accounts could take me only so far; it could not tell me directly how their experiences, as well as their interpretations of them, had been influenced by the social structures and institutions in which they were situated—how, that is, the experiences out of which political beliefs get forged are themselves *socially organized*. While staring at my transcripts, I began to imagine Durkheim insisting that I treat social facts as social facts and Marx chastising me, as he did the classical political economists, for taking as given what needs to be explained. My attempts at microsociology led me to the front door (or at least the breezeway) of macrosociology.

In what follows I attempt to steer between two types of methodological shortcomings. The risk of microsociology is that one's attentiveness to trees causes one to miss the forest. Close attention to the everyday world is critical for grasping why, phenomenologically, people think and act as they do and how they "produce" the world through their practices. But the systems of social relations that undergird immediate experience, as well as the cognitive categories through which it is apprehended, cannot be assumed to be transparent to the actors involved. The world is organized prior to and apart from the practices by which people continue to produce and reproduce it. Macrosociology, on the other hand, poses different dangers, particularly if used to account for what is observed at the social-psychological level. In attempting to see what factors influence people's beliefs and behavior that they themselves cannot see very clearly, one runs the risks taken, for example, by Freud when he explained observable psychological phenomena in terms of unobservable theoretical constructs. More important here, reductionism in all its sociological variants must also be avoided so as not to reduce people to products of circumstances that they in some measure choose and in many ways react to and thus shape.[1]

1. Whether or to what degree people can recognize the social structures that underlie their everyday worlds is both a theoretical and a methodological question (see Schutz 1953; Garfinkel 1967; Wright 1979, 11–14). My attempts to walk the tightrope between pure phenomenology and structuralist approaches has been aided immeasurably by Dorothy Smith (1974, 1975, 1978), who champions a structuralist phenomenology on the grounds that the "determinations" of the everyday world cannot be discovered within it; and by Pierre Bourdieu, who argues that "native experience of the social world never apprehends the system of objective relations" structuring it, and that even when informants are asked to do so they "leave unsaid all that goes without saying" because they are "inevitably subject to the censorship inherent in their habitus, a system of schemes of perception and thought which cannot give what it does give to be thought and perceived without *ipso facto* producing an unthinkable and an unnameable." People have, he argues, a *"learned ignorance,* a mode of

So, how to minimize such problems and still account in some systematic way for the sorts of affinities and estrangements described in earlier chapters? Research on the determinations of political consciousness may be caricatured as a century-long debate with Marx. There has been a tendency to reduce all the complexities and contradictions in the fifty-some volumes of Marx's oeuvre to the simple polemics found in *The Communist Manifesto*, a short pamphlet written to radicalize nineteenth-century European workers. *Das Kapital*, too, his masterwork, has been discredited for failing accurately to describe and predict the development of *particular* capitalist societies, when it is clear that, however error-ridden it has turned out to be in any specific case, he was constructing an ideal type or general historical model of capitalist development. Although there have been serious and silly criticisms of Marx's work on class consciousness, few studies of political ideology, theoretical or empirical, fail to ask some form of the question, "whither class consciousness?"

Class and Consciousness

Marx argued that the rise of industrial capitalism would lead to proletarianization of all workers. Facing growing impoverishment and immiseration under a ruthless wage system that deprived them of any alternative mode of livelihood, they would recognize their exploitation, develop common class interests and consciousness, and organize for revolutionary change. There have been a great many theories on why, especially in the United States, things have not worked out this way. There was the predominance of independent yeoman farmers held by Jefferson to be the precondition of democracy. There were the opportunities of an extensive frontier rich in resources and the absence of a traditional ruling class. And, on a more theoretical plane, there was Max Weber's insight that a common relationship to the means of production and a shared market position did not constitute a class. For Weber and many other theorists since, culture (for example, status groups) was autonomous from economic interests. Thus, the absence of class consciousness, which Marx saw as false consciousness, was neither false nor unexpected.

After unions succeeded in the 1930s in establishing the legal right to bargain

---

practical knowledge not comprising knowledge of its own principles" (1977, 18–19). Anthropologist Mary Douglas (1984) has also asked whether thought about the social order is possible. She argues that all societies have "structural amnesia" because reason cannot easily examine the categories of its own constitution. Bourdieu, however, charts a more hopeful course: "Only by constructing the objective structures . . . is one able to pose the question of the mechanisms through which the relationship is established between the structures and the practices or the representations which accompany them (1977, 21).

for higher wages—and particularly during the prosperity following World War II when the labor movement was characterized by "economism" or "business unionism" in which politics and working conditions took a back seat to higher living standards—many theorists argued that America's working class was no longer radical because it had been integrated into the middle class. This hypothesis, often called the embourgeoisment thesis, holds that capitalism's riches make available to more and more workers home ownership, automobiles, consumption goods, and suburban life-styles that place them in the middle class. Given their increasingly middle-class experience and stake in the status quo, workers will become more conservative and adopt middle-class values and political beliefs. Daniel Bell among others claims that such affluence entails the exhaustion of dreams for a more just society and thus the end of ideology. He quotes Sombart to summarize this argument: "On the reefs of roast beef and apple pie socialist utopias of every sort are sent to their doom" (1960, 277; cf. Marcuse 1964).

Despite its obvious explanatory appeal in the 1980s, when so many members of the working class voted for a conservative Republican president, there are problems with this argument. It assumes, for example, that workers *want* to emulate the middle class and that they will be accepted in middle-class worlds. It assumes that even if workers do so emulate that the meanings attached to middle-class consumption practices are the same for them. And it assumes that workers are unambiguously influenced by their participation in the sphere of consumption but not by their participation in production. A variety of empirical studies demonstrates that such assumptions are shaky and that the beliefs and behavior predicted by them are by no means the norm among industrial working classes. Lipset (1960), for example, has shown that while income equality has grown in many industrial democracies, so has electoral support for leftist labor parties. Since he wrote, there have been shifts to the right in Britain and West Germany, but there have also been a succession of strike waves, many in high-wage industries, and a persistence of labor and socialist electoral successes that fly in the face of the theory (cf. Mann 1973: Sabel 1982). Moreover, even at the peak of postwar affluence in the United States, most workers were never among the skilled craft workers who got the high wages that were supposed to make them more like the middle class.[2]

Although the embourgeoisment thesis is flawed, this does not mean it has no value for understanding the beliefs of the NDC workers. Greg Larson came

2. On the empirical and theoretical flaws of the embourgeoisment thesis, see, for example, Centers (1949), Lane (1962), Goldthorpe et al. (1969), Rinehart (1971), Hamilton (1972), Aronowitz (1973), DeFonzo (1973), Mann (1973), Levison (1974), Habermas (1975), Wright (1976), and Sabel (1982).

close to validating it with his own life when he admitted that he had been "bought off" with "good pay." Joe Demski swore he would quit if he were single and did not have a family in need of the economic security his wages offered. Others at NDC mentioned "mortgages and kids" as reasons their omnipresent resentments led only to sporadic and individualized resistance at the workplace. Clearly the NDC workers used their high wages to finance private suburban lives, and four of the six voted for Reagan in 1980.

The embourgeoisment process does not, however, account for their lack of contentment with the status quo—either at work or in political life. Most had not taken on a sense of self that was middle class. They saw themselves as blue-collar workers who were often exploited; indeed, even the most conservative among them bemoaned the speedup and the erosion of their craft along with the quality of their service. They may have become middle-class suburbanites empowered in the sphere of consumption, but they felt they were losing power over their labor process—and this was precisely what their union, like many others, traded to get their high wages and good benefits. Although preceding chapters made it apparent that there was no legitimation crisis for these workers, it was also apparent that for them there was little presumption of legitimacy. Their allegiance to private life and alienation from public life made for an ambivalent assent—rather than enthusiastic consent—to the American social order. Just as it would be a distortion to subsume their discontents under a rubric of class consciousness, so too would it be a distortion to find in their contradictory and often conservative beliefs no consciousness of class.

Rather than positing the caricatured abstract Marxian model of working people's consciousness as either wrong or revolutionary, I have leaned on a more concrete sensibility about class and consciousness among workers, like the notion of "ordeal" offered by Matza and Wellman:

> The necessity for livelihood, the authoritarian workplace, and the imminence of reprisal are material conditions of working class life. Each introduces elements of realism and prudence to working class thought which are often confused with an absence of consciousness or "false" consciousness. Yet it is these very material conditions that represent the *basis* for working class consciousness. . . .
>
> A typical way of suppressing an understanding of working class consciousness is [the] portentous distinction between [a class] *an sich* [of itself] and [a class that is] *fur sich* [for itself], insisting on the primacy of that which is not over the vulgarity of what is. Naturally, everything interesting (which is to say, history) occurs between the two types. (1980, 1–2)

The political beliefs and behaviors of the public-sector workers of CSS present similar problems for class-driven analyses. The coming of "post-industrial society" (Bell 1973) has brought with it increasingly technological and bureaucratic work organization as well as a service sector that is now larger than the manufacturing sector. Thus a "new class" of educated workers has arisen into which Gouldner (1979) among others reads much. He maintains that the power of this new class inheres in its control over human or cultural capital, as opposed to physical or financial capital, and that it therefore contends for power with the "old" (capitalist) class and tends to hold liberal and even oppositional political beliefs. The new class is said to want more money, status, professional auton-omy, and power, and the growth of the state is directly or indirectly one avenue for getting them. Barbara and John Ehrenreich (1977) complicate this thesis (correctly, in my view) by arguing that what they call the "professional-man-agerial class" (PMC), as it has arisen *within capitalism*, has developed along contradictory lines. This class sometimes resists capitalist or state-managerial attempts at rationalizing or deskilling their work and encroachments on profes-sional prerogatives; at other times (and often on the same grounds) it acts as a technocratic elite. Thus, the Ehrenreichs see two opposing tendencies in the PMC: a "long march" through society's institutions toward more democratic and just forms of social organization, and the growth of an elitist professional class that manages such institutions according to relatively undemocratic technical criteria that maintain the status quo.[3]

If the new-class thesis, however, is to help explain the beliefs and behavior of CSS workers, further complications and qualifications are required. More basic than questions about whether, to what degree, and in which segments the new class is oppositional is the issue of whether it can be said to constitute a class at all. Although all members may well share advanced education and thus have an interest in the value of cultural or human capital, the ideologies that might follow from this can vary considerably—for example, depending upon whether an individual chooses a career in business or in public service. According to a recent study by Brint (1984), it does seem to be the case that professional-managerial strata are more liberal than one might expect given their relative privilege. This suggests that new-class theorists have identified a new twist to the classical relationship between class position and political consciousness. But it is

3. Unlike Gouldner (1979), who holds that the new knowledge class is in opposition to the old propertied class, and unlike the Ehrenreichs (1977) who see this as one tension or possibility, Clarence Stone (1984) develops what he calls a "convergence scenario" in which knowledge and property are not competing bases of power but rather converge within large-scale organizations so that the same basic distribution of power is maintained, albeit in new forms. In contrast to Stone, Bell (1973, 1979) makes a cogent case for the idea that the professional class will be split by both interest and identity according to the type of work they perform and the type of organization within which they work (see Brint 1984). Management versus social workers, and private sector versus public come to mind as relevant here and support Bell's point.

also true that this liberalism is typically reformist rather than oppositional or antibusiness. What Gouldner saw as a potentially oppositional *class* of intelligentsia, Brint shows to be a combination of the general liberalizing influence of higher education and a generation exposed to uniquely delegitimating historical experience (that is, the 1960s cohort and, for example, Vietnam, Watergate, and so on). This points us away from class-based theories toward greater attention to matters like generation and historical context, which are discussed below.

For several reasons I am not convinced that new-class theories explain much about the beliefs of the six CSS subjects. First, I have noted the variation between social workers and eligibility workers in terms of salary, professional status and autonomy, caseloads, and to some extent even ideology. Thus, there is some question about whether most CSS workers may be said to belong to the new class. Second, their responses to bureaucratic workplace struggles did not revolve around the preservation of new-class professional prerogatives. O'Connor has noted that in the context of tax revolts and fiscal crises, "social work is everywhere being streamlined" and that as a consequence "service workers are being proletarianized" (1973, 241). Many social scientists have shown that such bureaucratic routinization and deskilling of white-collar service work lead either to efforts to professionalize or to withdrawal into careerist apathy (cf. Lipsky 1980; Ferguson 1984). Neither tendency was clear at CSS. Indeed, although the social worker Marc Driscoll wanted to protect his "professional judgment" from supervisors he found incompetent, and most of his coworkers mentioned the need for some of what Miguel White called "callousness" in the face of desperate clients who often resented and sometimes attacked them, their beliefs and behavior more closely resembled those of a labor struggle. They defended their sense of craft as social service workers more than their professional status and autonomy. Although it is true that the social workers in particular felt a certain pride in their professional skills, it is also the case that they eschewed elitism. Their pride, moreover, was given shape and political valence by their experience as discontented bureaucratic *workers*. In the face of budget cuts and layoffs their top priority was to preserve jobs rather than professional pay or privilege. They demanded of management better working conditions and a higher quality service to clients rather than large salary increases. They wanted power, yes, but only to do their jobs, not to run the agency, much less the state as a whole (recall that most had rejected promotions).

Most in the CSS group attempted to use what discretion they had to serve clients rather than using technical criteria to control clients by limiting their demands on the state, the latter objective, they seemed to agree, being what management was asking of them. And, rather than pushing for more professionalization, each of the six pushed for greater democratic participation in agency policy-making for both workers and clients. Finally, it must be said that although their identities varied, they were more apt to see themselves as white-collar proletarians than as members of a professional-managerial class; philosophically, most had thrown in their lot with the working class and the have-nots. They rather strongly and consistently supported the full panoply of state services and forms of regulation, but they did not do so uncritically. Moreover, such support can hardly be said to stem from their interests as members either of the new class or a class of state workers since most in the NDC group—despite any tendencies toward embourgeoisment—supported them as well.

In calling attention to both the limits of the embourgeoisment and new-class theories and the ways in which they do not fully account for the political beliefs of my two groups, I do not mean to imply that such class-based explanations of consciousness have nothing to offer. As will become apparent below, the fact that the NDC workers *were* members of a blue-collar middle class and that most CSS workers *did* belong to a white-collar working class is central to any understanding of their politics. I do mean to imply, however, that if "class" is understood as a *category* defined by relative position in the social structure and by the interests that purportedly flow from that position, then class is not enough to account for observed variations in the political beliefs of *individuals*.

What does work have to do, then, with the divergence in affinities and estrangements, and with the differences in formal ideological consistency and voting behavior described in previous chapters? During elections, media commentators often invoke the notion that people "vote their pocketbooks." Such folk wisdom has its social science analogue, the interest paradigm, which has long been dominant in political sociology (Bendix and Lipset 1966). Neither the embourgeoisment thesis nor the new-class thesis strays very far from this model, nor did I when I began my research. What I looked for were the ways in which the different interests of my two sets of workers informed their ideologies. What I found was something else again. Too slowly I reached the conclusion that there was simply too much fluidity to the beliefs I encountered and too much variability within groups belonging to the same basic class for the interest paradigm to account for individual belief patterns. Geertz provided a clue when he wrote that "the main defects of the interest theory [of ideology] are that its psychology is too anemic and its sociology too muscular" (1973, 202). Either I had to abandon the assumption that economic position and work role are important for explaining political consciousness or I had to enrich my conception of interests and my understanding of how they influence ideology. As will become clear below, I opted for the latter.

At the end of a long footnote in the back of his book *The End of Ideology*, Daniel Bell observed—astutely, I think, at least for that time—that "so far no Marxist theoretician has yet detailed the crucial psychological and institutional nexuses which show how the 'personifications' or masks of class role are donned by the individual as self-identity" (1960, 426n). Although Professor Bell might have noted that non-Marxist theoreticians had not done so either,[4] he did put his finger on a crucial issue: the necessity for understanding how the relationship between class position or work role, on one hand, and interests and ideology, on the other, is mediated by lived experience and cultural forms that do not necessarily correspond to class categories. This seems particularly important if what is to be explained are the beliefs and behaviors of individuals rather than classes, particularly individuals who occupy hybrid or "contradictory" class locations as is the case here (see E. O. Wright 1979, 61–64; Wright and Singlemann 1982).

I will try to show below that the sense one makes of one's economic position depends, among other things, on the expectations brought to the experience of class as encountered at the workplace. All human beings are socialized in childhood and adolescence with respect to hopes and fears, visions of the possibilities for and definitions of success and failure, which condition the expectations we bring to the world of adult work (Sabel 1982). Such expectations help constitute worldviews that are at once normative (how the world ought to work) and cognitive (how it actually does work). If we conceive of such world-views developmentally and interactively—understanding, for example, that one's sense of justice can be tempered by one's acceptance of social reality and/or that one's acceptance of reality can be tempered by one's sense of justice—then it is easier to see why worldviews are not easily attributable to any one set of experiences, either in childhood or at work. If we can assume that worldviews serve their holders as normative and cognitive maps of social reality, then it is safe to assume that they will be revised or even discarded according to experience (Geertz 1973, 193–233). Thus, even if all individuals sharing an economic or class niche had identical experiences, the interpretive significance attached to them and, therefore, the behavioral responses to them would vary with socialization and worldview.

Socialization and Generation

It should be obvious that political beliefs are not born when a person enters the workplace. Indeed, as was the case with most of the CSS workers, political beliefs often inform decisions about what sort of work to seek. As Lane notes, "The new

---

4. Since Bell (1960) wrote, neo-Marxists and non-Marxists alike have made various forms of headway on this question. See, for example, the works of Lane (1962, 1969, 1978), Aronowitz (1973), Geertz (1973), Gergen (1973), Sennett and Cobb (1973), Habermas (1975), Rubin (1976), Bourdieu (1977, 1984), Wellman (1977), Willis (1977), Botsch (1980), Hochschild (1981), Sabel (1982), and Horowitz (1983).

ideological item is not the first piece in a barren hall, but the last piece in a crowded, familiar room. It must fit. It must be congruent" (1962, 426). But congruent with what? The political values brought to one's adult working life clearly matter, although I think they remain malleable enough to be honed and shaped (as well as reinforced) by subsequent work experience.

Early election studies showed that family influence was central to voting decisions (for example, Berelson, Lazarsfeld, and McPhee 1954). Research since then has confirmed that *in the aggregate* there is a fairly high correlation between parents' political partisanship and their children's, but this association is far weaker for any given parent-child pair. In their review of the past thirty years of political socialization studies, Niemi and Sobieszek conclude that "young people are indeed reflections of their parents; however, they are very pale reflections, especially beyond the realm of partisanship and voting" (1977, 218). Where as recently as the 1960s it was assumed that political socialization was largely complete at the end of elementary school, there is now mounting evidence that the political beliefs of schoolchildren and their parents alike are affected by events and that there is change in even partisanship throughout the life cycle. The assumption that identity development was more or less complete by the start of adulthood, which therefore exaggerated the influence of the family in political socialization, has been largely abandoned.[5]

There are risks involved in inferring anything about early family life from later accounts. Even depth sociohistories such as I have presented are an archeological mode of sociology; they attempt to learn of whole civilizations from bits of a bone or bowl. As Goffman taught us, our presentations of self are edited, even censored. But in outline form, some basic facts may be discerned from what my subjects told me of their political childhoods, and these illustrate just how complex and contingent the influence of family can be.

From an early age Sally Jones bristled under her conservative parents and came to reject most of their political views well before her experience in and around the student protest movements of the 1960s. Her public-sector counterpart who was of the same age cohort, Karen Mullavey, watched the tennis ball of politics go back and forth from her mother's liberal court to her father's conservative one throughout the time she spent at home; she credited her priest and the ethos of the 1960s as the seeds of her current leftist ideology. Both Buford

---

5. Niemi and Sobieszek (1977) provide a sympathetic yet critical review of the progress of political socialization research. On the post-Freudian notion that identity development continues well into adulthood, see Erikson (1956), Strauss, (1969), and Gergen (1973). Lasch (1979) offers a historical analysis of why peers and the media have superceded the family as socializing agents. All this work suggests that the influence of the family on political and value orientations is historically specific.

Schmitt and Ron Jamison claimed to have been influenced by their mothers' religious orientations, although these led them in opposite ideological directions. Ironically, Ron's father was the sort of independent entrepreneur whom Ron eschewed as a career model and whom Buford revered as a model for humanity, whereas Buford's own father was a public worker of the sort he so often criticized. In his teens Joe Demski was surfing on southern California beaches while Kurt Wilson, a few miles away, was working in the Barry Goldwater presidential campaign. Joe accepted early his father's liberal worldview, but not his religious beliefs. Kurt moved at first to the right of even his conservative parents and then far to their left, although throughout he smoked marijuana (which would have morally offended them) and always retained a sense of duty to others (which they tried to instill in him and are doubtlessly proud of). José Bustamante and Miguel White were both raised in Catholic, working-class, Chicano families and retained their parents' liberalism. Yet, although Miguel remained, like his parent, a loyal Democrat, José was more apt to vote independently of party despite (indeed, often because of) the democratic values he said he got from his folks.

I do not offer these examples as evidence that the family is not important, but rather only to suggest that its influence on political beliefs is always mediated. Value orientations, character development, and the class-bound range of opportunities that inhere in family biography are all ingredients in the stew of ideological development. Yet what the individual will make of or do with these is another matter. Identity, political and otherwise, can be and often is forged in opposition to parents' beliefs as well as in accord with them.

Although the family is now seen as having more qualified influence on beliefs, research on political socialization has uncovered generational effects that further historicize and complicate the picture. For nearly a half century, the Democratic party drew a large proportion of its support from the "depression generation." There have been periods during the Eisenhower, Nixon, and certainly the Reagan years when this loyalty has ebbed, but the widespread suffering of the 1930s and Roosevelt's perceived success in alleviating it socialized a whole cohort of Democrats. Although the protest movements of the 1960s at no point involved a majority of either black people or college students, they too are often assumed to have achieved something like a generational consensus about racism and poverty and the Vietnam War. And there is some evidence that the decline in political trust in recent years (Nie and Andersen 1974; Nie, Verba, and Petrocik 1976) is rooted in such scandals as the Pentagon Papers exposé and Watergate. Although such events might lead to period effects that influence all generations, those who are coming of political age at such moments might become, for example, Watergate cynics.

Such broad patterns of generational influence become less clear, however, the closer one gets to individuals. Buford Schmitt and Ron Jamison shared the economic vulnerability of the depression but developed in opposite ideological directions. The younger subjects in both groups who came of age in the 1960s presented the same problem. Five of the six CSS workers entered adult work roles in that era. Some were from working-class families, others from middle-class families; Kurt Wilson claimed his family was in between. Some families were liberal, some conservative. There were Chicanos and WASPs. Some families talked a lot about politics, others not at all. In some families the parents were in political agreement, in others they were poles apart ideologically. How was I to make sense of the fact that such different individuals all ended up choosing social service careers and holding similar left-liberal political beliefs?

My first thought was of an intersection of unique biographies and shared history—that "the 1960s made them do it." It was an epoch, after all, characterized by affluence, by a trenchant questioning of a social order in which horrific social problems persisted in the face of sublime suburban consumption, and by a state reactivated by mass protests to address the problems and engender progressive social change. This conjuncture not only made it thinkable that social problems could and should be solved; it provided both opportunities and cultural sanction for doing so. One could make a living *and* a contribution, be involved in a creative career and still be "part of the solution" rather than "part of the problem."

The problems with this sort of analysis are many. In general, it is not methodologically kosher to infer direct causal links between the tenor of a time and individual experience and action. This was apparent among both groups. First, even among the young liberals of CSS there was variety. Marc Driscoll was not an activist but a detached graduate student in the 1960s. Kurt Wilson began the 1960s by enlisting in the service to "fight communism" and was converted to the Left not by the university but by his Vietnam experience. Chente Palacios began by being radicalized into and then alienated from the Chicano movement in community college. He was then drafted and ended up active in Vietnam Veterans against the War.

The notion that the peculiar intersection of biography and history in the 1960s could account for subsequent political beliefs and behaviors falls apart still more quickly when the younger NDC workers are examined. For Sally Jones, the culture of protest in which she moved helped her reject her parents' conservative values, but it also alienated her, so that she became and remained apolitical or even antipolitical. Her choice of a working-class life-style was in part a mode of opposition not only to her thoroughly professional family but also to the sorts of career decisions made by her age cohorts in the student movement and at CSS. Joe

Demski said his values were shaped by the 1960s, but he never felt comfortable with protests and was unable to find a way to integrate his liberalism and his livelihood. Rudi Ventura was of the same generation, but while most of the others his age in both groups were in college, he was working nights in a supermarket, taking business courses, *enjoying* his chosen stint in the army, and becoming a cop. His parents were middle-class liberal Democrats, and he had an early awareness of poverty and injustice, yet he was now a hawkish Reagan supporter, poised to leave NDC and join the ranks of the corporate lawyers and banker-developers with whom he played golf. Such beliefs and behavior were difficult for his coworkers Joe and Sally to relate to, and they seemed downright foreign to his generational cohorts at CSS.

The ways in which my specific cases failed to fit neatly under any 1960s generation umbrella suggests that it is a mistake to assume that "the 1960s" existed as such in the 1960s. The rapid-fire succession of the civil rights movement, assassinations, student protests, urban uprisings, and the women's movement certainly constitute a definable historical unit in retrospect. In lived experience, however, it was not at all monolithic. There were those who rebelled against "the 1960s" as well as those who reveled in them. Others abandoned this or that movement early, came to them late, or simply fell through any of numerous cultural cracks. In this light, it is little wonder why an epoch that had a profound effect upon the culture had less than a uniform permanent influence on the political beliefs of individuals.

At least as applied to my twelve subjects, then, traditional sociological notions of socialization and generation cannot take us all that far beyond two rather qualified assertions. First, the precise role of family is unclear. What is clear is that this influence is indirect insofar as one's family is something toward which one *takes a stance* and is therefore of *variable* significance with respect to its ideological consequences. Second, although generational influences are useful for understanding why *some* individuals are attracted to certain beliefs and career choices, their status as an explanatory variable at the individual level is indeed low. Just as the influence of early biography is contingent upon how it intersects with later history, so too the power of that history is contingent upon the biographies it touches. One's epoch, like one's parents, is resisted in some ways even while being accommodated in others.[6]

6. On the political socialization of the 1960s generation the classic work is by Flacks (1967, 1971, 1976). I am grateful to Bennett Berger for his helpful criticisms on the methodological weaknesses in generational analyses, and to Jack Whalen for his insights about the stance-taking character of human beings. For careful studies on the fate of radical ideals in the life course, see Whalen and Flacks (1981) and Berger (1981).

Entry into Adult Work

If the foregoing arguments have merit, then for all intents and purposes, world-views, visions of the social charter, and political beliefs in general are still potentially formative at the start of adulthood. In what follows here I describe how various facets of work experience—circumstances surrounding entry into the labor market, the social organization and culture of the workplace, and the relation between work and daily life—bear upon interests, identity, and ultimately ideology.

First, however, a necessary word as to what this section does not attempt to discuss. Occupational paths are the products of complex interactions between a multitude of personal and structural variables, and it is beyond the scope of this discussion to analyze them fully. The skills, education, personal preferences and capacities, and hopes and expectations carried from the family of origin to adulthood come face to face there with historically and regionally specific opportunity structures and labor market conditions. And of course this occurs under unique personal circumstances, perhaps foremost among them the presence or absence of children in one's family. As shown in the life histories in earlier chapters, the intentional or unintentional postponement of marriage and children helped public-sector workers pursue higher education and professional careers. The css workers tended to marry a bit later, if at all, and to have fewer children later in life than their NDC counterparts.

Although it is important not to underestimate the influence of such differences on subsequent work histories and ideological development, it is also important not to overemphasize them. If we look within age pairs across groups, it becomes apparent that marriage and family are of variable significance. Buford Schmitt began Bible college, but the financial responsibilities of his young and growing family made it too difficult to finish. Although there is nothing in his story to suggest that his beliefs would have been very different if he had, it is reasonable to assume that a college degree might have opened other career possibilities in which different work experiences might have tempered his ideology. As it was, he ended up choosing NDC because it offered the highest pay and best benefits he could then find. Ron Jamison, by contrast, postponed marriage and children longer than most in his generation—until he was well out of graduate school and established in his social work career.

José Bustamante was the oldest in a large Mexican-American family and planned to start his own family soon after getting out of the air force. While working full-time, he managed to complete two years of business training at a community college, but his family responsibilities led him to pursue a job at NDC for financial reasons. Although Miguel White was unable to complete his B.A.

owing to a different sort of family responsibility, he pursued his career in social services anyway, starting lower on the CSS ladder and taking a bit longer to climb it.

Both Sally Jones and Karen Mullavey came from middle-class professional backgrounds, attended universities, and were touched by the movement ethos of the 1960s. Each remained single. Yet, Sally dropped out of college after three years and actively chose a working-class existence in part because it was different from the service professional careers her comtemporaries chose, whereas Karen continued to pursue graduate training during her public service career.

Rudi Ventura's family was more or less middle class and he had two years of community college training in business. After his voluntary stint in the service, his sought-after career as a police officer led to the sort of desk job he dreaded, so he quit and chose NDC for the money. Chente Palacios, on the other hand, had a thoroughly working-class background, dropped out of community college, and was drafted. After knocking around in low-wage jobs, he used the GI Bill to complete a university degree in social sciences and start a social service career. Both were still single in 1983.

Marc Driscoll, the son of a serviceman, left home as the bright oldest son intent on college and upward mobility. He went immediately to graduate school, married a woman who had her own profession, and then obtained the additional graduate training in social work needed for his career at CSS. They had no children. Greg Larson, of Marc's age cohort, did not start a family as soon as he got out of the marines but took a job as a truck driver in part so he could stay in California. He was a bright and affable person whose lack of education and career had to do less with the responsibilities of children than with a sense of self and possibilities tied to his rural working-class background.

Like many in their generation, both Joe Demski and Kurt Wilson post-poned marriage until their late twenties and early thirties, respectively. Kurt left his upper-working-class/lower-middle-class family for the army; Joe left his middle-class family for the state university which he quickly left for world travel. After Kurt's right-to-left conversion experience in Vietnam, he earned his university degree and started a career at CSS before getting married. Joe found his subsequent nursing career frustrated by bureaucratic rules, took a job at NDC for the financial security, and for the same reason stayed there after his marriage and the birth of his son.

These few paragraphs cannot do justice to the complex contingencies that informed the sifting and sorting of these twelve individuals into six truck drivers and six social service professionals. They do suggest, however, that the results are not reducible to the presence or absence of children and family responsibilities, nor merely to the constraints of class background, armed services obligations, or educational opportunities. Personal volition was at work in each of these cases, although, as Marx reminded us, their choices were made "not of their own free will; not under circumstances they themselves have chosen but under the given and inherited circumstances with which they are directly confronted" (1974 [1869], 146).

Whatever combinations of structural and serendipitous factors, objective constraints, and subjective possibilities brought these people to their first adult work, I want to argue that the *form* that work took had crucial consequences for subsequent experience. By form of work I mean that over and above class position—one's role in the division of labor and one's relative income position—any given type of labor may be situated on a *commodity-career continuum*.

Each of the NDC workers, for example, ended up "choosing" *jobs* that brought the highest price for their labors. Their work took the commodity form. It thus implicated them in the laissez-faire moral economy in fundamental ways. The market under such circumstances was not merely the arena in which they, as consumers, purchased commodities needed for use; it was an arena in which they gained this purchasing power through the sale of their labor. The logic undergirding market institutions forms a primary axis within their habitus (so that, for example, although they often spoke of "big business," the concept of "the market" per se was inarticulable, taken for granted as part of the natural world).

Because they had built their lives in a system in which their labor took a commodity form, their sense of the social charter was subtly but I think profoundly affected. Sooner or later their expectations came to center on only the *opportunity* to exchange their labor for the highest price so as to finance maximally their private life. Any expectations, like those harbored by Joe Demski, for a way to make both what he called "a decent living" and a contribution to others were eroded. Rudi Ventura's hopes for work that would allow him to feel that he was "helping," that his work might entail similar meaning, grew faint under the NDC regimen. In their visions of the social charter, they came to reserve such hopes and expectations for the sphere of life outside work (see Flacks 1976; Moberg 1980). Whether they entered adult life with few such illusions (the older workers) or several of them (Joe and Rudi), their expectational set came to approximate a laissez-faire mean: the social charter offers no guarantees, only chances to exchange labor for the best price one can get. There are, then, no economic rights—to, say, a livelihood or shelter—that are part of citizenship.

The public-sector workers, in contrast, fell closer to the *career* end of the continuum. Whatever cultural or existential bargains they struck in order to pursue their work, the exchange of their labors for the highest price did not stand out among them. The quality of their work was not assessed principally by reference to economic success or income to finance a more fulfilling private life. The logic of the market was not a central organizing axis in their habitus; indeed, in some ways "the market" was a world outside. They worked in the state sphere, which, however bureaucratic and alienating, was a world where citizenship explicitly entailed more than just the opportunity to exchange labor for wages. Given their levels of higher education, they did not earn high salaries—the highest paid earned somewhat less than most NDC workers. Though they did not expect riches, they did expect their work to have some intrinsic satisfaction and meaning that would be rewarding to them and of use to others.[7] Such work experience, I submit, is one reason their sense of the social charter could continue to be broad, even if it was not when they started.

Although there are certainly careers that are not, for example, self-expressive or of value to the community and jobs that are or can be made so, this commodity-career distinction can have analytic value so long as it is recognized that most people experience their work as containing elements of both types and that what is likely to have determinative significance is the *proportion* of each type in any given work role. This said, the two ideal types may be summarized more formally.

If work takes a *commodity form*, workers' life-building strategies tend to be based upon the expectation that one has the right only to trade one's labor for the highest price in order to underwrite private life. There tend to be no expectations of intrinsic satisfactions in work itself; a job is a ready-made slot one fills, merely a means to satisfaction and self-determination in other spheres. Thus, there tends to be a marked split between work and life, the individual having little commitment to the work itself apart from its capacity to support private life.

If work takes a *career form*, life-building strategies tend to be based upon the expectation that one has the right to choose work that has meaning beyond its

---

7. Robert Bellah and his colleagues offer a similar, although threefold, typology of work, which is useful here: "In the sense of a 'job,' work is a way of making money and making a living. It supports a self defined by economic success, security, and all that money can buy. In the sense of a 'career,' work traces one's progress through life by achievement and advancement in an occupation. It yields a self defined by a broader sort of success, which takes in social standing and prestige, and by a sense of expanding power and competency that renders *work itself a source of self-esteem*. In the strongest sense of a 'calling,' work constitutes a practical ideal of activity and character that makes a person's work *morally inseparable from his or her life*. It subsumes the self into a community of disciplined practice and sound judgment whose activity *has meaning and value in itself, not just in the output or profit that results from it*. But the calling not only links a person to his or her fellow workers. A calling links a person to the larger community, a whole in which the calling of each is a *contribution to the good of all*" (1985, 66; emphasis added). In its ideal form, the social service work of the CSS subjects comes close to a calling, particularly its integration with other spheres of life, its valuation in nonoutput terms, and its link to community. In the reality of day-to-day practice, it is closer to a career.

ability to finance private life. There tend to be expectations that work will entail intrinsic satisfactions. A career is a form of work that affords self-expression and is not only a means to self-determination but also part of its end. Thus, there tends to be an integration of work with life or at least a muted split between them, the individual having a commitment to the work itself independent of its capacity to support private life.

I will return shortly to the notion that the relation between work and life may be marked or muted and that this influences political consciousness. First, however, it is necessary to point to differences in the workplaces themselves that are associated with (although not explained by) these two ideal types of work form and that help to account for the ideological differences between the two groups.

The Social Organization and Culture of the Workplace

Whether their work took the commodity or the career form, my subjects' accounts of speedups, productivity pressures, computerization, deskilling, and the erosion of craft and control over work were strikingly similar. The anxiety and exhaustion noted by the private-sector subjects was, arguably, the rough equiv- alent of the feelings of futility and burnout mentioned by their public-sector counterparts. Virtually all the workers in each group were upset about declines in the quality of their respective services, which they perceived to be the results of their managements' new productivity policies. Even the NDC workers, who took pride in their productivity, resisted the rigors of what management felt necessary for profitability. These people seemed to enjoy most (and work hardest at) those parts of their jobs that brought them into contact with their customers. Greg Larson put it best when he spoke of the satisfaction he got from "providing a quality service" and a "good value" to the public. Greg and his coworkers would all agree in principle to the importance of profits; but then each would more passionately bemoan the decline in the quality of their product. (In a sense, the NDC workers had their own tacit "ideal of service" not unlike the more explicit one invoked by CSS workers; it was as if their use-value ethic kept taking pokes at the exchange-value system in which they labored.)[8] A similar theme crept out of

8. It struck me that in both groups, but particularly at NDC, the workers' identities and their satisfactions with work depended upon at least the illusion that they had not been transformed, as James O'Connor puts it, from "concrete labor producing use values" into "social abstract labor producing exchange values" (1984, 107). Research on skill levels in the American economy (for example, Spencer 1983) shows that when industries are studied in the aggregate, there is little evidence of the sort of deskilling predicted by Braverman (1974). However, when industries and sectors are examined individually and in case studies, substantial, rapid deskilling is observable— especially the loss of what Spencer calls "substantive complexity" of tasks and of autonomy in and control over work processes. Thanks to Bennett Berger for noticing that the NDC workers, too, had their own sort of "ideal of service."

the complaints of css workers. They would quickly nod their acknowledgments to finite funds and fiscal crises, but then go on sometimes bitterly about how they were prevented from doing what was most needed for those most in need—the point, after all, of their work.

These parallel discontents led to rather parallel critiques of management and hierarchy. Most in both groups had refused promotions and had developed ways to resist the order under which they worked. Moreover, both the right-wing Republican and the democratic-socialist union president, along with everyone in between, voiced support for the principles of workplace democracy. But if both the levels and perceived sources of dissatisfaction and alienation were similar across work sites, then the rather distinct differences in the ideological inferences drawn from them and in styles of resistance beg for explanation. It is to be found, I believe, in the discrete forms of social organization and culture of their respective workplaces, which varied along a number of dimensions that bear upon political beliefs.

State and Market: Beyond the significance of their labor taking a commodity form, the NDC workers experienced the logic of the market as the defining axis in their workplace. The principles according to which their time, energy, and working lives were allocated had to do with the maximization of productivity and profitability. The laissez-faire moral economy *was* their social world, at least at work. The bottom line was the standard of rationality. Aside from the labor of the css workers taking a career form, the logic of state bureaucracy defined their workplace. Although they railed against regulations, the "business" the regulations organized was meeting human needs; the ostensible purpose of rules was uniformity of service provision acccording to professional criteria. Their social world at work was enveloped in a moral economy not really democratic owing to its bureaucratic aspect, yet not merely bureaucratic owing to the democracy implicit in the principle that citizens should have their basic needs met—if not regardless of cost, then at least without undue regard for costs. It struck me that the lived experience, day after day, of such different axes had something to do with their political beliefs and policy preferences. Although most in both groups supported more public spending, for example, on mass transit, the NDC workers tended to think it should, ideally, "pay for itself," whereas the css workers tended to feel that mass transit directly or indirectly meets so many needs that a fiscal self-sufficiency standard made little sense.

Social Relations: Marx once wrote of the "manifold relations" and "mutual intercourse" lacking among peasant farmers who shared the same structural niche in nineteenth-century France. This lack militated against the development of a feeling of community, awareness of common class ties, and political organization that would have made them into a revolutionary class (1974 [1869], 238–39).[9] Elements of such manifold relations were present at css and largely absent at NDC.

Most NDC workers remained atomized and isolated from each other by virtue of their individual routes. Time spent with coworkers at day's end was seen as time *not* spent fully away from their taxing work and with the families for whom they did it; thus it was minimized. Whatever bonds of solidarity they have felt were given scant opportunity for expression in such an organizational structure. Time pressures aside, communication itself tended to be constrained in the NDC work culture. Their version of the rugged individualist code required them to take whatever management dished out without "whining." Other norms steered conversations away from anything "too heavy" like politics and toward the jocular humor that lightened the pressure. Such facets of work organization and culture seemed to work against the formation of identities based upon work and against discourse that was political or ideological (see Lane 1962).

The css workers, conversely, shared common space in their group offices and were connected by the constantly buzzing telephone intercoms. They often shared coffee and lunch breaks. Doing their jobs required much consultation and collaboration on changing policies and on clients whose problems were parceled out among several workers. Communication was thus an inherent dimension of their work (apart from any white-collar tradition of schmoozing at the proverbial water cooler). In contrast to the cultural codes of NDC, collegial support was commonly given at css as the antidote to burnout. Such forms of work organization and culture were more likely to engender manifold relations, group-based identities, and a shop-floor discourse with ideological overtones.

There were also differences between work sites with respect to authority relations and the extent of autonomy granted workers. A substantial body of research shows that the necessity for conformity to managerial expectations and supervisorial rules at work makes for conformity outside of work (see especially Kohn 1969). Similarly, workers granted autonomy and discretion at work are likely to have, for example, higher self-esteem and confidence in their own critical judgments in all spheres. Thus, it seems important that NDC attempted to design their workers' every move and to monitor them rigorously for compliance,

9. Weber made much the same point in theoretical terms: "a class does not in itself constitute a community" (1946 [1925], 184). More recently, Gintis has explored why different groups with different capacities generate different forms of political discourse: "The power of a class and the content of its demands—and hence the changes it can bring about—depend on the forms of bonding it manages to achieve. Bonding, in turn, depends on the forms of *organization* and *communication* a class creates" (1980, 190; see also Shibutani 1955). It is worth noting that the quote from Marx was taken from one of his empirical studies in which he analyzed concrete episodes of political conflict and change that confounded his theories.

whereas css management, despite its overabundance of regulations, was more often required by both the nature of the work and workers' demands to grant them autonomy. Moreover, encroachments on that autonomy and management's authority on many issues were contestable and subject to relatively democratic and often intense negotiation, which was not the case at NDC.

Politicality: Workers at NDC had few opportunities or incentives for political discussion. Union meetings were rare and rarely attended. Their wages and benefits (with which they were largely satisfied) and their working conditions (with which they were largely dissatisfied) were negotiated nationally every third year by a distant bureaucratic union without participation by members. Thus there was no shared sense of union brotherhood. The workers confronted as individuals what most of them considered to be an omnipotent and intransigent management; their problems were dealt with route by route between supervisor and worker, if at all. Although work issues did find their way into locker room banter, public issues, which had little bearing upon day-to-day work, were rarely mentioned. The low politicality of the work culture was one more reason politics had low salience for the NDC subjects, and this, in turn, tended to limit further their appetite for political knowledge and their propensity for political participation. [10]

The css workers, in contrast, were apt to be talking about politics at any time; they were on the front lines of social policy. Their work lives and the lives of their clients were constantly and directly affected by Congress, the state legislature, and local government. In times past public agencies may have been more staid, but current political conflicts were in the air at css. Funding cuts, tightened eligibility rules, and the often ideological policy debates behind them were regularly discussed in the mass media and by those who had to implement and live with the resulting changes. Workers at css, moreover, elected union leaders and a committee of workers who annually negotiated a contract with city officials covering working conditions and client treatment practices as well as salary and benefit matters. The union local was active, responsive, and participatory in the extreme. Apart from whatever left-liberal sensibilities they brought with them to their careers, such features of workplace organization and culture tended to give politics much salience; it was in part for this reason that they were more knowledgeable about and active in political life.

10. Each of the twelve subjects was scored on the standard Political Participation Scale used in the national surveys of the Center for Political Studies at the University of Michigan. Although voting was the same across groups, the public-sector workers were more than twice as likely to engage in other forms of participation. Thus, the average raw scores on all seven items showed a marked difference—the NDC mean was 2.67 and the css mean was 6.17—although this cannot be attributed to variation in workplace politicality alone.

Worker Resistance: There was no collective, organized, or regular opposition to management at NDC. What resistance there was to corporate-level decisions tended to be ad hoc and covert; no theory or explicit ideology grounded it other than the commonsense assumption that "bosses screw workers." The workers did not believe they had the right to help define how the work would get done (despite their intricate knowledge of it) or the right to negotiate work loads. It was taken for granted, albeit begrudgingly, that the company paid them well and thus had the right as well as the power to determine the policy. They presupposed their own powerlessness; the notion that they as workers should discuss much less have a say in decisions was foreign to them, although liberals and conservatives, veterans and neophytes alike thought the company would be better off if they did.

At CSS, opposition to management was more regular, organized, and overt. Policy changes and problems were debated at frequent meetings with supervisors and between union leaders and workers. The belief that they had a right at least to argue in a quasi-democratic forum over management decisions was widely shared and grounded in the ideology that they had a professional obligation to watch out for their clients' interests (as well as their own). Thus, when management tried to streamline service delivery on the grounds of efficiency, workers tended openly to discuss and defend their craft, the quality of their service, and their professional autonomy. They did not actually have a lot of power, but they were not and did not feel powerless.

None of this is meant to imply that what workers experience at work is the only or even the principle source of their worldviews, policy preferences, or political behavior. Even if major significance, however, is granted to whatever preexisting ideological differences may have distinguished the two sets of workers at the start of their adult working lives, it is more than plausible that the sorts of variation in workplace organization and culture described here exacerbated and sustained them.

The Work-Life Relation

At the time of Marx's writing during the transition to full industrial capitalism in Europe in the last half of the nineteenth century, traditional forms of social life were being radically transformed by the new modes of production. A person's status in the community, social relations, and life chances increasingly had to do, Marx argued, with whether one owned means of production or worked for wages. The contradictions between the growing power and wealth of the former and the increasing exploitation and immiseration of the latter would, in his view, tear apart the system of social relations upon which capitalism depended. I cannot here summarize even the outlines of what has happened in capitalist societies since, much less the contentious competing interpretations of such developments, but I can assert that the *responses* to the very tensions Marx identified have altered them. A great variety of class and other conflicts has engendered state regulations on business, Keynesian macroeconomic policies, a cornucopia of welfare and social security programs, and other reforms that now constitute the genus (and, some would say, the genius) of modern *political capitalism*.[11]

As noted in the discussion of the embourgeoisment thesis, a central feature of such modern capitalist societies is the relative rise of living standards among working classes. The necessity for a mass-consumption market to absorb goods made available through the miracles of mass production, combined with Fordist strategies for class harmony that stressed the notion of worker as consumer, led to a historic trade-off. By bringing workers into full participation in the sphere of consumption, traditional conflicts in the sphere of production would be avoided, and the costs in full employment and higher wages could be offset by the stable and expanding market that would result. Rather than class combatants, workers would be consumers with a stake in the social order (see Marcuse 1964; Aronowitz 1973; Mann 1975; Ewen 1976; Bell 1976; Aglietta 1979). Crudely put, this sort of trade-off threw something of a monkey wrench into Marx's model of class consciousness and the transition from capitalism to socialism. Within modern political capitalism, then, the power of the sphere of production to shape consciousness now contends with that of the sphere of reproduction or consumption, and the cultural forms based upon it. Whereas Marx assumed not only that work under capitalist modes of production would become alien and exploitative but that it would make workers' lives in general increasingly difficult to sustain, neo-Marxian theorists generally concede that these very tensions have generated reforms that have put a floor under living standards.

In an effort to reformulate the determinants of political consciousness in light of such changes, Flacks (1976, forthcoming) has argued that it is commitment to one's private everyday life *outside of work* that stands as the pivotal principle around which political beliefs are now formed. The basis of overall political legitimacy, according to his conception, is the capacity of the political economic system to "deliver the goods"—that is, to make everyday life possible for the majority. Thus, contrary to Marx, alienating and exploitative work need

---

11. For a chronological sampling of interpretations of the fundamental shifts in modern industrial capitalism, particularly toward political capitalism and the promulgation of a mass-consumption culture, see Schumpeter (1942), Galbraith (1958), Marcuse (1964), Aronowitz (1973, 1981, 139–200), O'Connor (1973, 1984), Bell (1973, 1976), Crozier et al. (1975), Wolfe (1977), Wright (1979), Thurow (1980), Piven and Cloward (1982), and Calleo (1982).

not lead to resistance and radicalization so long as a relatively stable daily life beyond work remains intact.

This formulation seems empirically powerful, particularly with regard to the beliefs of the NDC subjects. Yet its *differential* relevance for the CSS subjects suggests an axis of variation. If it is not just work experience that informs ideology, but also, as Flacks shows, the experience of daily life in relation to it, then what I will call the *work-life relation* can be conceptualized as a critical dimension of the social organization of experience along which individuals may vary. For analytic purposes, it is useful to sketch two polar types of work-life relation, *compartmentalized* and *integrated*.

The lives of the private-sector workers leaned toward the compartmentalized end of the continuum. There tended to be a marked split between their work and their daily lives. Despite their differences, all six traded alienating and exhausting labor for the high wages that financed their relatively gratifying private lives. The more unpleasant the work, the longer the hours, and the fewer its intrinsic satisfactions, then the larger the pleasures of daily life loomed. This trade accentuates in lived experience the splits between production and consumption and between the economy and civic life that characterize reality *and* ideology in liberal democracies. The NDC workers said they "stuck it out" at their jobs, despite increasing discontents, not out of any fond adherence to the work ethic or allegiance to the company per se, but because of their fondness for and allegiance to the family satisfactions their paychecks underwrote.

Such a compartmentalized work-life relation provides structural support for privatism. By privatism I do not mean simply the urge to avoid or withdraw from public life but also the urge to become engaged in private pursuits where personal efficacy is highest. The phenomenon of privatization is often thought of in pejorative terms—people being "bought off" by the private pleasures of consumption (see, for example, Marcuse 1964). It is critical to recognize, however, that inaction has its causes just as action does and, indeed, that what is taken as inaction may be just another form of action. Privatism can also be, for example, an implicit critique of political institutions in which noninvolvement is an expression of delegitimation.[12] The assumption that privatized people have been

12. On the notion of "caused inaction," see Edelman (1977). See Wright's (1976) insightful analysis of survey data for evidence that what appears to be consent is more aptly described as *assent*. Survey data showing that privatized people tend to see political parties as dominated by "the establishment" may be found in Turkel (1980). In contrast to standard critiques of privatism, Moore's (1978) historical-comparative study of reactions to injustice suggests that the ability to adapt, to resign oneself to or ignore suffering, is a quality of mind essential to survival under harsh conditions and to psychic well-being in general. The Japanese concept of *Gaman*, or "silent suffering," for example, regards individual resignation and endurance as a sign of dignified strength rather than merely of domination, as in less flattering depictions of privatistic adaptations. In citing this I do not wish to

lured by consumption away from political protest they might otherwise under-
take may be a symptom of left-wing ethnocentrism. I have yet to meet a radical
activist who, if pressed, will not admit that political meetings are very often
frustrating (alternately boring and contentious) and that political organizing is as
difficult for committed door knockers as it is invasive for uninvolved door
answerers. On the other hand, private strategies for survival, problem solving,
and community building tend to be perceived as more organic, gratifying, and,
as an empirical matter, often more efficacious (see Botsch 1980). To the extent,
then, that people like the NDC workers want to "leave it all behind" at the end of
the day (and "it" seemed to include public issues as well as work matters), they are
less likely to perceive politics as interesting and salient to their daily lives.

A related point concerns the experience of class in everyday life. I asked
each of the NDC subjects what class, if any, they felt a member of or an
identification with. As might be expected of blue-collar, middle-class folks, their
answers amounted to equivocating shrugs. Ten hours a day they "busted ass,"
sweat, and swore about their supervisors. The rest of the time they lived pretty
much as do white-collar professionals with similar incomes. They were, in
effect, members of two distinguishable social worlds—with conflicting pulls,
contradictory loyalties, and competing perceptual schema. Their experience of
class thus may be said to have been *bifurcated*. This matters in the same measure
that ideological discourse is framed in class-based or ("material") interest-based
terms. (Of course, electoral discourse is more and more cast in homogenized
nonclass terms designed to appeal to if not help create nonclass-identified voters.)
Even if the form and the social organization and culture of their work, as well as
any tendencies toward privatism, had not already lowered the salience of politics
for them, class-based discourse could and did sound foreign or even incoherent
to the ears of those with bifurcated consciousness of class. A compartmentalized
work-life relation need not be associated with either a contradictory class position
or bifurcated consciousness, as it seemed to be among the NDC workers. But the
possibility that their interrelationships bore upon political beliefs and behavior is
worthy of further comparative and quantitative investigation.

Finally, a compartmentalized work-life relation also seemed bound up with
these workers' various strategies for dissociation from politics. Aside from the
impediments to and sanctions against serious political talk that stemmed from
the organization and culture of their workplace, most of the NDC workers made it
a point to steer clear of matters political. I have argued that this was not merely

---

glorify privatism, but to note its neglected features (see Flacks, forthcoming). I share with its critics a
concern over its implications for democratic participation because, among the NDC workers, the
privatism that seemed both to flow from and to facilitate compartmentalization worked against the
salience and knowledge of politics that might have given more coherent expression to their critical
beliefs about the existing social order.

due to alienation-as-affliction but to alienation-as-practice, that their apparent apathy about politics had as much to do with their radical critique of the system as with any self-conscious presumption of legitimacy granted it. Recall that with the partial exception of Buford Schmitt, they viewed the United States as a corporate plutocracy, its political system offering only an impoverished Tweedledum and Tweedledee choice. Political elites either were or would quickly become corrupt and ineffective. It was a system in which they placed little trust and felt little power. Thus, on ideological terrain bounded on one side by long hours and intellectual insecurities and on the other by private familial satisfactions, political life lacked both the lure and the utility to overcome these and other obstacles to salience.

Although the significance of such factors varied for each of the six subjects, they tended to lead toward similar consequences. José Bustamante avoided political discussions so as to "get along" with his friends and coworkers. Sally Jones actively refused even to pay attention to politics, much less actively participate. Joe Demski skirted political involvement to avoid both the taint he would feel from lending credence to a corrupt system and almost certain disappointment. Greg Larson kept public issues at arm's length because he did not "know enough" and because they inevitably seemed to entail an excess of "bad news." I am not suggesting that unique personality factors were not part and parcel of these ideological stances. Rather, I offer the hypothesis that a compartmentalized work-life relation was part and parcel of the similar dissociation strategies of six unique workers. And, as I hope to show later, this and the other shared structural features of their lives that seemed to go with it all helped make formal ideological consistency subjectively irrational and to keep their personal identities imbedded in the laissez-faire moral economy.

By comparison, the work-life relation of the public-sector workers tended to be *integrated*. To be sure, they were glad to leave the CSS offices at the end of the day, but the split between their work and their private lives was noticeably muted compared to that of their private-sector counterparts. Their many complaints notwithstanding, there were satisfactions in their work that had to do with making a contribution to the community. There was something of a fusion, therefore, between their values as citizens and their values as service professionals, rather than the more markedly distinct value realms found among the NDC workers—and probably most other workers as well (see Hochschild 1981). Although there was little doubt the CSS workers enjoyed the private family rounds their salaries financed, they gave no indication that they were "sticking it out" in their careers for that alone. And, although they expressed little allegiance to their agency per se, they often spoke of their allegiance to their clients and to social service work generally.

Thus, instead of facilitating privatism, their work contained various incentives for *immersion* into political life. They too had their private pastimes, but whereas none of the NDC workers engaged in any form of community or political work (aside from Buford's evangelical efforts in Sunday school), all of the CSS workers did or had. Was it George Bernard Shaw or Oscar Wilde who said that the trouble with socialism is that it takes too many weekends? No matter. All the CSS subjects would agree that the trouble with any civic or political work is that meetings usurp the free time needed to recuperate, to prepare for another day of tragic problems in the bureaucratic trenches. Yet each had done just such work.

Their political commitments varied. Kurt Wilson was involved in the rent control alliance, leftist electoral coalitions, and many other organizations on top of his union work. Chente Palacios had been active against the war and for rent control but was in a period of inactivity during my research. Marc Driscoll, more the professional than the protester, made donations like the others, occasionally testified at meetings of the city council, and sat on the board of a community youth organization. Karen Mullavey, like Chente, was in a less active phase; she had burned out on after-work political meetings when she had gone back to graduate school two nights a week. Whether currently active or taking a political respite, all the CSS workers took for granted the continuity between what they did at work and what they did in civic life: meeting more human needs, working for more social justice. With the exception of Driscoll and the ailing Jamison, the others often bumped into each other at various demonstrations and marches which none of the NDC workers attended. The unit of leisure for the NDC workers was the family outing. The leisure activities of the CSS workers were very likely to include community and political fund-raisers *as family outings*. Thus, in their world, politics was a more or less intrinsic feature of culture and leisure—its salience built in and its knowledge gained by osmosis if not always by design.

With respect to their experience of class, the comparison is again instructive, although less stark. For these public-sector workers, too, had something of a bifurcated consciousness. They were by education middle-class, white-collar, and ostensibly service professionals; but in reality their services were severely constrained by political-fiscal means, their profession was infringed upon by a bureaucratic mode of mechanization and deskilling, and they were paid less than many unionized blue-collar, less-educated members of the working class. If the NDC workers were part of the blue-collar middle class, then at least the eligibility workers at CSS may be seen as white-collar proletarians. If the NDC workers traded alienated labor for the high wages that supported small suburban splendors in private life, then perhaps the CSS workers were trading somewhat less alienated labor for a sense of altruism, with self-esteem serving as a substitute for higher salaries. (Thus, some might say they suffered from a different sort of "false consciousness" than the NDC workers.)

They were no more clear than the private-sector workers when asked about their class identities. Yet, even if they might be seen as having one foot in each of two social classes and—also like the private-sector subjects—enjoying parts of their work and not others, the ideological consequences were not the same. They had more liberal and formally consistent ideologies, participated more actively in politics, and engaged in collective overt opposition to management at the workplace. The structure of their lives may also have contained contradictory pushes and conflicting perceptual schema, but this did not seem to confuse them so much as to help their beliefs *congeal* around the ideal of service. Public and community life were accessible and made sense in their situation in the same way that family and private life were accessible and made sense to the NDC workers.

Whereas ideological ambivalence seemed to serve the NDC subjects, the public-sector subjects had several reasons for entertaining ideologies that leaned to the left. They had incentives (their clients, the attacks by the Right on the welfare state). They were situated in social networks where there were ideological traditions and resources available, such as a human needs standard and their visions of a new moral economy rooted in social justice (see Berger 1981, 195–200). Moreover, their workplace was such that there was power available to them and uses to which it fruitfully might be put. Thus, their ideological leanings made sense, given their goals, and in the process helped them make sense of politics as well. The NDC workers' discontents and critique led nowhere but home because their lives were organized in such a way that they had no shared ideological tradition or even a language with which to express them, and no institutional object was perceived as mutable to their ends via their efforts.

The Interplay of Identity and Ideology

A quarter-century ago Lane's (1962) in-depth study of thirteen men gave an account of why working-class consciousness and leftist ideology were so much less pronounced in the United States than in comparable European industrial democracies. The explanation hinged on his concept of "diffuse social identity," the absence of class or even group memberships that would provide a clear social identity and thus a single frame through which to view the political world. Despite his respondents' relatively low work status, they had experienced mobility: They were living better than their parents per the American dream. The economy then was strong and growth had not yet withered, so they experienced class boundaries as permeable, at least for their children. Each had conflicting memberships—churches, neighborhoods, bowling teams, unions, extended ethnic and family ties, friendships—which helped "morselize" the political issues over which others had fought. Such experiences engendered what Lane called a "low-density ideology," not dogmatic, passionate, or even necessarily consistent. Conditions are somewhat different at this writing, but if my NDC friends were any guide his portrait has aged well.[13] I observed and chose to analyze features of their lives that differed from those Lane stressed, but my private-sector subjects, like his, tended to have diffuse social identities and low-density ideologies. Buford Schmitt was the obvious exception, but Lane too found that a couple of his subjects held cabalist beliefs which did not easily fit his general pattern.

The differences, however, are telling. The bulk of Lane's subjects believed they lived in a just world where power was more or less democratically shared. Virtually no one at NDC held this view. In the intervening years they had witnessed too much national soul-searching over Vietnam, the Pentagon Papers, and Watergate, too much unpunished profiteering by the powerful, too many resignations of scandal-stained cabinet and corporate officers; thus they would have felt gullible to believe that America, though still a "great country," was not a corporate plutocracy. Their experiences—as workers in a national corporation, as members of a huge, distant, and, they were all sure, corrupt labor union, as consumers dependent upon the shoddy, overpriced products of "big business," and as citizen-voters who always had to choose among the lesser of evils for leaders who never seemed to change anything—all these experiences had convinced them otherwise. Although I found scant evidence of a legitimation *crisis* among them—for their lives "fit" (Mann 1975) at least adequately within the basic institutions of laissez-faire society—I did find that the *presumption* of legitimacy Lane's workers seemed to grant America in the late 1950s was not granted by my subjects in the early 1980s.[14]

One problem with Lane's snapshot of "the American common man" is just that—it is (as this study is) a snapshot, one taken at a moment in our history when the Great Depression had been overcome and a world war won. Leaders and heroes existed. Market and state seemed in harmony, and Lane's workers believed that government could and generally should cure all social ills. Postwar prosperity was proclaimed by elites and perceived by much of the electorate to be a permanent part of the American political-economic landscape. My snapshot

13. It would be an egregious methodological sin to imply that any rigorous longitudinal inferences can be drawn from a comparison of a dozen New Englanders circa 1960 and another dozen Californians circa 1980. Yet I am tempted to put myself in the occasion of such a sin because there are so many parallels between Professor Lane's questions, methods, and respondents and my own. Perhaps partial penance can be served by claiming merely heuristic purposes and by pointing, as have my predecessors, to the value of hypothesis-generating ruminations for subsequent hypothesis testing on more appropriate data sets.

14. See Lipset and Schneider (1983) for a comprehensive review of survey and opinion poll evidence that supports this point.

conveys a somewhat different image. The " American Century" seems to have lasted only a quarter-century. The economic boom and the optimism and end of ideology it supposedly engendered now seem more fleeting than Lane—indeed, most political observers—had imagined. The welfare state now seems more expensive and has been cast into greater ideological doubt.

At the start of 1984 my six NDC subjects assented to their niche in the social order—they were neither unpatriotic nor uncritical. The ethos of satisfaction that enveloped Lane's workers in many ways had dissipated for them, but it had not been replaced by any clear class consciousness. In lieu of ideology these men and women described only life-building strategies. They stayed centered in part by compartmentalizing conflicting spheres and experiences and getting on with their lives. Like Lane's men, and unlike their public-sector counterparts, they felt little in the way of a singular, strong, social identity around which issue positions might congeal; and because their lives were also compartmentalized, they had few clear group interests that might give political definition to apolitical selves and ideological valence to a web of hazy affinities and estrangements. Their ambivalence, then, was a form of rationality, one tailored to and rooted in the social organization of their lives. It seemed to help neutralize their discontents—both in the negative sense of giving them few political interests and outlets (cf. Hochschild 1981) and in the positive sense of allowing them contentment.

Only Buford had a well-developed formal ideology, but all of them had well-developed personal identities. In fact, I would suggest that Buford's ideology—like his coworkers' lack of one—helped shore up his sense of self. Strong personal identities allowed them to straddle the bifurcations in their world and in their experience of it. This offered them on a social-psychological plane a continuity and coherence made difficult by their social-structural situation. The consistent identities they carved from their laissez-faire habitus served them in ways a consistent ideology could not. If this set them adrift on the political high seas of the 1980s, it also gave them the sense, however illusory, that they were at the helms of their own boats.

For the public-sector six, conversely, personal identity in many ways seemed to depend upon the *development* of ideology. I came to this in trying to move beyond the values they had when they began their careers to an understanding of how six people from rather different backgrounds ended up sharing so many elements of leftist ideology and how their beliefs remained unshattered in light of subsequent experience. Even if the 1930s for Ron Jamison and the 1960s for the rest had provided hospitable circumstances for the choice of public-service careers, how could such choices and the values they imply be sustained in the more hostile political climate of the 1980s? Given their discontents at work, why had none seriously considered the more traditional life strategy of mobility in the market where the training and skills each had might command at least more money? Why did their beliefs appear impervious to attacks on the welfare state by the Right and abandonment of it by liberals? In the face of such shifts, how did they still exhibit less ideological ambivalence than the NDC workers?

The answers varied for each individual, but in each case, the notion of *identity needs* helped me make sense of their ideological trajectories, just as it had for the NDC workers. Psychohistorian Erik Erikson has argued that the very meaning of identity is "both a persistent sameness within oneself . . . and a persistent sharing of some kind of essential character with others." If this is so, as I believe it is, then the more social contexts shift under people, as the political changes of the early 1980s may be said to have done to the CSS workers, then the more important identity-sustaining memberships become. All six chose, each in his or her own way, to commit themselves to the ideal of public service—to helping those in need and addressing social problems. In their subsequent work they built identities around this ideal, which offered them positive status in the community and a favorable self-concept, much as the NDC workers had done with the laissez-faire, individualist codes according to which they had lived and succeeded. Although the rise of Reagan and the New Right may have shaken their status and sense of self, it may also have given them incentives for clinging to or shoring up rather than jettisoning those identities.[15]

Take, for example, their laundry list of complaints about work in their corner of the welfare state. If morale was low, management distrusted and disliked, resources chronically short, programs "set up to fail," and burn out endemic, why had there not been more change in identity and ideology? Beyond the need for "self-sameness," Erikson has stressed that identity also requires a persistent sense of *shared* character (see Shibutani 1955). What the CSS subjects

---

15. Erikson notes that the loss of such "sameness" can throw people off political balance and lead them to go to great lengths to restore it: "When established identities become outworn or unfinished ones threaten to remain incomplete, special crises compel men to wage holy wars . . . against those who seem to question or threaten their unsafe ideological bases" (1956; cited in Lane 1962, 400–401). A related yet more Freudian interpretation, G. William Domhoff points out, would see identity and ideology in defensive terms: That people will, for example, be inconsistent (NDC) or consistent (CSS) as either helps fend off anxiety over, say, powerlessness (personal communication, 1984). Thus, such defenses afford at least the sense of control over some sources of anxiety, and to the extent these strategies appear functional, people will be reluctant to entertain new ideologies or identities. See also Gergen's (1973) analysis of recent research, "Social Psychology as History," and Strauss's interactionist argument for historicizing identity: "A social psychology without a full focus upon history is a blind psychology. A concern with personal styles, strategies, careers—in short, with personal identities—requires a serious parallel concern with shared, or collective identities, viewed through time" (1969, 175).

shared was the constant need to cope with a fundamentally contradictory work experience. On one hand they confronted bureaucratic procedures that constrained their ability to help clients—to do their work, even if they had the resources they needed. It would be disheartening, too, when even their successes made no palpable ripple in the flow of troubled people and when they remained caught in the middle between the polar complaints of clients and taxpayers. On the other hand, what they did stood as the last resort for typically desperate people and the primary forum in which they could live their best beliefs, ply their trades, and make a living.

Out of such shared experience, and within a participatory union and politicized work culture, the CSS workers had forged a shared response: *critique and opposition, defense and commitment.* Their insiders' critique of and opposition to all that they found wrong with the welfare state as a workplace and a social institution was combined with a defense of the noble intent if not the effect of public aid programs, and a commitment to an ideal of service that was as critical to both their sense of craft and their clients' well-being as it was threatened. Rather than understanding such a stance as inconsistent or contradictory, I would argue that it is better seen as a mosaic of ideological work well suited to their material circumstances, much as was the case with the private-sector workers. With it they could defend the dignity and meaning of their efforts *and* acknowledge fully the pitfalls of the welfare state they knew too well existed.

Gestating within their work subculture was a set of values and practices with clear ideological themes. They were bound together as systematic ideology for some (Kurt Wilson), while for most of the others they remained a tacit web of related beliefs. Despite these variations, however, what the CSS workers shared was a stance toward their world in which ideology and identity supported each other. Their human needs standard of social rationality, the legitimacy they granted to a state sphere predicated on the production of use-values, and their general affinity for a new moral economy were all lines of reasoning that marked off an ideological terrain on which their identities could be sustained.

I have tried to show, in addition to the differences between the two groups in form of work, work culture and organization, and work-life relation, that the differential interplay of identity and ideology also had consequences for political beliefs. For the private-sector subjects whose more or less compartmentalized lives were implicated in the laissez-faire moral economy, identity was served by ideological ambivalence and dissociation from politics. Their diffuse social identities facilitated privatism just as the privatism stemming from the split between life and work militated against a focused social identity. Under such conditions, political salience was likely to be problematic and the desire for knowledge of and participation in politics diminished. The laissez-faire moral economy offered them a positive understanding of their struggles and successes and a sense of dignity and worth they found difficult to see in a moral economy rooted in the welfare state. Thus, the individualist codes by which they lived legitimated laissez-faire ideology just as that ideology seemed to them to legitimate their lives. Such forms of interplay between identity and ideology do not mean they had forgotten the injustices of the market system within which and against which they had struggled. It means only that their ambivalence was likely to remain characterized by a net affinity for laissez-faire worldviews. Thus, they could find Reagan and the Right appealing even as they continued to support a surprisingly broad social charter. And, just as the Left will have difficulty getting their unequivocal support for state programs, Reagan and the Right will encounter resistance to any attempt to scrap them.

For the public-sector subjects, whose more or less integrated lives were bound up with a new moral economy, identity was served by a relatively consistent leftist ideology and immersion into political life. Their more focused social identities militated against privatism just as the integration of their work and private spheres tended to focus their identities in social terms. Under these conditions, the salience of politics was likely to be greater and the desire for knowledge of and participation in politics enhanced. Insofar as they could continue to make their agencies meet human needs, their identities would be supported. The new moral economy offered them a positive understanding of their lives and conferred dignity and meaning to their labors, when the market system seemed to be overly hostile to them and their work. Thus, although they were far from uncritical advocates for expanded government, they continued to support the state and to grant little legitimacy to the market until and unless it met more of the needs of the have-nots.

Such a contrast surely is excessively stark, the work of the analyst's typifications rather than the words of his subjects about their lives and beliefs. There were a number of exceptions that also pointed to the necessity for qualification and attention to complexity or variation. Recall that Karen Mullavey was taking time out and that Chente Palacios, once a radical activist, found it as difficult to get energy up for the community organizing he thought necessary as it was rewarding to run in the evenings and renew himself for the next day's work. On the other hand, Buford's penchant for privatism did not keep him from penning passionate letters to the president. And although Joe Demski would rather spend his non-NDC time at a racetrack than at a political event, he attended a demonstration or two when he felt sure the issue was important and enough of his friends would be there to make it enjoyable. What I have described, then, are patterned tensions and tendencies rather than clear-cut certainties.

Such exceptions notwithstanding, I have sketched some of the empirically observable features of the social organization of lived experience that influenced the interplay of identity and ideology and, in so doing, made more understandable the variation in both the consistency and content of political beliefs among my two sets of subjects. Two theoretical inferences—one specific, the other speculative—flow from this. First, people may be said to have *identity interests* as well as material interests, and it is at best difficult to see the influence of one except through the lens of the other. In this study, for example, no amount of attention to class position, or even to variation in work form, work culture, and work-life relation, could have accounted for the variation in beliefs without also attending to how such features of social structure and organization impinged upon the self. Nor could such selves be made sense of apart from the social organization of the lives in which they were imbedded. To the extent that people themselves do not seem to perceive their material interests apart from how these look *given* their identity interests, and vice versa, then we who try to explain one without reference to the other will risk descriptive distortion and explanatory error.

This leads to a broader and doubtlessly more speculative point about the determinants of political consciousness and ideology. At the dawn of the post–World War II era, Richard Centers wrote of a "social cleavage" in the United States that had "grown almost to the proportions and maturity of a full-scale class war." Elites of both parties were alarmed by the widespread solidarity shown, for example, with striking railroad workers in 1946. Centers found in this "unimpeachable testimony of the workingmen's unity" (1949, 4), and his analysis of survey data supported the idea that clear working-class consciousness, if not a shared formal ideology, existed across the land. This consciousness looked rather different, however, a decade later when Lipset and Lane conducted their studies, just as I have found many new twists and turns in my subjects' answers to many of the same questions (see also Sennett and Cobb 1973; Botsch 1980; Hochschild 1981).

Of course, such differences may have had as much to do with the authors' methods, samples, and points of view as with changes in workers' ideologies. But even if that is so, the composition of classes in the United States is forever being reconstituted by the mechanisms of the capitalist market, the rapid growth and changing fortunes of the state and service sectors being two current examples. And since individual members of classes inevitably interpret and respond to changes in their social situations, classes *as they are lived* are not so much bounded categories constraining the beliefs and behavior of the people inhabiting them as they are social processes in which the systems of social relations that constitute classes get negotiated and renegotiated in everyday life. If "class" is examined with this sort of sensibility, it becomes easier, I think, to see why "interests" are not inscribed in work role or market position but rather are the products of how these interact with private life and personal identity.

Two of the lasting insights from Marx that (I hope) have made their way into the store of social scientists' common sense are the notion of historical specificity and the idea that the concrete practices of human beings (self-consciously or otherwise) produce the social world. However misguided or mistaken have been some of the uses to which his ideas have been put, I like to think Marx would be the first now to say that the "dominance" of "material" factors, too, is historically specific and will vary according to, say, what they are taken to *mean* by actors who are busy building lives and thus social life according to the symbolic prescriptions of their different cultures and subcultures.[16] Having said this, I am obliged to add that the significance of the relation between work and private life and of the interplay between identity and ideology is probably not unique to my subjects, although perhaps it is unique to their epoch.

16. On this final speculation I have drawn upon and recommend Geertz (1973, 1983), Smith (1974, 1978), Sahlins (1976), Berger (1981), and Aronowitz (1981, 139–200, 1985).

9

The Disarticulation
of Political Beliefs

ITH scarcely 5 percent of the November 1980 vote in, America's
three major television networks projected in nearly perfect unison
that Ronald Reagan would win the presidency. The political
beliefs of the populace, the anchormen all proclaimed, had
shifted dramatically to the right (cf. Burnham 1981; Ferguson
and Rogers 1981). Reagan and a chorus of conservative commentators immediately proclaimed their "mandate" to radically curtail the social charter that had
evolved over the past half-century. The people described in this book contributed
in different, often paradoxical ways to the voting tallies on which these proclama-
tions were based. This chapter begins with a look at the patterns in their electoral
decision making. It then ties together various strands of analysis and speculation
on how the *means* of articulating and measuring political beliefs affects the
meaning they are taken to have and what this might imply for the future of
American politics.

How did the ideological affinities and estrangements described in earlier
chapters manifest themselves in political behavior? I have discussed my subjects'
basic values, beliefs, and policy preferences, their community activism or lack of
it, and their very different styles of resistance at the workplace. But for better or
worse, the preeminent mode of political participation and expression in the
United States is electoral. How, then, did these twelve workers translate their
values into votes—particularly votes affecting the social charter?[1]

---

1. Dozens of increasingly sophisticated studies of voting behavior have not taken us all that far
toward answering such questions. On the lack of progress and on deficiencies in theory, see Niemi
and Weisberg (1976), and Wright (1976).

Clearly there is no methodologically sound way to determine how representative my dozen respondents are, and they could never stand as a true sample of the 1980 electorate even if randomly selected. Yet, as most large-scale representative surveys suggest, in-depth research on a small number of cases is valuable for exploring *how* beliefs come to be expressed in behavior. Such exploration seems critical because, given the apparent lack of support for a conservative mandate among ten of my twelve subjects, I am left with political behavior that is puzzling indeed. For if, despite their net affinity for the laissez-faire moral economy, the values of the new moral economy were alive among the NDC workers, then how did the registered Democrats Ventura, Larson, and Bustamante come to vote for Reagan in 1980? Similarly, if the CSS workers were all more or less committed to the new moral economy under explicit attack by Reagan, how could leftists Wilson, Mullavey, and Palacios fail to cast an effective vote against him in defense of their vision of the social charter? If the mandate inferred by Reagan from the margin of his victories in some sense was, to borrow from Gilbert and Sullivan, skim milk masquerading as cream, then answers to these questions are essential for understanding the masks involved.

Table 1 shows my subjects' voting behavior across four elections, two statewide and two presidential, from 1978 through 1984. The clearest pattern is the consistently liberal voting of the public-sector respondents. Across issues and candidates in each of the elections their votes constituted a consistent defense of the post–New Deal social charter. The CSS workers all rejected Proposition 13 cutting property taxes and Proposition 9 cutting income taxes (both billed by their backers as a means of striking back against government and the welfare state as well as lowering tax rates). Home owners and renters alike also supported local rent control initiatives in both 1978 and 1980. There were three reluctant votes for President Carter in 1980 as well as two admittedly symbolic or protest votes for the more leftist Citizens' party candidate, Dr. Barry Commoner. Chente Palacios did not vote in 1980, in part because he had moved and found it difficult to reregister and find a new polling place and in part to protest the effort it would take just to choose among "bought and paid for" contenders. In 1984, all voted for Mondale except Kurt Wilson, who was "so disgusted by Mondale's attempt to move to the right of Reagan on Nicaragua and foreign policy issues" that he left the presidential column blank on his ballot. The only ostensible exception to the liberal voting pattern was Marc Driscoll's "no" vote on Proposition 11, the proposed state tax on oil companies. Marc, who found the muddled complexity of much legislation an impediment to democratic politics, rejected this measure because "it wasn't clear." He had supported Carter's similar national windfall profits tax, however, and noted that his vote implied no opposition to the idea of taxing or regulating the oil industry. In short, they each voted, year after year, in favor of a strong welfare regulatory state, a new moral economy.

TABLE 1 Voting by Individuals and Groups on Selected Issues and Candidates—1978, 1980, 1982, 1984

| | 1978 | | 1980 | | | | 1982 | | | 1984 | |
	Proposition 13 "Tax Revolt" Property Tax Cut	Local Rent Control	President	Proposition 9 State Income Tax Cut	Proposition 11 "Tax Big Oil"	Local Rent Control	Governor	Senator	"Bottle Bill" Mandatory Container Recycling	Nuclear Weapons Freeze	President
NDC											
B. Schmitt	Yes	/No/a	Reagan-R	Yes	No	/No/	Deukmejian-R	Wilson-R	No	No	Richards-AIPb
G. Larson	Yes	/No/	Reagan-R	No	Yes	/No/	Deukmejian-R	Wilson-R	Yes	Yes	( )
R. Ventura	Yes	Yes	Reagan-R	No	Yes	Yes	Bradley-D	Wilson-R	No	No	Reagan-R
J. Bustamante	No	/Maybe/	Reagan-R	No	Yes	/Yes/	Bradley-D	( )	Yes	Yes	Mondale-D
S. Jones	( )a	(Yes)	(Anderson-I)	( )	(Yes)	(Yes)	(Bradley-D)	( )	( )	(Yes)	
J. Demski	No	Yes	( )	No	Yes	Yes	Bradley-D	Brown-D	No	Yes	Mondale-D
CSS											
R. Jamison	No	/Yes/	Carter-D	No	Yes	/Yes/	Bradley-D	Brown-D	Yes	Yes	Mondale-D
M. Driscoll	No	Yes	Carter-D	No	No	Yes	Bradley-D	Brown-D	Yes	Yes	Mondale-D
C. Palacios	(No)	(Yes)	(Commoner)b	(No)	(Yes)	(Yes)	(Bradley-D)	(Brown-D)	(Yes)	(Yes)	Mondale-D
M. White	No	Yes	Carter-D	No	Yes	Yes	Bradley-D	Brown-D	Yes	Yes	Mondale-D
K. Mullavey	No	Yes	Commoner	No	Yes	Yes	Bradley-D	Brown-D	Yes	Yes	Mondale-D
K. Wilson	No	Yes	Commoner	No	Yes	Yes	Bradley-D	Brown-D	Yes	Yes	( )

a. Symbols: ( ) = did not vote; preference, if any, indicated.
  / / = could not vote—rent control on city ballots only; preference indicated.

b. Bob Richards, American Independent party (ultraconservative); Dr. Barry Commoner, Citizen party (democratic socialist).

Little of this liberalism or consistency was found in the voting patterns of the private-sector subjects. Buford Schmitt was the only one whose votes were uniformly conservative. He even voted against Reagan in 1984 for not being conservative enough:

> He didn't do what he promised to do. His shooting down of the Libyan planes was just a macho show which he hasn't followed up on. He's put us further in debt than any other president in history. . . . He should've gotten the Academy Award for his grandstanding at the Republican convention. He was appealing to Americanism and patriotism and that shouldn't have been the issues. It should've been his record, which wasn't very good. In fact, he didn't do what he said he was gonna do—lower taxes and balance the budget, and so forth.

Buford's dissatisfaction did not, of course, tempt him to turn Democratic. When I asked him in January 1986 whom he had voted for, Buford paused and said, "Oh, his name escapes me at the moment. Used to be on the Wheaties box. Richards . . . that's it, Bob Richards, the candidate of the American Independent party." He characterized his vote as a "protest": "I knew he didn't have a chance, . . . but I wanted to show Reagan that there were people who were conservative and who weren't going to be fooled by him."

At the other end of the ideological spectrum, Joe Demski's votes were nearly as uniformly liberal. But the four NDC workers in between present voting histories that are more difficult to grasp. Sally Jones expressed some liberal preferences, but continued to abstain in protest. The other three joined Buford in voting for Reagan in 1980, although only one of them leaned toward conservatism on other issues and candidates. Greg Larson, for example, voted for Reagan and the Republican candidates for governor and senator and, like these candidates, favored Proposition 13 and opposed both rent control measures. Yet unlike these candidates, he voted against Proposition 9 and for the tax on oil companies, the bottle recycling bill, and the nuclear freeze. In a follow-up interview in 1983, Greg said he had "soured" on Reagan because he had "screwed" working people while "rattling sabers." To whom was he looking in 1984? "Nobody. I don't even know who's running yet. I just know I wouldn't vote for Reagan again."[2] In a subsequent follow-up interview after that election, his view had softened. He told

---

2. Greg's turnaround on Reagan during his first term and the subsequent softening of his criticisms were mirrored in poll findings. After a year in office, a Yankelovich/Time magazine poll found a majority doubting Reagan's trustworthiness, opposing his military spending, and hoping he would not seek a second term (San Francisco Examiner & Chronicle, March 21, 1982). After eighteen months in office, a Los Angeles Times poll (August 8, 1982) found that a third of Reagan voters "would not support him again." This tendency was strongest among blue-collar workers, union members, and middle-income groups whose switch to Reagan in 1980 was critical to his winning. At the midpoint of his first term, a Gallup poll showed that six times as many voters favored

me that Reagan was "not doin' all the things I'd like," but that he was, "well, all right." Greg, however, was not inspired enough one way or the other to vote: "I just didn't make it, kept puttin' it off. I almost got down to the feeling that you don't really have any choice—like it was all cut and dried before you even voted."

José Bustamante voted against Proposition 13 and Propostion 9 because he felt they would "hurt the schools," even though he felt he paid unfairly high taxes compared with the wealthy and even though his own children were in Catholic schools. He voted in favor of the tax on oil companies, the bottle bill, the nuclear freeze, and the Democratic candidates for governor and senator, who felt the same way. He also favored rent control, although it was not on the ballot in his district. Why then, in 1980, did this lifelong Democrat vote for Reagan? In July 1981 he told me he thought Carter had not shown "enough initiative on his own" and that he was "always backing down":

> I got really disillusioned with Mr. Carter. . . . My philosophy is . . . if someone gets in there you gotta give 'em a chance. No matter who it is, you know, you gotta see what they're gonna do. And [Carter] just went on and I just got disillusioned with him. . . .

> Q: So at some point you decided to vote for Reagan?

> Yeah. The way I felt about it is that, let's give somebody else a chance. It couldn't get any worse, or it couldn't get screwed up any more than it already is. . . . What's to say this guy [Reagan] might [not] turn out halfway decent or whatever?

By April 1983 José was again disillusioned. He found Reagan "not looking out for his own people" (Americans in need) and "spending too much on the military and not enough on other things." Too many people were "still out of work" despite the Reagan recovery. José felt that "if things don't change, I don't think he oughta run again. I know I won't vote for him." Indeed, in 1984, he returned to the Democratic camp he had been in his whole life and voted for Mondale.[3]

---

cuts in military spending to balance the budget than cuts in social programs (*Los Angeles Times*, February 14, 1982). Obviously, none of this apparent dissatisfaction proved consequential by the end of Reagan's term. He captured most of the senior vote (despite his attempts to cut Social Security), half the blue-collar and union vote (despite union busting, plant closures, lower wages, and high unemployment), and a majority of women (despite his cuts in social services affecting women, his jocular, cowboyish style, and his militarism, and despite Democratic attempts to win the alleged gender gap with a female vice-presidential nominee). See, for example, Robert Bendiner, "Reagan an '84 Dewey?" (*New York Times*, March 20, 1984); G. Gallup, "Reagan Agenda Gets Mixed Review," (*Los Angeles Times*, November 18, 1984).

    3. I am duty bound to readers—and particularly to José Bustamante, whom I value as a person as well as a most helpful respondent—to report that as of a follow-up interview on January 14, 1986,

Rudi Ventura offered a good many antigovernment anecdotes in each interview and invoked them as the reason for his vote for Proposition 13. He also supported Reagan in 1980, and Republican candidates for governor and senator. Yet he opposed the Proposition 9 tax cut as too damaging to the necessary services government must perform, voted for rent control in 1978 and 1980, and for the tax on oil companies. In 1984, Rudi again voted for Reagan, although this time he was alone among his five coworkers. He did so, he told me, because Reagan is "no worse than anyone else" and because Mondale had been "trying to win by putting a woman in there." After twice voting for America's most conservative modern president, was he a confirmed Republican? Unlike the more conservative Schmitt, Rudi believed that Reagan deserved his support because he "doesn't back down," "means what he says," and therefore, "scares Russia." But beyond this he seemed to have little sense of loyalty to a conservative cause or party. He still voted "for the man," still saw all politicians as "bought and paid for," and still thought we need the state to take care of people "who hustle and still can't make it." Rudi was a foreign policy hawk and at most a lukewarm liberal on the welfare state, but he did not see himself as an unequivocal part of any broad mandate.

If the 1980 election was in fact a watershed election signaling a radical shift back to laissez-faire precepts, there is little clear evidence of it among these three Democratic switchers. It may be fair to put Ventura mostly in Reagan's camp, but neither Larson nor Bustamante supported much of what Reagan stood for in 1980, and neither voted for him again.

Reagan's margin of victory in 1984 clearly suggests that others, if not these men, came to support Reagan or continued to do so. Whether this was due to his personal appeal or his policies is still hotly debated. In 1981 it was possible for political scientist Walter Dean Burnham to argue that for the mass of voters, the 1980 election "had become a question of throwing Jimmy Carter and the Democrats out with whatever alternative was available. In a room with only two exits, people will surge toward one, wherever it leads, if the other is blocked in some way" (1981, 109). For a time it was possible to say that economic distress, a failed incumbent, and an unknown "lesser evil" with clear convictions and promises of profits aplenty could account for Reagan's first victory. Exit polls and postelection surveys found about two in five Reagan voters citing simply "the

José had no recollection of having voted for Reagan in 1980. When I probed him about my recollection of his statements to the contrary in our earlier interviews, he explained that "I thought [Reagan] might be a nice change, but I've never voted Republican. I liked some of the things he was saying, but when it came right down to it, I couldn't do it." In fairness to him I must note the possibility that he misconstrued my 1981 questioning and was thus offering a hypothetical set of answers rather than an account of his actual voting behavior. After checking both transcript and tape, however, and after much anguish and advice, I decided to quote José exactly as I had recorded him.

need for change" as the basis of their votes, whereas only about one in five cited his conservatism. Reagan's short coattails and the Democratic gains in Congress in 1982 also lent credence to the argument that 1980 did not constitute a true realignment of the electorate under the Republican banner.

Yet, the resounding win in 1984 demands further accounting. It is well beyond the scope of this work to address, much less settle questions about the real meaning of Reagan's 1984 landslide, but it is important to note two factors that clearly played a part. First, as early as 1983 and even after the election, poll after poll showed that it was possible for a majority of voters to oppose many if not most of Reagan's policies, or even to believe that his foreign policies were dangerous and his domestic policies unjust, and still like him personally as a leader. Thus we saw the remarkable if common phenomenon of voters voting for a candidate with whom they fundamentally disagreed for perceived lack of an attractive alternative. Most analysts, I think, would agree that both Reagan's victories show that a candidate's convictions need not be fully endorsed for him to be popular; they need only be strongly felt and clearly articulated. Whereas both Carter and Mondale tried to move to the ideological center, to distance themselves from the once heartfelt liberalism they had come to see as a campaign stigma, Reagan took the ideological gamble of staking out a more radical right-wing stance. Whatever its substantive appeal, its relative clarity seemed alluring by comparison (as Greg Larson put it, "At least he's sayin' *somethin'* ").[4] More on this below.

Second, it seems critical not to overlook the other, related ingredients in Reagan's winning electoral stew—abstention and defection—which tell us something about our political life at this moment in history. Chente Palacios was a leftist who had long been disappointed with the choice of candidates and disheartened by the results of U.S. elections. Even if he had overcome such feelings and found his new polling place in 1980, he either would have joined Wilson and Mullavey in voting for the Citizens' party candidate or voted for the Socialist party candidate as a protest over the absence of genuine alternatives. Here he was in agreement with his more moderately liberal CSS coworker, Marc Driscoll, who voted Democratic yet derided the two-party system as offering "a distinction without a difference."

Both Sally Jones and Joe Demski also abstained—Sally entirely and Joe in 1980 when he could not bring himself to vote *for* Carter. As much as he detested Reagan, Joe felt it would be "immoral" to imply approval of Carter's creeping Republicanism with a positive vote. Thus, Sally's frequently leftist beliefs as well

---

4. See, for example, Robert G. Kaiser, "The Democrats Are Missing One Small Thing: Convictions," *Washington Post Weekly*, November 28, 1983, and Ross K. Baker, "Party Realignment (Continued)," *New York Times*, October 14, 1984.

as the consistently leftist beliefs of Joe and Chente did not yield a single effective vote against Reagan in 1980. Similarly, Kurt Wilson could not bring himself to vote for Mondale in 1984, despite his antipathy to everything Reagan stood for and everything his policies would mean. His voice too was lost. For what seemed to these voters good solid reasons, abstention became the best moral choice. [5] When seen as drops in the larger political stream, however, the significance they intended was swallowed up by the significance that would be inferred from their nonvotes, namely tacit support for, or at least the absence of opposition to, a candidate and policies they passionately opposed.

A related point may be made with regard to defectors. In 1984, Buford broke ranks with the Republican party to register a protest vote. Although his choice was both sincere and strategic, there is no reason to believe it will be noticed much less pull Reagan further to the right. In 1980, both Karen Mullavey and Kurt Wilson defected from the Democratic party. Neither felt "right" about voting for Carter, a man who barely had won their tepid support in 1976 and who in their view had consistently failed to defend Democratic principles and back-pedaled toward the political center for most of his term. Despite their knowledge of the damage Reagan would likely do to the welfare state—evident to them from his two terms as governor and his campaign rhetoric—they could not in good conscience cast a positive vote for Carter even to effect a negative vote against someone, as Karen put it, "far worse." They were caught in the two-party catch-22: they saw no real competition, so they in effect contributed to Reagan's win by failing to vote for his only real competition.

The forms of reasoning behind abstention and defection evident here suggest a proposition about the *expression* of political beliefs that is discouraging for democratic processes. At best, the act of voting does not necessarily constitute an articulate rendering of even limited preferences, much less basic beliefs; at worst, the two-party system as it currently operates can seriously distort voters' intentions. The delegitimation implicit in the actions of the abstainers (and, arguably, of a substantial proportion of America's largest party, what Burnham calls "the party of nonvoters") is lost to view for all intents and purposes.

5. According to the Elections Research Center of the U.S. Census Bureau, voter turnout has been declining steadily since 1960, when it was 62.8 percent, through 1980 when it was 52.6 percent, and even the 1960 figure was well below that of comparable industrial democracies. See, for example, G. Gallup, Jr., "There'll Be More Voters" (*San Francisco Chronicle*, October 15, 1984). These figures do not include those eligible but unregistered to vote (*New York Times*, November 10, 1982). Poor turnout was often interpreted in the past as a sign of consensus and basic satisfaction, but that view is now changing (cf. Nie et al. 1976; Wright 1976; Burnham 1980, 1981). The accounts of my abstaining subjects, as well as declining turnout and poll data showing steep drops in party identification, suggest that this reinterpretation is warranted.

Similarly, the delegitimation expressed by Buford, who defected from the Republican party for more conservative pastures, and by Karen and Kurt, who left the Democratic fold for a democratic socialist third party, is also lost. Although these two types of dissatisfaction with electoral choices had drastically different ideological implications, they are much alike in their lack of political implications for the larger political arena. To be true to their beliefs, these voters had to make themselves inarticulate if not mute.

To be sure, these examples of electoral reasoning may be some distance from those of the mainstream electorate. My subjects in both groups were in certain ways atypical. It is doubtful, for example, that one or two of every six welfare workers could be called socialists of any stripe and equally unlikely that one or two of every six truck drivers would be born-again evangelicals or place themselves to the right of Reagan. Each group also voted somewhat against the grain in 1984—the CSS workers showing more support for Mondale in 1984 than they had for Carter in 1980 and the NDC workers being less apt to vote for Reagan again than they had been four years earlier.

If we hold aside the abstainers and defectors, however, and listen only to those in both groups who voted for one of the two mainstream candidates, no clearer expression of legitimacy is heard. For at least two of the four NDC workers who voted for Reagan in 1980, there was little if any *intention* of endorsing the bulk of his policies. Larson and Bustamante never understood their vote for Reagan as signaling a shift in party loyalty, and neither Larson nor Ventura felt much loyalty to the Democrats from which they might shift. The same point can be made about the Democratic voters at CSS. Ron Jamison may have been a committed old-line Democrat, but the others made it clear that theirs were reluctant anti-Reagan votes rather than positive votes of support for Carter or Mondale and their policies.

The idea that political participation through voting is in itself a measure of legitimacy may be quite misleading to judge from the degree of disarticulation evident among these dozen citizens. Although their voting patterns were different, members of both groups shared a conviction that their political ideas lost something in the voting booth (it was almost as if the lever that marked the ballots served as an ideological scalpel, severing voting behavior from the beliefs that animated it). All one need do to test this empirically is to talk with voters at length about what they believe and how they bring their basic values to bear upon their ballots. If other investigators also find this to be so, then the celebration of democracy in America that began before Tocqueville and is repeated each time network anchormen close their coverage of another election will come to sound increasingly anachronistic.

The Embeddedness of Beliefs

Critical readers may now be wondering how much of this disarticulation is really new and noteworthy and how much is merely the lament of a Democrat disappointed with elections in the early 1980s. In this section I will try to show that there are very good theoretical reasons for believing that beliefs *by their nature* do not easily lend themselves to consistent and categorizable expression and measurement. I will also argue, however, that there are observable features of this epoch—the political technology with which beliefs are made publicly available and the historically specific experiences and modes of discourse from which they are forged—that make this particularly so.

The nuggets of electoral reasoning described above seemed quite rational from a subjective point of view, and yet they led to sometimes unexpected and often ironic voting behavior. José the liberal Democrat, for example, voted for Reagan in 1980 not because he was drawn to the right but because he felt pushed from the left—a core theme in his comments being his disappointment over Carter's failure to help the poor. More important, without understanding José's understanding of the way corporate power influences candidates and why, in part for that reason, he felt the need to dissociate himself from politics, it would be difficult to make sense of his decision to simply "give somebody else a chance." The meaning of this vote and many others discussed in this study are indecipherable apart from the values, reasoning, and situation of which they are part; and these in turn are indecipherable apart from the life history or biographical context in which they are inevitably embedded.[6]

Attempts to infer ideological meaning from isolated opinions or lone policy preferences are fraught with similar difficulties, as was clear in each of the twelve biographical sketches. To look, for example, at Ron Jamison's response to a poll question on growth control regulations, one might not guess he was a lifelong liberal Democrat and thirty-year member of the Sierra Club and that he opposed such regulations only because he felt they inhibited the production of housing for the poor. Ron reasoned from what he felt were liberal values and arrived at what is usually taken as a conservative poll response. Ideological principles, then, do not necessarily imply anything in practice about specific issue positions. Whatever partisan political valence an opinion may have for its holder is neither apparent from nor intrinsic to its expression.

6. A useful discussion of the problem of the embeddedness of economic action is offered by Mark Granovetter, who writes, for example, that "what looks to the analyst like nonrational behavior may be quite sensible when situational constraints, especially those of embeddedness, are fully appreciated" (1985, 506). His insights apply equally well to political action.

This point came crashing home to me when I was tabulating my subjects' responses to poll questions on public security spending. Preferences on police and prison issues have been found to fall neatly along the traditional liberal-conservative continuum (see, for example, Citrin 1978). Yet Kurt Wilson, a committed democratic socialist, local union president, and the most consistent leftist among the public-sector six, opted for *more* spending on police and prisons. When I asked why, he explained that the "capitalist crisis" was increasing social hardship and, therefore, violence and crime, that working people were "most often the victims," and that despite his opposition to the existing distribution of property and privilege ultimately defended by the police and to many of their methods, he felt obliged *as a radical* to support increased spending for police. He applied a similar logic to the prison question. He worked with "crazies" everyday and was acutely aware of both the need for institutions and the damage they can do. Thus he favored more spending for prisons in the hope that they might be made "less brutal and dehumanizing." Interestingly, two of his liberal coworkers preferred less spending on prisons precisely because they saw such institutions as "brutal" and "dehumanizing."

At the opposite ideological pole was Buford Schmitt who repeatedly stressed the need for "law and order" and saw "protection" as one of the very few legitimate functions of the state. Yet he favored *less* spending on police because "liberal judges just let all the criminals go anyway" and less spending on prisons on the grounds that they were too much like "country clubs" that "we wouldn't need if we used the death penalty more often, as we should."[7] Here Buford reasoned from what he very much believed were right-wing premises; and if his issue positions were being tallied into an ideological scale he would have liked very much to be scored on the conservative end. Kurt, on the other hand, would be equally misunderstood in the opposite direction.

The fact that I was doing a content analysis of a mere twelve transcripts rather than a regression analysis of twelve hundred questionnaires gave me no greater ability to predict these opinions on the basis of their holders' party identifications, self-professed ideologies, or other beliefs. These last examples were taken from the person in each group with the most consistent ideology, the two respondents whose beliefs seemed to have been subject to the most constraint or to be most likely to cohere with one another. The fact that the others, more apt

7. To hear Schmitt lament lenient jurists and the lack of punishment, one would not imagine that the United States had been on the biggest binge of incarceration in its history—more than doubling the prison population since 1970. For a solid analysis of criminal justice policy shifts and the ideological debates that shaped them, see Currie (1985).

to entertain conflicting or multiple belief systems, were at least as likely to offer such misinterpretable responses, suggests the strong possibility that the ideological valence and political implications of a given belief can be quite autonomous from its expressed form, whether a poll or survey response or a vote.

These illustrations and others I have given throughout the case studies show that the fluid features of beliefs that make them difficult to grasp analytically are integral to the subjective significance and intended political meaning attached to them by their holders. In fairness it must be said that my colleagues who design polls and surveys make no pretense of taking such things into account or of measuring the full complexity of opinions and policy preferences. Indeed, it may be argued that at the aggregate level there is little *need* to know all the intricacies of context and reasoning that help account for *why* any one citizen believes this or that and what this may signify about U.S. politics, because citizens are asked only for a thumbs up or a thumbs down on a limited array of limited issues and candidates. Thus, the need is only to know how many up and how many down. Yet, if the data offered here are any indication, it is also fair to suspect that such aggregate frequencies can mean more, less, and other than what they are often taken to mean.[8]

One important reason for this is that political beliefs are embedded phenomena; they are context-dependent in various ways. To the extent this is so, then the traditions of symbolic interactionism and ethnomethodology have much to offer in the way of a theoretical sensibility about them. Drawing on both these schools of thought, Wilson (1970) outlines an "interpretive paradigm" in which definitions of the situation, roles, norms, meanings, and actors' senses of social structure are all seen as negotiated in the course of the ongoing interpretive procedures of everyday interaction. Within this paradigm verbal behavior indicates or indexes the particular context in which it occurs. In this sense political beliefs are, in Garfinkel's (1967) phrase, "indexical"—they take their meaning from the concrete elements of the interactional context in which they are evoked and uttered. They are "occasioned" rather than stable phenomena (Zimmerman and Pollner 1970) and so may well not constitute an ideology per se even if they appear rigorously consistent. Rather than being a predictable feature of everyday consciousness, beliefs are more likely to remain amorphous and inchoate until elicited.[9]

8. I cannot here do justice to the methodological debates that have raged for years over what surveys measure, how well, and with what effects on the responses they call forth. Survey scholars have grappled in great detail and with some success over such problems. See, for example, the useful text by Schuman, Presser, and Rossi (1981) on experimental evidence regarding the effects of question form and context.

9. Cressey and Elgesem (1968) offer related insights on how working police officers are often

From the interpretive point of view, ideological consistency—usually defined in terms of formal, abstract ideologies, party platforms, and political theories—may not be empirically warranted in everyday life. Converse's (1964) classic study, based upon a cognitive perspective, found that few members of the electorate hold political beliefs that are consistent, at least in this formal or abstract sense, with one another. At least ten of my subjects supported this finding. I did not find, however, that their inconsistencies had anything to do with the lack of cognitive sophistication many analysts believe is necessary to organize rationally political information into consistent belief systems. In examining beliefs in detail and closer to how they operate in daily life, I found various forms of rationality behind most inconsistency. In a general theoretical way Egon Bittner makes a strong case that inconsistency *is* rational, even cognitively sophisticated. He shows that in contrast to "the outlook of common sense," any archetypal ideology seeks "a unified and internally consistent interpretation of meaning in the world," which simply will not serve its holder well under ordinary circumstances:

> One of the most widely accepted ideas about culture and normatively governed conduct in complex social setups concerns the existence of a heterogeneity of enforceable cognitive and evaluative standards. The objects and events that an ordinary person encounters, recognizes, judges and acts upon in the course of his everyday life do not have unequivocally stable meanings. This is not to say that recognition, judgment and action are not normatively governed, but that the ordinarily competent person is *required* to use practical wisdom to interpret the relevance of a rule to a particular instance of the typified situation to which it presumably pertains. . . .
>
> The ordinarily competent person . . . must know that what under some circumstances could be a lie may in the next context be a required expression of tact; and he must be able to live with such ambiguities in relative comfort. (1963, 930)

Through Bittner's theoretical frame, the ambiguity, ambivalence, and contradiction so visible in my subjects' accounts look rational rather than anomalous. The exigencies of the everyday world virtually demand multiple value systems, although with respect to political beliefs it seems likely that some

---

conflicted over whether to enforce the "law enforcement ideology" or the "adjustment ideology" in a given trouble situation. More generally, the contextual sensibility I have tried to develop here about political beliefs has been theorized by Knorr-Cetina and Cicourel (1981), who argue for a cognitive understanding of social order, and against both collectivism and individualism in method. They propose instead the promising notion of "methodological situationalism" so as to be able to integrate micro- and macrolevel analyses.

historical contexts (for example, the days of "dealignment" in the early 1980s) as well as some situational contexts (such as the locker room at NDC) make more forceful demands than others (say, the depression or a union meeting at CSS). In this light, it is less puzzling to find that Marc Driscoll's views ranged from those of a moderate Republican to those of a populist Democrat and that Greg Larson's ideological proclivities ran the gamut from social Darwinism to social democracy. In contrast to Converse and cognitive dissonance theory, my subjects' accounts of their lives and beliefs suggest the proposition that contradictory experiences impose logical and psychological constraints of their own, under which seemingly conflicting values make sense. Bittner drew upon totalistic ideologies to make his point, but Becker and his colleagues reached much the same conclusion in their study of culture and socialization in medical school:

> People find it possible to maintain two sets of values between which there are possible contradictions and incompatibilities, at the same time. Immediate situational pressures constrain behavior in the present and play an important part in shaping the values participants make use of. But this influence need not have any effect beyond the situation in which it operates. Values operate and influence behavior in situations in which they seem to the actors to be relevant. When that relevance is not clear, the values are not used and others, more appropriate to the problems to be faced, are brought into play. But this does not mean that the original values are gone forever. Instead, those values may simply lie dormant, ready to be made use of as soon as an appropriate situation presents itself. (1977, 430–31; see also Edelman 1977)

After reading a draft of this book, my colleague Rob Rosenthal wrote to ask, "So what *are* you saying about ideological consistency and how people's beliefs relate to the liberal-conservative continuum?" We had spent hours together in fascination over Converse's belief system surveys, so I had to confess to him that I was trying to say several things that do not add up to a simple answer. My data suggest that the continuum may be useful as one analytic typology, but that it is a precarious act to place a belief on a single point along it. Some of my twelve were more consistent and thus easier to place in liberal or conservative camps than the others, but even the most consistent ideologues of the Left and the Right hold anomalous beliefs. Some were more consistent than they looked in strict liberal-conservative terms, others less. Some said they were conservative and appeared so on many issues, but held many radical-left beliefs as well. On most issues most of my subjects' beliefs were neither consistent nor easy to place along the continuum. Indeed, their beliefs seemed to sit simultaneously on points along several different continua. If these twelve are any indication, the liberalism-conservatism index is but one dimension of belief systems among many and therefore misses as much as it measures.[10]

I rummaged through two theoretical closets looking for tools that would help organize the vagaries of valence I had uncovered. In the first, I found Marx's work and a concept of ideology defined as a system of ideas and beliefs that distort or misrepresent contradictions in the social world in ways that serve the dominant class (Larrain 1983). The ideal-typical belief systems that are said to characterize epochs may fit this definition. I found, however, that the belief systems of situated actors often serve, for example, contradiction containment functions (for example, Wexler 1983; Geertz 1973), which allow them to compartmentalize or otherwise manage what they may well recognize as unjust or injurious to their interests but which they feel, often accurately, they are powerless to change. Insofar as beliefs are resources developed or left dormant, honed by or harbored from experience, and invoked or withheld by stance-taking actors who have purposes in their immediate circumstances, then however mystifying of social structure they may be by "objective" or historical standards, beliefs as *practices* are not reducible to ideology in the traditional Marxian sense (cf. Larrain 1983; Wexler 1983; Geertz 1973, 193–233).

In the second, I found the interpretive perspective of interactionists, ethnomethodologists, and cultural anthropologists summarized above. This helped force my attention to the social processes by which ideological consistency is *situationally achieved*. This was as true in my formal interview situations as it seemed to be at the workplaces where my observations were informal. Each time I probed for an explanation of what appeared to be a contradictory opinion, my respondents provided one; and in each instance their reasoning produced not only the appearance of consistency among beliefs and continuity of values but a critical explication of their meaning. When situations call for it, people strategize and struggle to achieve the sense and the appearance of consistency. Whether prompted by a problem at work or a probe from me in their living rooms, inconsistencies to which attention was called provided occasions for what Berger has called ideological work:

---

10. In a very complex analysis of qualitative interviews, Neuman (1981) identifies two discrete dimensions of political thinking—differentiation and integration—and makes a clear case that ideological consistency can stem, for example, from mere repetition of slogans rather than from deduction from abstract political principles. Thus, consistency may not reflect cognitive complexity, just as cognitive complexity may allow differentiation that leads to *inconsistency*. He argues that to grasp the nature of belief systems a more sensitive method than forced-choice surveys are necessary. See Phillips (1982) on how modern populism and cultural conservatism demand a reformulation of the liberal-conservative typology.

Local social contexts can usually be relied upon to generate (by interactions with their larger environments) unanticipated conditions or situations that further exacerbate the practical ambiguity of ideas, make them difficult to "live up to," and hence make the ways in which they will be interpreted difficult to predict or anticipate. . . .

Ideas are human creations, and they are created *for purposes, in contexts, and are definable in time and place,* by living people who invested themselves in *these* (rather than *those*) ideas for discoverable reasons. . . .

If they have to, [people will] accommodate their ideas to recalcitrant circumstances, while at the same time they attempt to maintain some semblance of consistency, coherence, and continuity in what they believe they believe they believe. That is what ideological work is all about. (1981, 16–22)

Although Berger's is a study of the "microsociology of knowledge," he is always sensitive to how, for example, "local social contexts" interact with their "larger environments" and to how humanly created ideas are "definable in time and place" and take their form from "recalcitrant" and other "circumstances." For me this leads back toward a Marxian perspective from which situations are themselves seen as situated in historical and social-structural context. This suggests the possibilities for an *interpretive Marxism* capable of doing justice to both the historically contingent and the situationally contingent aspects of beliefs and behaviors. From this perspective, structurally situated actors bring mutually informing material and identity interests to bear upon their purposes in more or less emergent interactional contexts. It seems to me that there is nothing intrinsic to the ethnomethodologists' notion of indexicality that prevents it from incorporating such broader facets of context. Similarly, there is nothing intrinsic to historically grounded, neo-Marxian studies of cultural practice that prevent analysis of microcontexts. If both theoretical stances hold that human actors produce the world through their material and symbolic practices, then a structurally informed indexicality could take into account features of an actor's habitus (such as work-life relation) that influence both the sorts of situations in which the person is likely to become enmeshed and the frames through which these will be perceived.

I have tried to show that there is much disarticulation of political beliefs and that this stems in part from their embedded, emergent, and therefore indeterminate character. In the foregoing theoretical digression, however, I derived a perspective that calls for attention to the ways in which such characteristics are historically informed and specific. I now want to describe some features of our current political culture that make what Berger calls "the practical ambiguity of ideas" particularly acute and that both lead to and exaggerate the disarticulation of political beliefs.

The Social Construction of "Public Opinion"

For more than a century there has been a debate over production technology. Marx, Lenin, and many others who opposed capitalism's tendency toward exploitation, alienation, and degradation of both labor and nature were great admirers of its revolutionary technology. Technology's ill effects, according to this school, stemmed from its ties to the capitalist system of social relations in which the surplus generated by labor was privately appropriated and used to further exploit and even replace workers. Once these social relations were replaced by socialism, they imagined, this great productive technology could be put to progressive use, reducing human toil and poverty. The technology itself was seen as politically and socially *neutral*. Against this view, others argued that technology was fundamentally predicated upon reducing the importance of human skill and effort (for example, Braverman 1974). Thus, the machines *themselves* as developed under capitalism embodied a system of social relations that degraded human labor and alienated people from the very processes that produced what they needed to live. Technology, then, could not simply be put to nonexploitative use, for technology was *not neutral* (see Aronowitz 1978, 1981).

I hope the same sort of debate is now emerging over how the stuff of political life—policy ideas and candidates, parties and platforms—get produced, and I want to argue that the "not neutral" position with respect to production technology is an apt metaphor for modern politics. Two-party elections, computerized direct-mail fund-raising, mass media, and the marketing and advertising and campaign image consultants spawned by them, as well as voter surveys and opinion polls, together constitute the hardware and software of modern *political technology*. It is decidedly not neutral insofar as it embodies a system of sociopolitical relations in which the values, beliefs, preferences, efforts, and intellectual capacities of the citizenry tend to be expropriated and degraded by it.

To be sure, nostalgia for the egalitarian participatory democracy of nineteenth-century town meetings tends to paint a romantic patina over our political past. George Washington most assuredly did not sleep everywhere, and the political elite of preelectronic eras no doubt could manipulate public opinion with the best of today's master image makers. Moreover, participatory democracy of lore has obvious limitations in the age of national states and international corporations and markets. Such objections cannot, however, erase evidence suggesting that modern political technology has contributed to the erosion of mass political trust, efficacy, and participation in and identification with our political institutions.

At the dawn of the media age, David Riesman noted clinical symptoms of "technological unemployment in politics" (1952). If we had begun to see the end of ideology, he seemed to say, then it had its dark side. The paradigm-setting studies of the American voter in the 1950s began large-scale research on electoral decisions with methods developed to measure consumer choice among competing brands of product. While advancing the scale and scope of knowledge, the drive toward measurement precision in these studies also tended to narrow the operational definition of the political, so that the meaning of democracy came more and more to be seen as the choice between two competing elites (cf. Berelson, Lazarsfeld, and McPhee 1954; Campbell et al. 1964; Gitlin 1978). The portrait of a passive electorate sketched in these studies bears scant resemblance to the informed active citizenry of democratic theory found, for example, in Thomas Paine's writings and *The Federalist* papers. People voted out of habit rather than rational reflection. Low enthusiasm was often taken for high satisfaction, and the resulting low-temperature political culture was frequently conceived as a positive sign since predictable party attachments and the absence of passion lent themselves to order and stability (for example, Lipset 1960; Huntington 1968). The increasingly ritualized major-party competition of the postwar era made for just enough voter participation to legitimate top-level decisions without stirring up much fuss. Meanwhile, research on electoral behavior, focusing its considerable methodological prowess on the determinants of such voting, helped structure an intellectual debate in which voting patterns *stood* as politics.

Most political writers inferred from all this that whatever cleavages remained in U.S. society were safely incorporated by political parties and that a basic consensus reigned. By the 1960s this inference seemed shaky. Mann reviewed some two dozen empirical studies of democratic political systems and found "not a value consensus which keeps the working class compliant, but rather a lack of consensus in the crucial areas where concrete experiences and vague populism might be translated into radical politics" (1970, 436; cited in Lindblom 1977). As was the case with most of the NDC workers, ambivalence can make for a muffled voice, so that what is heard sounds like real rather than residual conservatism.

Alford and Friedland (1974) reviewed the dominant traditions in political sociology and found that insufficient attention had been paid to what they described as a "dialectic of mass participation and electoral impotence." The potential instabilities of increasing democratic suffrage, they demonstrated, had been tempered by the growth of nonpartisan offices and bureaucratic-administrative agencies, and the power of the executive branch over the legislative. In the process of fostering a stability of sorts by managing overt conflicts, these

developments in political infrastructure reduce popular identification with political institutions. Democratic struggles for universal suffrage and for a government that insulated the populace from the most severe swings of the market
succeeded in changing the structure of the state; the resulting state structures,
however, in turn succeeded in changing if not capturing the terrain on which
such struggles were fought (see also Mills 1956; Esping-Anderson, Friedland,
and Wright 1976; Kesselman 1982). What such trends have meant for political
culture and process was well expressed in *The Symbolic Uses of Politics* by Murray
Edelman:

> Mass publics respond to currently conspicuous political symbols: not to
> "facts," and not to moral codes embedded in the character or soul, but to the
> gestures and speeches which make up the drama of the state.
>
> The mass public does not study and analyze detailed data about
> secondary boycotts, provisions for stock ownership and control in a pro-
> posed space communications corporation, or missile installations in Cuba.
> It ignores these things until political actions and speeches make them
> symbolically threatening or reassuring, and it then responds to the cues
> furnished by the actions and the speeches, not to direct knowledge of the
> facts.
>
> *It is therefore political actions that shape men's political wants and
> "knowledge," not the other way around.* The common assumption that
> what democratic government does is somehow always a response to the
> moral codes, desires and knowledge embedded inside people is as inverted
> as it is reassuring. This model, avidly taught and ritualistically repeated,
> cannot explain what happens; but it may persist in our folklore because it so
> effectively sanctifies prevailing policies and permits us to avoid worrying
> about them. (1964, 172–73: emphasis added)

Is this any different than the politics of any other society or era? Although it
is probably true that Edelman's points might be made about many societies, past
and present, current political culture in the United States seems so different in
degree from the past as to constitute a difference of kind. Although published
more than two decades ago, Edelman's thesis seems even more true today (even
his examples sound strangely current). Leaders with access to mass media, now
more than then, shape and even create "public opinion" by naming the issues
and crises about which people come to have opinions. Political events are
experienced, if at all, at third hand. "Newsworthy" events are defined if not
staged by elites, interpreted by other elites and journalists, and then reinterpreted
by editors whose job it is to sell news. Although such news must be cast so as to fit
the existing frames and experiences of the public and hence cannot be manipulated any way its authors please, those with media access seem to have dispropor-

tionate ability to construe if not totally construct its significance. If Edelman's argument has even some merit (and I believe it has much), then the beliefs and preferences thought to make up "public opinion" are hardly naturally occurring democratic phenomena.

Public opinion seems to me constructed in a second and more subtle way by the mechanisms that purport to measure it. Political attitude surveys and opinion polls have proliferated in the last decade to the point where they are a central feature of political culture. No other society has had its pulse taken so often on so many issues. Polls were always routine news items for what they purportedly told us about ourselves, but now all the major television networks and many major newspapers and magazines have their own polling arms. Major political candidates would sooner do without substantive policy advisers than campaign poll-sters—indeed, for many the pollster *is* the substantive policy adviser. Back when the Gallup poll was the only game in town, Blumer (1948) asked if "public opinion" actually existed apart from what polls elicit and measure, and wondered whether such opinions were measured as they are organized and operate empirically in social life. Although polls have certainly grown in both precision and prestige and have made more information about everyone available to everyone, I have yet to find an adequate answer to his question.

In fact, the oddities and anomalies, concealed consistencies, and vagaries of valence I found in my subjects' accounts of their beliefs, as well as the multiple possibilities for disarticulation and misinterpretation that occur when these are severed from their context, lead me to believe that Blumer's critique must be broadened. I think that the polls, surveys, ballots, voting tallies, and media reports on them that make up the political technology that makes "public opinion" available to us as such all in some measure expropriate the means of making meaning and alienate us from the voice with which we speak in political life. This process entails at least four stages:

1. *Decontextualization:* The policy preferences, political beliefs, and behaviors of individual citizens are abstracted by means of forced-choice questions from the biographies, life strategies, value systems, forms of reasoning, and social settings in which they originate and "live" and in relation to which they derive their particular meaning and significance.

2. *Aggregation/Analysis:* Once abstracted, such newly constituted units of political significance are quantified into aggregates and reorganized so that they become emblematic of social categories (for example, race or region) and trends, the empirical character or even existence of which prior to these procedures is unknown.

3. *Inference/Interpretation:* Mass media and political leaders then reanalyze,

reabstract and report, in accordance with *their* purposes, aggregate findings and trends as phenomena occurring independently of the procedures that have produced them, attributing to them one or more meanings and locating them structurally as properties of one or more social categories or groups. One core consequence is the further construction and negotiation of political reality in which the role of those said to be the authors of that reality becomes at best increasingly limited and at worst lost altogether.

4. *Recontextualization:* Such measures of, and trends in, public opinion—having been rendered socially available as "facts" scientifically arrived at and signifying something "objective" about "voters" or "the public"—become part of the political culture from which they were said to have originated; thus, as part of the social world, these facts influence not only the political behavior of elites toward the electorate but also the various contexts and processes from which the original individuals derive the very political self-understanding and knowledge shaping preferences, beliefs, and so on. [11]

I offer these stages as a stop-action look at the routine procedures of modern political technology most of us take for granted. Through such a lens it is easier to see how what are implicitly or explicitly understood to be the autonomous acts or attitudes of individuals are more likely the artifacts of our means for apprehending them. I do not mean to suggest (speaking of ideological work) that we who study and interpret public opinion may as well stare at ink blots or read tea leaves as peruse our printouts. There are regularities in aggregate patterns of belief that do have social meaning apart from the individual idiosyncrasies and interpretive anomalies to which I have pointed. Yet I have been so struck by the radical differences between the responses found in my own earlier survey work and the more discursive statements of these depth interviews that I think we know far less about what political beliefs are and mean than we think. If so, one way to learn more is by methodological reflexivity, by remaining alive to the ways in which our methods (to say nothing of our theories) both affect and effect our findings. It may be that Edelman's inversion of democratic theory has its parallel both in the polls and at the polls.

11. In formulating these four stages I have benefited greatly from the theoretical work of Dorothy Smith (1974, 1978). Todd Gitlin's study of the role of mass media in "the making and unmaking of the New Left" was also instructive, for example: "The process of making meanings in the world of centralized commercial culture has become comparable to the process of making value in the world through labor. Just as people *as workers* have no voice in what they make, how they make it, or how the product is distributed and used, so do people *as producers of meanings* have no voice in what the media make of what they say or do" (1980, 3).

Debased Discourse

I have tried to describe some of the ways in which political beliefs can be disarticulated, manipulated, mismeasured, and misinterpreted through the processes of political technology. There is another feature of political culture that should be mentioned, and it has to do with the loop back from technology to citizenry: what are voters given in the way of content? On what sorts of debate and discussion of what manner of political ideas do we develop our positions and preferences in the first place? Of course, here one comes up against the chicken-or-egg dilemma in that it is difficult to say whether the technology or the content come first. It seems preferable to understand them both as part of a whole.

A theme running throughout the comments of each of my subjects was the perception of a poverty of real choice among candidates and policies. Each seemed to take it for granted that all candidates simply said what they needed to say to get elected and that the nature of mass media politics unfortunately demanded this. Although none of the twelve ever used the term, I submit that each was commenting upon the *debased discourse* that characterizes modern American politics. If, as I have tried to show, all political beliefs are contextual or indexical in both the situational and the historical senses, then surely debased discourse constitutes a core feature of the metacontext from which my subjects' beliefs were derived. It was bound up with their strategies for dissociating themselves from politics and for protesting the absence of alternatives via abstention and defection to third parties, which in effect led to electoral disarticulation. It also makes measurement of beliefs and preferences still more precarious insofar as measurement presupposes that political terms have invariant meanings when such discourse makes it less and less likely that political terms have any clear meaning at all.

Examples of debased discourse abound. Issues are made into slogans suitable for the six-second quip on the nightly news, the principal means for knowing candidates. That technology then turns slogans into issues when, for example, media commentators discuss not so much the problems besetting the country as campaign tactics. [12] Our leaders often succeed or fail on the impression-management abilities of their media consultants. Personality tends to replace principle, so that voters must become armchair psychoanalysts. Campaign contributions replace party participation as the means of getting a message across. Positions and platforms are not sculpted to the contours of the crises we face; rather, the crises

---

12. If "to speak less than discursively is to sloganize," then virtually all news reports and survey responses distort to the degree they prevent by definition discursive ("adult") speech; thought, premise, reasoning, inference, and so on are all eclipsed by the eliciting and presentational devices (Gibson 1980, 100).

we face are sculpted to suit what will "sell in Peoria." Religion becomes a public relations resource; a candidate's proximity to religion (rather than his distance from it) stands as a "good selling point." A logic of electability rooted in marketing theory is the axis along which political discourse is organized.

None of this is necessarily new. Diggins (1984) and Bellah and his colleagues (1985, 27–51), for example, argue that such debasement really began not when the mass media emerged but when the modern politics of liberal capitalism and self-interest triumphed over the classical politics of virtue and community. For them, the trouble did not start in the television age; that age was merely the extension by technological means of a process that began in the nineteenth century, when Democrats justified patronage and Whigs rationalized private greed. Whenever it began, the result has been if not the "lost soul" of American politics (Diggins) at least the loss of a "common language" with which to speak of the larger good (Bellah).

I suggest that these processes have in the 1980s taken a quantum leap forward, if that is the word. As noted earlier, part of Reagan's initial appeal had to do with the clarity of his radical-right platform in relation to Carter's failed attempts to move toward a Republican-leaning center while still speaking enough traditional Democratese to retain the support of liberals. Such clarity, however, should not camouflage the shrewd marketing magic behind its success. This became perfectly clear, so to speak, in 1984. Reagan's campaign strategists designed what they called an "operation," tellingly titled "the Great American Fog Machine," which would "fog the issues with images" (cited in Germond and Witcover 1985). Having approached new Orwellian heights in his first term by labeling the MX missile a "peacekeeper" and appropriating the auras of many political and folk heros whose policies were opposed to his (Franklin D. Roosevelt, John F. Kennedy, and Bruce Springsteen are a few examples), Reagan in the 1984 campaign surpassed these by proclaiming, to cite but one case, that rising poverty rates were declining. The campaign's guiding spirit was a vacuous smoke-and-mirrors nationalism as outlined in a June 1984 strategy memo by top Reagan adviser Richard Darman: "Paint RR as the personification of all that is right with, or heroized [sic] by, America. Leave Mondale in a position where an attack on Reagan is tantamount to an attack on America's idealized image of itself—where a vote against Reagan is, in some subliminal sense, a vote against a mythic 'AMERICA.'"[13] A political culture that consists of such tactics draws not from James Madison but from Madison Avenue.

13. The memo was disclosed by Goldman and Fuller (1985). A prototype of the "misspeakings" for which Reagan became legendary was contained in David Shipler's article, "The View from America" (New York Times Magazine, November 10, 1985): "Important national perceptions can be

Were the Democrats any less likely to debase discourse? Hardly. While Mondale strategists claimed that huge rallies and the "pizzazz factor" were consciously sacrificed to the laying of an "issues foundation" in "classroom-like settings," they quite unselfconsciously spoke of better camera angles and the appearance of "conviction" and "passion" on the front page of the *New York Times* (September 16, 1984): "The use of such settings as school gymnasiums rather than outdoor sites is intended to cast him as, well, the more accessible candidate." It was as if they had discovered the pitfalls of the logic of marketing and the electability trap only to use them to design a cleverer sales gimmick. Mondale himself admitted as much in his postmortem address to the AFL-CIO, when he attributed his crushing defeat to "a failure in marketing and packaging."[14]

Hitting on the record deficits of Reagan the fiscal conservative may have seemed a natural tactic, but coming from Democrats long perceived as profligate welfare state spenders, it seemed to yield only more disbelief. By avoiding a defense of Democratic party traditions of social and economic justice on the debatable assumption that the electorate had shifted to the right, both Carter and Mondale tailored their policy rhetoric to the center-right. It may be that in the process they lost both overall credibility and the support of the Democratic Left. This timidity tacitly let Reagan and the New Right choose the terrain of battle. It was a terrain on which the Democrats were ill equipped to succeed; instead of "letting Reagan be Reagan" and criticizing him for it, the operative goal seemed to be to out-Reagan Reagan. Pollster and Democratic consultant Patrick Caddell put the point starkly in a speech on why the Democrats could not win without articulating a clear vision of their own: "In any contest between the ersatz and the real, the real will win every time."

After failing miserably with such a strategy in two national contests, a reorganizing Democratic party seems at this writing to be more than ever

shaped by a well-turned phrase or dramatic image, even when the underlying facts are in doubt. Describing Soviet intentions, for example, President Reagan . . . used a quotation that he ascribed to Lenin: 'We will take Eastern Europe. We will organize the hordes of Asia. And then we will move into Latin America and we won't have to take the United States; it will fall into our outstretched hands like an overripe fruit.' It turned out to be a phoney, contained in a 1958 book by Robert Welch of the John Birch Society" (36). Habermas speaks of such tactics as "a manipulation of mass loyalty which is both perfected and passed off as respectable, administered by political parties. . . . At an earlier stage it was still said that the parties . . . procured the *acclamation* of the voting public. That is a touchingly old-fashioned expression for the staged performances, barred against all spontaneity, which run according to scenario and bring literally everything under control. . . . *that* was the new quality which the last American presidential election attained—with an actor playing a president whose office is increasingly restricted to presenting this office to the outside world as fictive reality" (1985, 97).

14. Mondale's speech was quoted by Richard Reeves ("It Wasn't the Medium, It Was the Message," *San Jose Mercury News*, February 26, 1985). See also the *Washington Post* article under the headline, "Mondale Says His TV Image Caused Defeat" (February 19, 1985).

indentured to the logic of electability. Democratic National Committee chair Paul Kirk told state leaders in November 1985 that to win back power they had to stress "the shared aspirations of average Americans," by which he meant "the unifying common interest themes of family, of work, of education, of fiscal pragmatism and economic opportunity, of equality and competitiveness, of patriotism and a more secure future." Such themes emerged not from party principles or national need but from public opinion research on what would sell in the age of Reagan. Conspicuously absent from his list were many themes Democrats have stressed since Roosevelt. There are no signs in the party mainstream that future presidential candidates will gamble as Reagan did in 1980 on staking out a clear ideological claim. How much the "shift to conservatism" became self-fulfilling when the Democrats acted as if it were a fait accompli is difficult to know. What is less difficult to know is the effect on political discourse, captured here by Norman Birnbaum: "Political debate about economic issues, within the Democratic Party and between the Democrats and Republicans, has become an exercise in staying off the point. It is not simply a matter of a public cretinized by vapid slogans, misleading definitions and fraudulent rhetoric. The purveyors of this stuff have already cretinized themselves" (1984, 197).

One critical link between modern political technology and debased discourse is campaign finance. The notion that massive spot advertising on television is the sine qua non of electoral success is now unquestioned truth in political circles. In addition to reducing platforms to media-sized morsels and character and career to split-second images, television advertising requires massive campaign contributions. A recent report by the Center for Responsive Politics showed that between 1974 and 1984 the costs of a congressional campaign increased fivefold and for a senate race sixfold. In the same period the number of corporate political action committees (PACs), whose primary function is to disburse contributions so as to influence politicians, grew by more than 1,700 percent—outnumbering labor PACs ten to one—and increased their campaign spending by a factor of ten. Meanwhile the proportion of campaign financing that comes from small donors dropped by half. To be competitive in national politics, then, candidates must attract large contributions. At a minimum this inhibits them from taking the sort of stands and running the kind of campaigns that might alienate large contributors. And such stands and campaigns, in turn, inhibit untold numbers of voters from political learning and genuinely partisan participation.[15]

15. The research report of the Center for Responsive Politics was summarized in "The High Cost of Campaigning" (San Francisco Chronicle, December 17, 1985). Successive reports by the California Fair Political Practices Commission support the same point for state and even local races, in which campaign spending doubled between 1978 and 1982.

What sort of political culture does all this money underwrite? News articles commenting upon how often candidates slander each other are commonplace in every election season. In one of these, a campaign consultant explained the trend by saying, "Because there is so much skepticism, campaign managers find it easier to make a credible negative point rather than a positive point. It's the suspicion abroad in the land about politicians."[16] A fair description, but his theory puts the sociological cart before the horse by claiming that skepticism and suspicion are the source of negative political advertising. A similar debasement is evident in the television ads for or against various ballot initiatives. A sampling of California political advertising during the last week of the 1982 election campaigns showed scenes of a flowing mountain stream while a narrator asserted that a water conservation initiative will cause the state to "run out of water"; a uniformed police officer claimed that gun control is "too dangerous"; and an esteemed physicist who helped invent the atomic bomb told voters that an advisory plebiscite recommending a verifiable bilateral freeze on nuclear weapons would *lead* to nuclear war. I am not convinced that it is sociologically necessary to explore class, sex, race, and voter psychology in order to understand why citizens might wish to "tune out" or "turn off" politics after listening to a confusing barrage of such ads.

These anecdotes are offered to illustrate the proposition that changes in political technology and culture—television advertising, corporate PACs and campaign financing, media pseudoevents, computerized direct-mail fund-raising, and platforms designed according to marketing strategies—have commodified and debased political discourse and that this helps account for the low regard in which more and more voters, including *all* of my respondents, hold politics and politicians.[17] If the name of the game is maximizing market share

16. "A Nasty Campaign—Insults and Cynicism" (*San Francisco Chronicle*, November 1, 1982). In an earlier article on campaigns an insider similarly observed that "the race has boiled down to money and paid media. It's a shame but the candidates are caught in a vicious cycle. . . . They have to purchase the attention of the voters. That in turn imposes a heavy financial burden, which requires adjustments in schedule to raise more money to buy the time." The point was underscored by pollster Mervin Field: "The American public really doesn't hold the process in high esteem anymore. The whole wisdom has become 'Dump it on TV' and everything has become slick and artificial" (*San Francisco Chronicle*, October 10, 1982).

17. When money and media push out party and populace, political trust and party identification will suffer; this in turn facilitates dealignment among the electorate. See, for example, Nie et al. (1976) on the "principled rejection of parties," and Himmelweit, Humphries, and Katz (1981) who show that declining party allegiance in Britain was not due to indifferent and inconsistent "floaters," but to the political context within which voters decide. Nie and Andersen's (1974) insightful reanalysis of American voting through 1972 shows that inconsistency was not due to enduring characteristics of the public because levels of consistency *increased* among low-education voters who grew disenchanted in the late 1960s.

With respect to the term *discourse*, note that Willis and Corrigan take to task discourse theorists

across social groups, then the process is the same whether Democrats or deodorants, presidents or pickles are being sold. When the goal is "product name recognition," then we will see crossover politicians just as we have seen crossover popular music that blends rock and country or jazz in order to sell records to many audiences. In the commodity form, both politics and music must soften the sharp edges of ideals and sever roots in order to sell to new segments. This is troubling insofar as political "consumers" tend to garner less and less information about how the world works and might be made to work better, or what role they might have in either.

Even if we correct for any tendency toward caricature in this description, commodified politics and debased discourse remain. They make understandable my subjects' practice of political alienation, their low trust and lack of loyalty to parties, and their shared assumption that the two-party system offers only a Tweedledum and Tweedledee choice between different candidates beholden to the same corporate plutocracy. I cannot here demonstrate which part of the process came first, but it is at least arguable that a dynamic of debased discourse, ideological drift, electoral dealignment, secondary debasement, and so on characterizes American political culture. For my subjects as least, the perception of politics as corrupt seemed to support their strategies for dissociation manifest in weak party identification and low political trust. Politicians, Democrats in particular, seemed to perceive this sort of phenomena more broadly in terms of dealignment and attempted to redress it via a market share–electability calculus, which in turn required the very same large campaign contributions, elite ideological drift, and manipulation of increasingly vague symbols that contributed to voters' negative perceptions in the first place.

If all such phenomena are somehow of a piece, then who can blame, say, Sally for her refusal through five elections to even listen to news of politics, much less vote? Was Chente's decision to jog instead of find a new polling place some kind of aberration? Is it so puzzling that most of the others in both groups— liberal, conservative, or a little of both—held politicians in a contempt so taken for granted that it no longer entailed affect? Who can blame Greg or José for skipping to the sports section or for not having much desire after a ten-hour day to

---

and semioticists for assuming that discourses exist apart from subjects. Like Althusser's subjectless history, they claim, such theories smuggle in an assumed working-class passivity by showing only how discourses structure experience. If it is "idealist" to assume volition, surely it is idealist "to posit a discourse abstracted from the historic and continuing social relationships which . . . make it observable at all" (1983, 87). Willis and Corrigan show, as I have tried to, that working-class cultural forms are capable of "turning back," mocking, or resisting what they call "hegemonic discourses." Among my subjects, it is possible to see what is taken as alienation, low political trust, or cynicism about politicians as strategic forms of dissociation, and thus, perhaps, an inchoate "counter-hegemonic cultural form."

delve into the political quagmire of the front page to retrieve consistent issue positions about which they might again feel a partisan clarity? Is it an act of political irrationality to avoid the labor involved in sorting through the half-truths and hyperbole, the pap and the propaganda, in order to forge truly informed decisions and take a stand behind one of the major parties when experience suggests it matters little anyway? Given their views of the American political system, perhaps what begs for explanation is not the way they voted but the fact that they did so at all.

A Curious Convergence: Notes on the Democratic Current

In drawing this analysis to an end, I want to return to the core questions raised in the beginning about the American moral economy or social charter. What can be seen of the political landscape by gazing simultaneously through all twelve of the windows my subjects provided? Two themes stand out for me. Although neither was explicitly named as such by any one subject, each of them talked around and about both. My terms for these are *democracy of work* and *populist delegitimation*.

I chose the awkward term *democracy of work* to distinguish it from the more commonplace *workplace democracy* because what I heard was a longing broader and deeper if more ineffable than that. But I do mean the term to encompass fully the principles of workplace democracy—having a real say over the pace of work, how it should be done, who supervisors ought to be, and how they should supervise. In private and public sector alike, all these workers were certain, though not at all in immodest ways, that they knew how to do their jobs better than those who directed them, that they could solve problems better than "management" without increasing costs or decreasing productivity. They were neither asked for their knowledge nor listened to when they offered it.[18] Even the

18. See Moberg (1980) on the drop in the 1970s in the percentage of people reporting satisfaction with hours, pay, security, their interest in their work, and the opportunity to develop their abilities. A recent Hart poll found that half its national sample believed that if workers chose managers and set policy, performance would improve; two-thirds would prefer to work in employee-owned firms; three-fourths favored consumer and community representation on corporate boards; and that a presidential candidate advocating such changes would be preferred two to one. These findings cut across the liberal-conservative continuum, but were strongly and inversely related to class (see Hart et al. 1975; Rifkin 1977). There is also evidence that morale, commitment, and productivity all increase under participatory management. See the *Harvard Business Review* for case studies and surveys since 1965; Weatherly (1981) for a list of such articles; *Monthly Labor Review* for research showing that employee-owned firms achieve higher productivity; Conte and Tannenbaum (1978) on how productivity rises in proportion to democratization; and Martin (1983) for the same evidence on public agencies. However, Weatherly shows the obstacles to participatory management in public agencies (for example, political unpopularity of welfare has led to managerial toughness, high turnover, worker resistance owing to lack of control over resources by even management, and thus perceived high costs in effort relative to cloudy benefits).

few who had doubts hesitated only insofar as they feared workplace democracy might be misused by management or not really implemented. Kurt Wilson had been actively involved in increasing participatory democracy in all spheres for a decade, but he was wary of workplace democracy at css because he had seen participation and input initiated and manipulated by management in such a way that the result was more work and less power for the workers. Joe Demski was all for workplace democracy as national policy, but he feared that within the corporate hierarchy of NDC it would destroy fellowship by inducing workers to exploit each other. This reverence for fellowship and the democratic work ethics it implies was cited by most in both groups as one important reason they had refused promotions. Individual career mobility was not alluring enough to overcome their desires to remain among peers and avoid becoming part of the hierarchies they hated (see also Sennett and Cobb 1973; Aronowitz 1973). In this sense Republicans and Democrats alike lived a rarely articulated democratic ethic.

Their broader belief in a democracy of work was manifest in their public policy preferences. Most in both groups had doubts about the use of tax funds to bail out Chrysler because they understood Chrysler's bankruptcy to be a function of management's decision to stick with "gas guzzlers" on which there were higher profit margins. Most supported the decision "only to save the workers' jobs." All twelve, however, supported the idea of similar loans to a worker-community group trying to buy and run Youngstown Sheet and Tube, which its parent conglomerate was intent on closing for a tax write-off. That the federal government in this case rejected the loans only confirmed their modal suspicion that the state favored "big business" at the expense of workers and communities.

Although there were clear differences between private- and public-sector workers and conservatives and liberals on the nature of the *obligation* to work, only Buford had any reservations about government doing whatever was necessary to ensure that people had the *opportunity* to meet that obligation. They did not mean merely letting the market loose as in Reagan's "opportunity society." Most agreed that the state should be the "employer of last resort," and even Buford supported employment and training programs as "benefiting the whole." Similarly, all of them shared both a belief in meritocracy and a belief (Schmitt excepted) that under the banner of meritocracy some gaping inequalities having nothing to do with effort or skill had been perpetuated. Most of the NDC workers were more likely to argue that rewards should stem from effort and ingenuity than were most of the css workers. Yet, most in both groups cited examples of how the effort-reward link had been severed routinely in the marketplace (lawyers, speculators, and auto industry executives were favorite examples).

This broader belief in a democracy of work also showed up in their complaints about their jobs. All had managed to find meaning and satisfaction in jobs that were often alienating and frustrating, and their criticisms made it clear that they wanted work that would challenge their creativity and provide something of value to society. It galled Buford and the other NDC workers when management's response to competition was to keep hiring down and work loads up. They all said this bothered them not only because it forced them to work harder and longer in jobs already legendary for that but because it hurt "the quality of our service." Most made mention of the pride they took in their product even as they were complaining about other aspects of the company. What they did not say directly was that corporate decisions that impinged on this felt unjust, undemocratic. Similarly, when the CSS workers felt most useful, most proud, was when they managed to get a troubled client "on his feet," in a job, off welfare—in a sense, into full citizenship. It bothered them that the new eligibility rules made this more rather than less difficult. They expected the Reagan reforms to cut against their ideal of service and to reduce the time they could spend helping people. But what disturbed them more was that the new rules also cut against the very laissez-faire ideals invoked to justify them by making it far more difficult for anyone to work his way off public assistance. None of the CSS workers actually used the term, but such policies seemed to strike them as un-American, undemocratic. There is, I submit, a work ethic running through such comments that encompasses many more dimensions than the individualist notion that livelihood is up to the person alone.

A second and related form of convergence between the two groups may be called *populist delegitimation*. Just as most in each group had a range of criticisms of management, there were striking similarities in complaints about the master institutions of both state and market spheres, and these tales of discontent appeared all across the ideological and voting spectrums. Four of the private-sector subjects opposed not the principle of a welfare state or state regulation of the market but rather the bureaucratic, inept, or undemocratic practices with which this was financed and carried out. There was surprisingly little disagreement on this from the public-sector workers. Although they might argue that the intent of alienating bureaucratic procedures was uniformity and thus fairness, they would admit more or less readily that individual differences got short shrift. Indeed, they spent much of their time trying to bend the bureaucratically rigid boxes on their forms to fit the unique details of damaged lives. There would be full agreement on the regressive character of taxation and the need to do a better job of building individual self-sufficiency for the poor. What united the complaints of both groups was not the idea that the state *tries* to make up for what the market fails to do but that it too often fails to do this—fails, that is, to enhance people's capacities for achieving the ends of the laissez-faire moral economy. This was precisely the criticism leveled at CSS by Driscoll, one of its leading social workers, and the theme expressed more vaguely by most NDC workers.

The state, then, doesn't work very well. Most CSS workers attributed this to the constraints placed upon it by business interests; their private-sector counterparts—both less familiar with the politics of the welfare state and less self-interested—tended to believe that government is often generically inept. Where they converged was on the notion that "big business" gets pretty much what it wants from both politicians and thus government in general. This shared populist critique tended to mean that the state was not seen as an arena from which hoped-for change was likely to emerge.

Market institutions, then, generally fared no better. Clear distinctions were made in both groups between small business and corporate America. Social relations with local merchants were personal and participatory and were experienced as democratic. Bank of America and Dow Chemical, the utilities and the oil companies, were another matter entirely. The inviolability of private property applied more to family homes and firms in which owners work than to faceless conglomerates that know no national boundaries or that come from other states to invest in condominium developments along *their* public beaches. Even Buford the evangelical believer in capitalism bemoaned "international bankers" who send America's capital, jobs, and, therefore, parts of its "sovereignty" abroad. Rudi the would-be capitalist felt the same way about "the big boys" of the corporate world. All had complaints that may be seen as indictments for violations of an unwritten code of capitalist conduct. What market mechanisms and the commodity form had done to health care (according to Sally), to fuel prices (Rudi), and to housing (Joe) was nothing short of disgraceful. Most of these people did not conceptualize such beliefs so abstractly, but all of them made arguments that there are moral limits on market forces, a greater good to which market institutions should be held accountable. Indeed, this idea has always lain at the heart of capitalist ideology. Not even the most nakedly greedy maintain that the market is moral in and of itself simply because it allows them riches. The market's legitimacy depends fundamentally upon its capacity to serve society and its citizens with those riches. Of my twelve subjects, only Buford took it as an article of faith that capital accumulation by itself serves as its own legitimation apart from its social consequences. For the others, this was more or less an empirical question. Most had their doubts about the notion that the market's raison d'être—that it does a better job at meeting human needs than any other imaginable arrangement—still has moral validity.

I do not wish my inferences to gloss over the many individual and group differences I spent several chapters describing. Yet, running through these differences was a gut-level populism, shared sentiments that consistently took the side of "the little guy" against both the bureaucracy of the state and the plutocracy of the market. Central to such sentiments was an undifferentiated or generalized delegitimation. G. William Domhoff (1978), one of the preeminent scholars of the structure of power in America, has described four concrete processes by which corporate elites shape politics: special interest group pressures (for example, industry PACs, high-powered law firms hired as lobbyists); policy formation organizations (Council on Foreign Relations, Trilateral Commission, Business Roundtable); candidate selection (choosing, grooming, promoting, and financing); and the "ideology process" (mass media promotion of probusiness frames and definitions of problems and the national interest that skirt questions about the distribution of wealth and power). None of my subjects had ever read Domhoff's books, but all twelve intuitively understood at least the first three of these processes. The specifics were often only vaguely grasped, the consequences sometimes oversimplified, and the processes themselves differentially interpreted. But all three were part of their commonsense notion of how the world works, part of political folklore. This does not mean that some of them did not still feel that the United States was "a great country" or even, for Buford and Rudi, "the greatest." It is likely that most Americans see our political system as pluralistic, but this does not prevent them from understanding that some interests have far greater power than others (see Form and Rytina 1969). In short, most of my respondents found it quite possible to see America in the late twentieth century as simultaneously good relative to most other nations and bad relative to its ideals—to what it should or could be.

Does such populist delegitimation have significant political ramifications? For Habermas (1975), advanced capitalist societies are sustained by "legitimating beliefs" about the justness and validity of institutions and practices that are repressive and exploitative. Thus it is the false attribution of legitimacy to master institutions—the mistaken belief in their validity and fairness, and the false consciousness within which people believe their well-being depends upon them—that support capitalist social formations. As it pertains to the beliefs of the people in this book, however, there is a certain awkwardness to this theory. Most of them granted only tepid and contingent legitimacy to either state or market, so their "mode of conformity" (Riesman 1952) did not appear to rest upon wholly mistaken beliefs. Further, my subjects were usually well aware of the exploitative aspects of master institutions, yet nevertheless perceived that their well-being did, as an empirical matter, depend upon them. Thus, false consciousness defined in such terms cannot easily be applied to them in that they seemed to acknowledge both the injustice of such institutions and that what was good in their lives had occurred within them. If this was a form of false consciousness, it was so only relative to a standard extrinsic to their lived experience. That few of them assessed their situation by more ideal or ideological standards seemed to have less to do with being fooled by legitimations than with the fact that ideologies were either unavailable or failed to help them make sense of their experience. And an ideology that does not work well cognitively seems unlikely to have strong normative appeal.[19]

Habermas argues that the inequalities and injustices of capitalism will be challenged when contradictions in the economic sphere are displaced onto the political-administrative sphere. There, they can no longer be portrayed as the results of some invisible hand but rather will be perceived as caused by the concrete policy decisions of officials. Thus, such decisions will be opened up to democratic scrutiny, critique, and demands. For most of my respondents the invisible hand was increasingly visible and decreasingly part of "nature"; "the system" was seen as mostly the work of a dimly perceived corporate-plutocratic "them." However, most remained unaware of or disconnected from the cultural resources with which they might have effectively scrutinized, criticized, or made demands. For the NDC workers there was little in the way of language, organization, or precedent; for the CSS workers there was some of each, but these generally got spent just keeping matters from getting worse at their small station within the state. For both groups, there was little faith that either the state or politics generally was a forum more hospitable to them than the market, a forum in which their criticisms and potential demands might be heard or have consequence.[20]

One view of politics through these twelve windows, then, is irony: It is in part the very generalized character of delegitimation that militates against a legitimation crisis, and their populist critique is so wide-ranging that it leaves no arena untainted enough to seem appealing or effective for populist political ends.

19. See Lane (1978) on how the market influences personality. My reading of Habermas has benefited from McCarthy's (1978) lucid synthesis of his oeuvre and from the useful overview of *Legitimation Crisis* by Flacks and Turkel (1978).

20. Habermas himself complicates the thesis of *Legitimation Crisis* in his *The Theory of Communicative Action*. In a recent interview he outlined his conception of a "crisis of the welfare state" from that work in a way that speaks directly to the ambivalence about the state I encountered: "The project of the welfare state has also become problematic in public consciousness, insofar as the bureaucratic means with which the interventionist state aimed to bring about the 'social restraint of capitalism' have lost their innocence. . . . The bureaucratization of the life-world . . . is experienced by broad strata of the population as a danger. . . . These new attitudes are exploited by neoconservatism, in order to sell the well-known policy of shifting the burden of problems back from the state onto the market—a policy which, Lord knows, has nothing to do with democratization, which rather effects a further uncoupling of state activity from the pressure for legitimation emanating from the public sphere, and understands by 'freedom' not the autonomy of the life-world, but a free hand for private investors" (1985, 99).

Another is offered by Mann (1975), who argues that the very notion of legitimation crisis is a viable part of linguistic currency only for intellectuals. What matters most for the continuation of capitalist societies, he argues, is the fit between ordinary people's daily lives and capitalist institutions (jobs, housing, stores). As I've tried to show, such a fit did exist for my subjects, alongside their discontents. What *might* have occurred if the language, culture, and organizations of an authentically democratic politics were to fit their everyday lives seems as intriguing a question as any answer I might offer would be speculative (see Flacks 1976, forthcoming). It seems fair to say, however, that Joe Demski and José Bustamante, and maybe even Sally Jones would have looked politically much more like Kurt Wilson than they did. I can also say, if these twelve workers are any guide, that the persistence of residual conformity in capitalist societies does not necessarily require false consciousness. Although most felt little in the way of a legitimation crisis, most felt little legitimacy. Their conformity, as Schaar has argued in general terms, seemed to rest on pragmatics rather than passion:

> The philosophical and experiential foundations of legitimacy in modern states are gravely weakened, leaving obedience a matter of lingering habit, or expediency, or necessity, but not a matter of reason and principle, and of deepest sentiment and conviction. (1969, 280–81)

It does not seem accurate to say that such populist delegitimation along with the shared support for the ideal of a democracy of work constitute a democratic *movement*. I would argue, however, that together they can be understood as a democratic *current*, an inchoate phenomenon embedded in mundane practices and sentiments, intermediate between nothing and a movement. Such a formulation, I hope, names the evidence without reading too much into it. As Studs Terkel has said of his respondents' lost and found American dreams, "something's happening, as yet unrecorded on the social seismograph. . . . There are signs, unmistakable, of an astonishing increase in the airing of grievances: of private wrongs and public rights. . . . In unexpected quarters, those, hitherto quiescent, are finding voice . . . [and] the last communiqués are not yet in" (1980, xxv).

My respondents' last communiqués are most certainly not yet in, but I am not certain what sort of voice they are apt to find or even, for many of them, if one will be sought at all. One danger in asking such large questions of such a small number of subjects is that the time frame is too constricted to take in many of the possible answers. It is worth remembering that in the 1980s virtually everyone is a small-d democrat, whereas less than two centuries ago democracy was feared to be as subversive of civilization as communism is said to be by many today.

Democracy's success, however, has depended in no small way on its dilution from, say, the Greek or Jeffersonian conceptions to modern elite conceptions that hold that participatory democracy can avoid anarchy only via a functional oligarchy of professionals. In the former, the lack of informed and active participation and clear articulation was disaster; in the latter, a sizable amount of apathy is "good for the system."[21]

If in fact such a democratic current exists, the question becomes whether it will be damned up or overflow its banks—or neither. In O'Connor's seminal formulations (1978, 1984), the American capitalist state came to a critical juncture in the 1970s: the loss of U.S. economic dominion in the world market had produced pressures on the state to reduce regulation and welfare spending in favor of capital accumulation. Democratic demands for increased participation (implicit in regulation) and for improved mass living standards (implicit in welfare and education spending) have become too expensive for the market's tastes. Against these, demands by business for untrammeled growth and profitability that began before Reagan have found their voice in him. O'Connor thinks this clash will set in motion a popular movement to democratize the state, transform it from an agent of the market to one whose purpose is to meet human needs. Such a movement would be about a defense of the rights and living standards accumulated since the New Deal and embodied, however precariously and contradictorily, in the state. Here O'Connor's case coincides with that of Piven and Cloward (1982), who maintain that state intervention in the market on behalf of both business and the polity has rendered the economy transparently political. Because such precedents now are part of historical experience, they say, a new moral economy is afoot in which the state is expected to ensure the right to a livelihood. Accordingly, attempts by Reagan and the Right to dismantle democratic sides of the state and reimpose the primacy of the laissez-faire moral economy will, *in the long run*, be doomed by the demands of the many whose everyday lives have been insulated by the state from the ravages of the market.

"In the long run," Keynes once said, "we're all dead." What evidence is there that the democratic current is turning into a democratic movement in defense of the state, the social charter, and the new moral economy? As of this writing, Democrats in Congress apparently have discerned enough popular support for the vast bulk of what the state does to hold the line against an extremely popular president bent on cutting back the state. Although fiscal crisis

21. In a report to the Trilateral Commission, Huntington makes this view rather explicit: "Some of the problems of governance in the U.S. today stem from an *excess of democracy*. . . . The effective operation of a democratic political system usually *requires* some measure of apathy and non-involvement" (Crozier et al. 1975, 113–14; emphasis added). Well-argued alternative views may be found in Alford and Friedland (1974, 1985), Macpherson (1977), and Finley (1985).

and budget cuts persist and the discourse of the New Deal and the Great Society is nowhere heard, there is little evidence the Right has succeeded in dismantling most of the regulatory and welfare functions of the state.[22] Yet if the consensus behind the new moral economy was socially constructed, it can be socially deconstructed—particularly when fundamental economic restructuring has shaped a political context of fragmentation and dealignment and when the political language and organization with which this might be resisted is as distrusted as it is impoverished.

If I have understood my subjects correctly, there are openings for and obstacles to a democratic movement. Their different leanings and modes of ambivalence notwithstanding, the debate that might ensue should these two sets of workers be convened would not center on *whether* there is a legitimate role for the state in meeting human needs. It would be about where to draw the lines: who should be eligible for how much after what level of effort and for how long? How many reins should government put on business and how tightly should they be held? Taken together, their transcripts may be read as a *discourse that presupposes the legitimacy of the state in all its basic welfare and regulatory aspects.* Eleven of my twelve favored, for example, health care as a right, guaranteed employment, stronger public education, assistance for the needy, and regulatory restraints on the freedom of capital that take explicit account of social costs. In this sense, my data provide some measurable support for Piven and Cloward: these eleven share a bottom-line belief that here, in the late twentieth century, nostalgic notions of an individualism that leaves each citizen's fate to the market alone and the public interest to unfettered competition will not suffice as the basis of a decent society.

These shared sentiments might serve as support for a democratic movement in defense of the new moral economy. If they are often latent and mixed up with other, conflicting sentiments at this historical juncture, they might become manifest and unmixed by events. The abstract-sounding structural shifts mentioned previously have had concrete consequences in working lives at both NDC

---

22. Although Americans have long bristled at "big government," particularly when mobilized to do so in the era of slow growth, tax revolts and the Reagan presidency, there is surprising support—as Piven and Cloward contend—for the vast bulk of state programs. For example, soon after Reagan's second landslide and at the peak of his popularity, twice as many in Gallup's national sample said "too little" was being spent on social programs as said "too much" (G. Gallup, Jr., "Big Defense Budget Opposed," *Los Angeles Times*, March 3, 1985). See also M. Oreskes, "Poll Finds Majority in U.S. Are Fearful of Budget Cutbacks" (*New York Times*, March 7, 1985), D. Rosenbaum, "20 Years Later, the Great Society Flourishes" (*New York Times*, April 17, 1985), R. D. Hershey, Jr., "Spending Rose Sharply in 'Reagan Revolution'" (*New York Times*, February 2, 1986), Palmer and Sawhill (1982), and Reeves (1985) who says the liberal consensus that guided the development of the welfare state still holds.

and CSS. The fit between everyday lives and market institutions may loosen. In follow-up interviews, for example, Greg and José complained of the unwritten company policy of "getting rid of the older guys" who "cost 'em more," a policy implemented as one strategy for dealing with deregulation and heightened competition in the transport industry. If this policy were to be applied to these twenty-year veterans, threatening their family lives, their affinity for the laissez-faire moral economy might weaken along with their estrangement from the new moral economy.

It is not at all certain, however, that such openings as might occur would overcome the obstacles already visible. The "crisis ideology" (O'Connor 1981) justifying wage concessions at both NDC and CSS and lower living standards for most Americans has had some impact on expectations. Sally Jones told me in 1983 that she was satisfied with a new NDC-union contract that for the first time in history offered no pay raise because "It's no time to strike, too many people are out of work." The CSS workers did strike, but to no avail. Their caseloads were up, their clients were in worse shape, and, as Karen Mullavey said, "Morale is really down. I can't see either [political] party pulling somebody out of the fire to build a working economy—one that feeds people, employs people, educates them. That dream has been squashed. . . . it's heretical to even bring it up." In the scenarios of O'Connor and Piven and Cloward, public workers like those at CSS would bond with their clients and lead the movement to democratize the state. But low morale, squashed dreams, and mere liberalism as heresy are not the elements of an effective defense of the post–New Deal social charter. Such obstacles suggest that political economic conditions and the Right's response to them have dampened democratic expectations and capacities.

It is not possible, of course, to predict the political direction of a nation— with any amount of data, much less a dozen case studies. The value I place on reflexive candor requires my admission that I would *like* to be able to argue that the reassertion of market supremacy by Reagan and the Right will engender the first overt defense of the state as a democratic haven and that this defense will democratize rather than further bureaucratize it. Such support for this tendency as I found in my private-sector subjects' was too tepid and contingent to support this argument, so the value I place on fidelity to their accounts requires that I not make it. Moreover, the value I place on not appearing foolish in light of the margin of victory enjoyed by Reagan in 1984 virtually demands that I conclude on a different note. It does seem safe to say that if there is any semblance of a mandate for radically restricting the social charter, then there is always the risk that this will mobilize the constituencies behind past mandates for broadening it (the civil rights, environmental, and women's movements, for example, do not seem to have disappeared in the face of a changed political climate).

It seems even safer to say that there are very likely multiple mandates, just as there are multiple value systems, that can and do coexist. Despite what I had hoped, as a citizen, I might find in my subjects' beliefs, I cannot deny that among many of the NDC workers reaction and radicalism seemed to float rather handily around the same ideological space.[23] I do not know a more humane or charitable chap than Greg Larson, yet he was at times capable of justifying conservative policy preferences with what he himself saw as inhumane and uncharitable opinions. Even some of the more consistently liberal CSS workers seemed able to entertain anomalous ideological strains. Marc Driscoll more than once espoused his respect for Barry Goldwater, who appealed to him not for the substance of his beliefs but for the principled honesty with which they were held, particularly as compared to "wishy-washy liberals." If the polity at large is as capable of entertaining multiple value systems and harboring support for multiple mandates as my subjects seemed to be, then there exists an *ideological indeterminacy* capable of surprises for everyone. Republicans and the Right may be surprised by the enduring character of basic support for a broad social charter even among those who voted for them. Democrats and the Left may be surprised by the degree to which people can be *already radical*—not because of some affinity for imported European ideological traditions but because of a continuity with traditional American values—albeit in ways that militate paradoxically against a movement in support of them. Yet if basic economic changes have dissipated the political consensus that once made liberalism seem transcendent, then the end-of-ideology theorists also may have spoken too soon.

If I have been accurate and fair in my attempt to cull themes from the ongoing discussions I had with my dozen very different subjects, then the populist delegitimation and the ideal of a democracy of work expressed by all of them do suggest the existence of a democratic current. For most of the Americans whose ideas compose this book, socialism remains stigmatized, New Right nostalgia seems senile, and postwar liberalism appears increasingly moribund. But *democracy*, despite and perhaps because of its apparent distance from daily reality, seems to have meaning that cuts across differences in experience, education, and income that are thought to push people into different ideological camps.

The existence and character of this democratic current is, as we social scientists like to say about phenomena we think we are clever enough to measure, "an empirical question." I hope subsequent investigators look for it. Although I cannot offer empirical predictions, my theoretical speculations lead me to

---

23. I am indebted to Troy Duster and Bennett Berger for not allowing my optimism to overshadow my analysis on this point; personal communications, 1984.

suggest that we should look in all the least likely lacunae of the body politic. For if there is a democratic current out there, it is embedded in the infrastructural practices of daily life, taking on this or that ideological valence according to the historical and situational exigencies of lived experience. It will not be easy to detect and describe because its channels have been chosen in part as paths of resistance to the very political technology by which "public opinion" is constructed and political discourse debased.

References

Aglietta, M. 1979. *A Theory of Capitalist Regulation: The U.S. Experience.*
London: New Left Books.

Alcaly, R. E., and Mermelstein, D. 1977. *The Fiscal Crisis of American Cities.*
New York: Vintage.

Alford, R. R., and Friedland, R. 1974. "Nations, Parties, and Participation: A
Critique of Political Sociology." *Theory and Society* 1.

———.1975. "Political Participation and Public Policy." *Annual Review of
Sociology* 1.

———.1985. *Powers of Theory: Capitalism, the State, and Democracy.* Cambridge: Cambridge University Press.

Aronowitz, S. 1973. *False Promises: The Shaping of American Working Class
Consciousness.* New York: McGraw-Hill.

———.1978. "Marx, Braverman, and the Logic of Capital." *Insurgent Sociologist* 8.

———.1981. *The Crisis in Historical Materialism: Class, Politics and Culture
in Marxist Theory.* South Hadley, Mass.: Bergin.

———.1985. "Why Work?" *Social Text* 12.

Barnet, R. 1980. *The Lean Years: Politics in the Age of Scarcity.* New York:
Simon & Schuster.

Beardsley, P. L. 1980. *Redefining Rigor: Ideology and Statistics in Political
Inquiry.* Beverly Hills, Calif.: Sage.

Becker, H. S. 1970. *Sociological Work.* Chicago: Aldine.

Becker, H. S., Geer, B., Hughes, E. C., and Strauss, A. L. 1977. *Boys in White.*
New Brunswick, N.J.: Transaction.

Bell, D. 1960. *The End of Ideology.* New York: Free Press.

———.1973. *The Coming of Post-Industrial Society.* New York: Basic Books.

————.1976. *The Cultural Contradictions of Capitalism.* New York: Basic Books.

————.1979. "The New Class: A Muddled Concept." In *The New Class?* Ed. G. Bruce Briggs. New Brunswick, N.J.: Transaction.

Bellah, R., Madsen, R., Sullivan, W. M., Swidler, A., and Tipton, S. M. 1985. *Habits of the Heart: Individualism and Commitment in American Life.* Berkeley: University of California Press.

Bendix, R., and Lipset, S. M. 1966. "The Field of Political Sociology." In *Political Sociology.* Ed. L. Coser. New York: Harper & Row.

Berelson, B., Lazarsfeld, P., and McPhee, W. 1954. *Voting.* Chicago: University of Chicago Press.

Berger, B. M. 1981. *The Survival of a Counterculture: Ideological Work and Everyday Life among Rural Communards.* Berkeley: University of California Press.

Birnbaum, N. 1984. "Some Points of Light." *Nation,* July 21–28, 1984.

Bittner, E. 1963. "Radicalism and the Organization of Radical Movements." *American Sociological Review* 28.

Blumer, H. 1948. "Public Opinion and Public Opinion Polling." *American Sociological Review* 13.

Botsch, R. 1980. *We Shall Not Overcome: Populism and Southern Blue Collar Workers.* Chapel Hill: University of North Carolina Press.

Bourdieu, P. 1977. *Outline of a Theory of Practice.* London: Cambridge University Press.

————.1984. *Distinction: A Social Critique of the Judgment of Taste.* Cambridge: Harvard University Press.

Braverman, H. 1974. *Labor and Monopoly Capital.* New York: Monthly Review Press.

Brint, S. 1984. " 'New Class' and Cumulative Trend Explanations of the Liberal Political Attitudes of Professionals." *American Journal of Sociology* 90.

Burawoy, M. 1979. *Manufacturing Consent.* Chicago: University of Chicago Press.

Burnham, W. D. 1980. "The Appearance and Disappearance of the American Voter." In *Electoral Participation.* Ed. R. Rose. Beverly Hills, Calif.: Sage.

————.1981. "The 1980 Earthquake: Realignment, Reaction, or What?" In *The Hidden Election.* Ed. T. Ferguson and J. Rogers. New York: Pantheon.

————.1982. *Current Crisis in American Politics.* New York: Oxford University Press.

Calleo, D. P. 1982. *The Imperious Economy.* Cambridge: Harvard University Press.

Campbell, A., Converse, P., Miller, W., and Stokes, D. 1964. *The American Voter.* New York: Wiley.

Castells, M. 1980. *The Economic Crisis and American Society.* Princeton, N.J.: Princeton University Press.

Centers, R. 1949. *The Psychology of Social Classes.* New York: Russell & Russell.

Citrin, J. 1978. *Do People Want Something for Nothing? Public Opinion on Taxes and Government Spending.* Berkeley: University of California, Survey Research Center.

Conte, M., and Tannenbaum, A. 1978. "Employee-Owned Companies: Is the Difference Measurable?" *Monthly Labor Review,* July.

Converse, P. 1964. "The Nature of Belief Systems in Mass Publics." In *Ideology and Discontent.* Ed. D. Apter. New York: Free Press.

Cressey, D. R., and Elgesem, E. 1968. "The Police and the Administration of Justice." *Scandinavian Studies in Criminology* 2.

Crozier, M., Huntington, S. P., and Watanuki, J. 1975. *The Crisis of Democracy: Report on the Governability of Democracies to the Trilateral Commission.* New York: New York University Press.

Currie, E. 1985. *Confronting Crime.* New York: Pantheon.

de Certeau, M. 1980. "On the Oppositional Practices of Everday Life." *Social Text* 3.

DeFonzo, J. 1973. "Embourgeoisment in Indianapolis." *Social Problems* 21.

Della Fave, L. R. 1980. "The Meek Shall Not Inherit the Earth: Self-Evaluation and the Legitimacy of Stratification." *American Sociological Review* 45.

Denitch, B., ed. 1979. *Legitimation and Regimes.* Beverly Hills, Calif.: Sage.

Diggins, J. 1984. *The Lost Soul of American Politics: Virtue, Self-Interest, and the Foundations of Liberalism.* New York: Basic Books.

DiTomaso, N. 1978. "Public Employee Unions and the Urban Fiscal Crisis." *Insurgent Sociologist* 8.

Domhoff, G. W. 1978. *The Powers That Be: Processes of Ruling Class Domination in America.* New York: Vintage.

Douglas, M. 1984. "Is Thought about the Social Order Possible?" Paper presented at the annual meeting of the American Sociological Association, San Antonio, Texas.

Durkheim, E. 1933 [1915]. *The Division of Labor in Society.* New York: Free Press.

Edelman, M. 1964. *The Symbolic Uses of Politics.* Urbana: University of Illinois Press.

———. 1977. *Political Language.* New York: Academic Press.

Edsall, T. B. 1983. *The New Politics of Inequality.* New York: Norton.

Edwards, R. 1979. *Contested Terrain: The Transformation of the Workplace in the Twentieth Century.* New York: Basic Books.

Ehrenreich, J., and Ehrenreich, B. 1977. "The New Left: A Case Study in Professional-Managerial Class Radicalism." *Radical America* 11.

Erikson, E. 1956. "The Problem of Ego Identity." *Journal of the American Psychoanalytic Association* 4.

Esping-Andersen, G. 1982. "After the Welfare State." *Working Papers for a New Society*, May-June.

Esping-Andersen, G., Friedland, R., and Wright, E. O. 1976. "Modes of Class Struggle and the Capitalist State." *Kapitalistate* 4–5.

Ewen, S. 1976. *Captains of Consciousness: Advertising and the Social Roots of Consumer Culture*. New York: McGraw-Hill.

Ferguson, K. E. 1984. *The Feminist Case against Bureaucracy*. Philadelphia: Temple University Press.

Ferguson, T., and Rogers, J., eds. 1981. *The Hidden Election: Politics and Economics in the 1980 Presidential Campaign*. New York: Pantheon.

Field, M. 1978. "Sending a Message: Californians Strike Back." *Public Opinion*, July-August.

Finley, M. I. 1985. *Democracy Ancient and Modern*. New Brunswick, N.J.: Rutgers University Press.

Flacks, R. 1967. "The Liberated Generation: An Exploration of the Roots of Student Protest." *Journal of Social Issues* 23.

———. 1971. *Youth and Social Change*. Chicago: Markham.

———. 1976. Making History vs. Making Life: Dilemmas of an American Left. *Sociological Inquiry* 46.

———. Forthcoming. *Making History vs. Making Life*. New York: Columbia University Press.

Flacks, R., and Turkel, G. 1978. "Radical Sociology: The Emergence of Neo-Marxian Perspectives in U.S. Sociology." *Annual Review of Sociology* 4.

Flanigan, W., and Zingale, N. 1979. *Political Behavior of the American Electorate*. Boston: Allyn & Bacon.

Form, W. H., and Rytina, J. 1969. "Ideological Beliefs on the Distribution of Power in the United States." *American Sociological Review* 34.

Free, L., and Cantril, H. 1967. *The Political Beliefs of Americans*. New Brunswick, N.J.: Rutgers University Press.

Friedrichs, D. 1980. "The Legitimacy Crisis in the United States: A Conceptual Analysis." *Social Problems* 27.

Fromm, E. 1941. *Escape from Freedom*. New York: Rinehart.

Galbraith, J. K. 1958. *The Affluent Society*. New York: Mentor.

Garfinkel, H. 1967. *Studies in Ethnomethodology*. Englewood Cliffs, N.J.: Prentice-Hall.

Geertz, C. 1973. *The Interpretation of Cultures*. New York: Harper's.

———. 1983. *Local Knowledge*. New York: Basic Books.

Gergen, K. 1973. "Social Psychology as History." *Journal of Personality and Social Psychology* 26.

Germond, J., and Witcover, J. 1985. *Wake Us When It's Over: Presidential Politics of 1984*. New York: Macmillan.

Gibson, W. 1980. "Network News: Elements of a Theory." *Social Text* 3.

Gilbert, N. 1983. *Capitalism and the Welfare State: Dilemmas of Social Benevolence*. New Haven: Yale University Press.

Gintis, H. 1980. "Communication and Politics: Marxism and the 'Problem' of Liberal Democracy." *Socialist Review* 50–51.

Gitlin, T. 1978. "Media Sociology: The Dominant Paradigm." *Theory and Society* 6.

———. 1980. *The Whole World is Watching: Mass Media in the Making and Unmaking of the New Left*. Berkeley: University of California Press.

Glaser, B., and Strauss, A. 1967. *The Discovery of Grounded Theory*. Chicago: Aldine.

Goffman, E. 1959. *The Presentation of Self in Everyday Life*. New York: Doubleday.

———. 1974. *Frame Analysis: An Essay on the Organization of Experience*. New York: Harper & Row.

Gold, D., Lo, C., and Wright, E. O. 1975. "Recent Developments in Marxist Theories of the State." *Monthly Review*, October-November.

Goldman, P., and Fuller, T. 1985. *Quest for the Presidency*. New York: Bantam.

Goldthorpe, J. H., Lockwood, D., Bechhofer, F., and Platt, J. 1969. *The Affluent Worker in the Class Structure*. Cambridge: Cambridge University Press.

Gough, I. 1979. *The Political Economy of the Welfare State*. London: Macmillan.

Gouldner, A. 1979. *The Future of Intellectuals and the Rise of the New Class*. New York: Seabury.

Gramsci, A. 1971 [1930]. *Prison Notebooks*. Ed. Q. Hoare and G. N. Smith. New York: International Publishers.

Granovetter, M. 1985. "Economic Action and Social Structure: The Problem of Embeddedness." *American Journal of Sociology* 91.

Habermas, J. 1971. *Knowledge and Human Interests*. Boston: Beacon Press.

———. 1973. "Wahrheitstheorien [Theories of truth]." In *Wirklichkeit und Reflexion: Festschrift fur W. Schulz*. Ed. H. Fahrenbach. Frankfurt, West Germany: Pfullingen.

———. 1975. *Legitimation Crisis*. Boston: Beacon Press.

———. 1985. "A Philosophical-Political Profile." *New Left Review* 151.

Hamilton, R. F. 1972. *Class and Politics in the United States*. New York: Wiley.

Hart, P., and Associates. 1975. *American Public Opinion and Economic Democracy*. Washington, D.C.: Peter D. Hart Associates Survey Report.

Himmelweit, H. E., Humphries, P., and Katz, M. 1981. *How Voters Decide*. London: Academic Press.

Hochschild, J. L. 1979. "Redistributing Wealth: Positions, Payments, and

Attitudes." In *Public Policy and Public Choice*. Ed. D. W. Rae and T. J. Eismeier. Beverly Hills, Calif.: Sage.

————. 1981. *What's Fair: American Beliefs about Distributive Justice*. Cambridge: Harvard University Press.

Horowitz, R. 1983. *Honor and the American Dream: Culture and Identity in a Chicano Community*. New Brunswick, N.J.: Rutgers University Press.

Huntington, S. P. 1968. *Political Order in Changing Societies*. New Haven: Yale University Press.

————. 1981. *American Politics: The Promise of Disharmony*. Cambridge: Harvard University Press, Belknap Press.

Ignatieff, M. 1985. *The Needs of Strangers*. New York: Elisabeth Sifton Books.

Irwin, J. 1970. *The Felon*. Englewood Cliffs, N.J.: Prentice-Hall.

Irwin, J., and Cressey, D. R. 1962. "Thieves, Convicts, and the Inmate Culture." *Social Problems* 10.

Janowitz, M. 1976. *The Last Half Century*. Chicago: University of Chicago Press.

Janowitz, M., and Marvick, D. 1956. "Competitive Pressure and Democratic Consent." In *Political Behavior*. Ed. H. Eulau, S. J. Eldersveld, and M. Janowitz. Glencoe, Ill.: Free Press.

Jencks, C. 1983. "Discrimination and Thomas Sowell." *New York Review of Books*, March 3; and "Special Treatment for Blacks?" *New York Review of Books*, March 17.

————. 1985. "How Poor Are the Poor?" *New York Review of Books*, May 9.

Kamieniencki, S. 1985. *Party Identification, Political Behavior, and the American Electorate*. Westport, Conn.: Greenwood.

Katz, J. 1982. "A Theory of Qualitative Methodology: The Social System of Analytic Field Work." In *Poor People's Lawyers in Transition*. New Brunswick, N.J.: Rutgers University Press.

Katznelson, I. 1981. "A Radical Departure? Social Welfare and the Election." In *The Hidden Election: Politics and Economics in the 1980 Presidential Election*. Ed. T. Ferguson and J. Rogers. New York: Pantheon.

Kesselman, M. 1982. "The Conflictual Evolution of American Political Science: From Apologetic Pluralism to Trilateralism and Marxism." In *Public Values and Private Power in American Politics*. Ed. D. J. Greenstone. Chicago: University of Chicago Press.

Knorr-Cetina, K., and Cicourel, A. V. 1981. *Advances in Sociological Theory and Methodology*. Boston: Routledge & Kegan Paul.

Kohn, M. 1969. *Class and Conformity*. Homewood, Ill.: Dorsey.

Konrad, G. 1976 [1969]. *The Case Worker*. New York: Bantam.

Kuttner, R. 1980. *Revolt of the Have's: Taxpayer Revolts and the Politics of Austerity*. New York: Simon & Schuster.

Kuttner, R., and Kelston, D. 1979. *The Shifting Property Tax Burden*. Washington, D.C.: Conference on Alternative State and Local Policies.

Ladd, E. C. 1978. "Is America Going Right?" *Public Opinion*, September-October.

Lamb, K. 1974. *As Orange Goes: Twelve California Families and the Future of American Politics*. New York: Norton.

Lane, R. E. 1962. *Political Ideology: Why the American Common Man Believes What He Does*. New York: Free Press.

———.1969. *Political Thinking and Consciousness*. Chicago: Markham.

———1973. "Patterns of Political Belief." In *Handbook of Political Psychology*. Ed. J. Knutson. San Francisco: Jossey-Bass.

———.1978. "Autonomy, Felicity, Futility: The Effects of the Market on Political Personality." *Journal of Politics* 40.

Larrain, J. 1983. *Marxism and Ideology*. Atlantic Highlands, N.J.: Humanities Press.

Lasch, C. 1979. *The Culture of Narcissism*. New York: Norton.

Lazarsfeld, P., Berelson, B., and Gaudet, H. 1948. *The People's Choice*. New York: Columbia University Press.

Levison, A. 1974. *Working Class Majority*. New York: Penguin.

Lindblom, C. E. 1977. *Politics and Markets*. New York: Basic Books.

Lipset, S. M. 1960. *Political Man*. New York: Anchor.

Lipset, S. M., and Raab, E. 1978. "The Message of Proposition 13." *Commentary*, September.

Lipset, S. M., and Rokkan, S. 1967. *Party Systems and Voter Alignments*. New York: Free Press.

Lipset, S. M., and Schneider, W. 1983. *The Confidence Gap: Business, Labor, and Government in the Public Mind*. New York: Free Press.

Lipsky, M. 1980. "The Welfare State as Workplace." *Working Papers for a New Society*, May-June.

———.1981. *Street-Level Bureaucracy: Dilemmas of the Individual in Public Services*. New York: Russell Sage.

Livingston, D. L., and O'Donnell, C. 1980. "Accumulation Crisis and Service Professionals." In *The Capitalist Crisis in the Public Sector*. Ed. Union of Radical Political Economists. New York: Monthly Review Press.

Macpherson, C. B. 1977. *The Life and Times of Liberal Democracy*. London: Oxford University Press.

Magney, J. 1979. "Mountains, Molehills, and Media Hypes: The Curious Case of the New Conservatism." *Working Papers for a New Society*, May-June.

Mann, M. 1970. The Social Cohesion of Liberal Democracy. *American Sociological Review* 35.

———.1973. *Consciousness and Action among the Western Working Class*. London: Macmillan.

———.1975. "The Ideology of Intellectuals and Other People in the Development of Capitalism." In *Stress and Contradiction in Modern Capitalism*.

Ed. L. Lindberg, R. Alford, C. Crouch, and C. Offe. Lexington, Mass.: D. C. Health.

Marcuse, H. 1964. *One Dimensional Man.* Boston: Beacon Press.

Martin, S. 1983. *Managing without Managers: Alternative Work Arrangements in Public Organizations.* Beverly Hills, Calif.: Sage.

Marx, K. 1967 [1867]. *Capital: A Critique of Political Economy.* Vol. 1. New York: International Publishers.

————. 1974 [1869]. "The Eighteenth Brumaire of Louis Bonaparte." In *Karl Marx: Surveys from Exile, Political Writings.* Vol. 2. Ed. D. Fernbach. New York: Vintage.

Marx, K., and Engels, F. 1964 [1847]. *The German Ideology.* Moscow: Progress Publishers.

Matza, D., and Wellman, D. 1980. "The Ordeal of Consciousness." *Theory and Society* 9.

McCarthy, J., and Zald, M. 1978. "Resource Mobilization and Social Movements: A Partial Theory." *American Journal of Sociology* 82.

McCarthy, T. 1978. *The Critical Theory of Jurgen Habermas.* Cambridge, MIT Press.

Mead, M. 1953. Introduction to *The Study of Culture from a Distance.* Ed. M. Mead and R. Metraux. Chicago: University of Chicago Press.

Mepham, J. 1977. "The Theory of Ideology in *Capital.*" *Cultural Studies* 6.

Merton, R. K. 1968. *Social Theory and Social Structure.* Rev. ed. New York: Free Press.

Miliband, R. 1969. *The State in Capitalist Society.* New York: Basic Books.

————. 1977. *Marxism and Politics.* London: Oxford University Press.

Mills, C. W. 1940. "Situated Actions and Vocabularies of Motive." *American Sociological Review* 5.

————. 1956. *The Power Elite.* New York: Oxford University Press.

————. 1959. *The Sociological Imagination.* New York: Oxford University Press.

Moberg, D. 1980. "Work and American Culture: The Ideal of Self-Determination and the Prospects for Socialism." *Socialist Review* 10.

————. 1981. "Recession a Third Party to Contract Talks in Trucking." *In These Times,* November 18–24, 1981.

Moore, B. 1978. *Injustice: The Social Bases of Obedience and Revolt.* White Plains, N.Y.: M. E. Sharpe.

Mosley, H. 1981. "Corporate Social Benefits and the Underdevelopment of the American Welfare State." *Comtemporary Crises* 5.

Nelson, J. S. 1977. "The Ideological Connection." *Theory and Society* 4.

Neuman, W. R. 1981. "Differentiation and Integration: Two Dimensions of Political Thinking." *American Journal of Sociology* 86.

Newfield, J., and Dubrul, P. 1977. *The Abuse of Power: The Permanent Government and the Fall of New York.* New York: Viking.

Nie, N., and Andersen, K. 1974. "Mass Belief Systems Revisited: Political Change and Attitude Structure." *Journal of Politics* 36.

Nie, N., Verba, S., and Petrocik, J. 1976. *The Changing American Voter*. Cambridge: Harvard University Press.

Niemi, R. G., and Sobieszek, B. 1977. "Political Socialization." *Annual Review of Sociology* 3.

Niemi, R. G., and Weisberg, H. F., eds. 1976. *Controversies in American Voting Behavior*. San Francisco: W. H. Freeman.

O'Connor, J. 1973. *The Fiscal Crisis of the State*. New York: St. Martin's Press.

————. 1978. "The Democratic Movement in the United States." *Kapitalistate* 7.

————. 1981. "Accumulation Crisis: The Problem and Its Setting." *Contemporary Crises* 5.

————. 1984. *Accumulation Crisis*. Oxford: Basil Blackwell.

Offe, C. 1985. *Disorganized Capitalism*. Cambridge: MIT Press.

Owen, H., and Schultze, C. L. 1976. *Setting National Priorities: The Next Ten Years*. Washington, D.C.: Brookings Institution.

Palmer, J. L., and Sawhill, I. V., eds. 1982. *The Reagan Experiment*. Washington, D.C.: Urban Institute Press.

Phillips, K. 1982. *Post-Conservative America: People, Politics, and Ideology in a Time of Crisis*. New York: Random House.

Piven, F. F., and Cloward, R. 1971. *Regulating the Poor: The Functions of Public Welfare*. New York: Pantheon.

————. 1982. *The New Class War: Reagan's Attack on the Welfare State and Its Consequences*. New York: Pantheon.

Poulantzas, N. 1973. *Political Power and Social Classes*. London: Verso Press.

Reeves, R. 1984. "The Ideological Election." *New York Times Magazine*, February 19.

————. 1985. *The Reagan Detour*. New York: Simon & Schuster.

Riesman, D. 1952. *Faces in the Crowd: Individual Studies in Character and Politics*. New Haven: Yale University Press.

Rifkin, J. 1977. *Own Your Own Job: Economic Democracy for Working Americans*. New York: Bantam.

Rinehart, J. W. 1971. "Affluence and the Embourgeoisment of the Working Class." *Social Problems* 19.

Rubin, L. 1976. *Worlds of Pain: Life in the Working Class Family*. New York: Basic Books.

Rude, G. 1980. *Ideology and Popular Protest*. New York: Pantheon.

Sabel, C. F. 1982. *Work and Politics: The Division of Labor in Industry*. Cambridge: Cambridge University Press.

Sahlins, M. 1976. *Culture and Practical Reason*. Chicago: University of Chicago Press.

Schaar, J. 1969. "Legitimacy in the Modern State." In *Power and Community.* Ed. P. Green and S. Levinson. New York: Random House.

Schneider, W. 1984. "Running on Empty." *New Republic,* March 5.

Schuman, H., Presser, S., and Rossi, P. 1981. *Questions and Answers in Attitude Surveys.* New York: Academic Press.

Schumpeter, J. 1942. *Capitalism, Socialism, and Democracy.* New York: Harper Colophon.

Schutz, A. 1953. "Common Sense and Scientific Interpretations of Action." *Philosophy and Phenomenological Research* 14.

Sears, D., and Citrin, J. 1982. *Tax Revolt: Something for Nothing in California.* Cambridge: Harvard University Press.

Seeley, J. 1967. *The Americanization of the Unconscious.* New York: International Science Press.

Sennett, R., and Cobb, J. 1973. *The Hidden Injuries of Class.* New York: Vintage.

Shibutani, T. 1955. "Reference Groups as Perspectives." *American Journal of Sociology* 60.

Shoch, J. 1985. "Analyzing Reaganism." *Socialist Review* 79.

Simon, W. 1978. *A Time for Truth.* New York: Readers' Digest Press.

Skocpol, T. 1979. *States and Social Revolutions.* London: Cambridge University Press.

Skocpol, T., and Orloff, A. 1984. "Why Not Equal Protection? Explaining the Politics of Public Spending in Britain 1900–1911, and the U.S., 1880–1920." *American Sociological Review* 49.

Smith, A. 1937 [1776]. *The Wealth of Nations.* New York: Modern Library.

Smith, D. 1974. "The Ideological Practice of Sociology." *Catalyst* 8.

———. 1975. "What It Might Mean to Do a Canadian Sociology: The Everyday World as Problematic." *Canadian Journal of Sociology* 1.

———. 1978. "On Sociological Description: A Method from Marx." Mimeographed.

Smith, E., and Citrin, J. 1978. "The Building of a Majority for Tax Limitation in California: 1968–78." Berkeley: University of California, Survey Research Center, State Data Program.

Spencer, K. I. 1983. "Deciphering Prometheus: Temporal Changes in the Skill Level of Work." *American Sociological Review* 48.

Stack, S. 1978. "The Effect of Direct Government Involvement in the Economy on the Degree of Income Inequality." *American Sociological Review* 43.

Stephens, J. 1979. *The Transition from Capitalism to Socialism.* London: Macmillan.

Stone, C. 1984. "New Class or Convergence?" *Power and Elites* 1.

Strauss, A. 1969. *Mirrors and Masks: The Search for Identity.* San Francisco: Sociology Press.

Thompson, E. P. 1971. "The Moral Economy of the English Crowd in the Eighteenth Century." *Past and Present* 50.

———. 1978. *The Poverty of Theory and Other Essays.* London: Merlin Press.

Thurow, L. 1980. *The Zero-Sum Society.* New York: Basic Books.

Tilly, C. 1985. *The Contentious French.* Cambridge: Harvard University Press, Belknap Press.

Turkel, G. 1980. "Privatism and Orientations toward Political Action." *Urban Life* 9.

Veblen, T. 1899. *The Theory of the Leisure Class.* New York: Macmillan.

———. 1904. *The Theory of Business Enterprise.* New York: Scribner's.

Vidich, A. J. 1980. "Inflation and Social Structure: The U.S. in an Epoch of Declining Abundance." *Social Problems* 27.

Wallerstein, I. 1976. *The Modern World System: Capitalist Agriculture and the Origins of the European World-Economy in the Sixteenth Century.* New York: Academic Press.

Walzer, M. 1983. *Spheres of Justice: A Defense of Pluralism and Equality.* New York: Basic Books.

Weatherly, R. 1981. "Participatory Management in Public Welfare." Paper presented at the annual meeting of the Society for the Study of Social Problems, Toronto, Canada.

Weber, M. 1946. [1925]. *From Max Weber: Essays in Sociology.* Ed. H. Gerth and C. W. Mills. New York: Oxford University Press.

———. 1953 [1920]. *The Protestant Ethic and the Spirit of Capitalism.* New York: Scribner's.

Wellman, D. 1977. *Portraits of White Racism.* London: Cambridge University Press.

Wexler, P. 1983. *Critical Social Psychology.* Boston: Routledge & Kegan Paul.

Whalen, J., and Flacks, R. 1980. "The Isla-Vista 'Bank Burners' Ten Years Later: Notes on the Fate of Student Activists." *Sociological Focus* 13.

Wilensky, H. 1975. *The Welfare State and Equality: Structural and Ideological Roots of Public Expenditures.* Berkeley: University of California Press.

Willis, P. 1977. *Learning to Labor: How Working Class Kids Get Working Class Jobs.* Westmead, Eng.: Saxon House.

Willis, P., and Corrigan, P. 1983. "Orders of Experience." *Social Text* 7.

Wilson, T. P. 1970. "Conceptions of Interaction and Forms of Sociological Explanation." *American Sociological Review* 35.

Wolfe, A. 1977. *The Limits of Legitimacy: Political Contradictions of Contemporary Capitalism.* New York: Free Press.

———. 1981. *America's Impasse: The Rise and Fall of the Politics of Growth.* New York: Pantheon.

Wright, E. O. 1979. *Class, Crisis, and the State.* London: Verso.

Wright, E. O., and Singlemann, J. 1982. "Proletarianization in the Changing

American Class Structure." *American Journal of Sociology* 88 (supplement).

Wright, J. D. 1976. *Dissent of the Governed: Alienation and Democracy in America*. New York: Academic Press.

Wriston, H. M. 1960. *Goals for Americans: The Report of the President's Commission on National Goals*. Englewood Cliffs, N.J.: Prentice-Hall.

Yankelovich, D. 1972. "A Crisis of Moral Leadership." *Dissent* 21.

————.1974. *The New Morality*. New York: McGraw-Hill.

Yankelovich, D., and Kaagan, L. 1979. "Two Views on Proposition 13: One Year Later: What It Is and What It Isn't." *Social Policy*, May-June.

Zimmerman, D. H. 1974. "Fact as Practical Accomplishment." In *Ethnomethodology*. Ed. R. Turner. Middlesex, Eng.: Penguin.

Zimmerman, D. H., and Pollner, M. 1970. "The Everyday World as a Phenomenon." In *Understanding Everyday Life*. Ed. J. Douglas. Chicago: Aldine.

Index

255